D1860487

THE YOGA PHILOSOPHY

THE YOGA PHILOSOPHY

BEING THE TEXT OF PATANJALI, WITH BHOJA RAJA'S COMMENTARY; WITH THEIR TRANSLATIONS IN ENGLISH BY DR. BALLANTYNE AND GOVIND SHASTRI DEVA, AN INTRODUCTION BY COL. OLCOTT AND AN APPENDIX.

Revised, Edited and Reprinted for the Bombay Theosophical Publication Fund.

By

TOOKARAM TATYA, F.T.S.

GYAN

Published by

GYAN

Gyan Publishing House
5, Ansari Road
Daryaganj, New Delhi-110002
Phone: 011-47034999, 9811692060
E-mail: books@gyanbooks.com

Distribution Network
gyanbooks.com
India, USA, Canada, UK, Australia, France

© Publisher

All rights reserved. No part of this work may be reproduced, stored, adapted, or transmitted in any form or by any means, electronic, mechanical, photocopying, micro-filming, recording or otherwise, or translated in any language, without the prior written permission of the copyright owner and the publisher.

ISBN : 978-81-212-9792-9 (PB)
First Published, 1885

2nd Impression 2023

Printed at: Gyan Press, Delhi.

The book is sold subject to the condition that it shall not, by way of trade or otherwise, be lent, resold, hired out, or otherwise circulated without the prior publisher's written consent.

THE YOGA PHILOSOPHY
Author: TOOKARAM TATYA

The Theosophical Society's Publications.

THE YOGA PHILOSOPHY,

BEING THE TEXT OF PATANJALI, WITH BHOJA RAJA'S COMMENTARY; WITH THEIR TRANSLATIONS IN ENGLISH BY DR. BALLANTYNE AND GOVIND SHASTRI DEVA, AN INTRODUCTION BY COL. OLCOTT AND AN APPENDIX.

Revised, Edited and Reprinted for the Bombay Theosophical Publication Fund.

BY

TOOKARAM TATYA, F.T.S.

SECOND EDITION.

1885.

PREFACE TO THE SECOND EDITION.

PATANJALI'S work on the philosophy of *Yoga*, having been written in Sanskrit, is generally inaccessible to the public who are not conversant with that learned language. With a view to remedy this want, the work was some years ago translated into English, partly by the late Dr. Ballantyne and partly by Govind Shastri Deva. But these translations were not collated and, consequently, the whole work was not easily accessible. Their reprint therefore, in one complete volume, has become necessary at the present day, when interest has been revived in the study of the *Yoga* philosophy throughout India by the Theosophical Society.

This book having gone through a first edition within four months, and there still being a great demand for it, the Managers of the Theosophical Publication Fund have thought it best to issue this second edition. Care has been taken to ensure accuracy in the text by comparing it with the Bhoja Vriti in Sanskrit, and in some places the translation into English by Dr. Rajendralala Mitra has been consulted. But the original text of Dr. Ballantyne has been principally followed.

The Society is much indebted to Mr. Janardan Damodar Kolatkar for having assisted in passing the work through the Press.

The Edition now offered is calculated to help to counteract the materialistic tendencies of the present age, and to re-open the path of the true spiritual philosophy and science of the ancient Aryans. The Managers of the Theosophical Publication Fund hope that it will be acceptable to the religious and philosophic world, especially to such thinkers as are engaged in the solution of the great problem of human life, and thatit will lead to a proper understanding of the Infinite in the true and scientific sense.

Bombay, 1st October 1885.

INTRODUCTION.

THERE existed in Ancient India six schools of Philosophy, which in subsequent ages had their counterparts in Greece. These schools were known as the six Shastras or Darshanas, denoting six different aspects of the spiritual knowledge. They were known by the designations of: 1. Nyaya philosophy(Logic); 2. Mimansa philosophy (Ritual), 3. Vyshashika philosophy (Atomic); 4. Sankhya philosophy (Materialistic); 5. Patanjali philosophy (Yoga); and 6. Vedanta philosophy (Pantheistic). The object of all these schools of philosophy has been to prescribe rules for freeing the soul from the miseries of rebirth, and to enable man by following the prescribed discipline, to reach the highest spiritual development.

Patanjali, the founder of one of these schools of philosophy, has been justly recognized both in this country and in Europe as a profound thinker. The tenets of this philosopher will, to an unbiassed mind, appear similar to those of certain metaphysicians of Greece and modern Europe. His views regarding the soul and its nature are corroborated by some of the best scholars and thinkers of the Western World. His claims as a sage propounding the clearest and most original views on the laws which govern the visible universe and the invisible within it have been frankly acknowledged. With the object of introducing, therefore, his philosophy more generally to the Indian public, the compilers have deemed it advisable to give at the end of this preface extracts from the Introduction to an English Translation of the Bhagvat Gita by Mr. J. C. Thompson. This gentleman has taken great pains to understand this subject, and having been, as it would seem, a born philosopher himself, has been able to present a very clear summary, the reproduction of which will, the compilers trust, form an appropriate Introduction to this volume. It will enable the reader to obtain at a glance an insight into the nature of the difficulties he may have to encounter in these pages, and facilitate the comprehension of many passages.

A short sketch of the life of Patanjali is reproduced from "A View of the History, Literature, and Mythology of the Hindus," by the late Rev. William Ward of Serampore.

The compilers would recommend the students of this work to study also the Wákyasudhá, Aparokshánubhuti, and other works on the practical parts of the Vedanta incorporated in the works of Ràja-yoga by Shrimat Shankaráchàrya and other writers. They also recommend a study of the Bhagvat-Gita, Yoga Váshistha, the Sànkhya Kàriká of Gowdapáda, the Hatha Pradipika, the Shaiwàgama, and similar other books on the Yoga Philosophy. The perusal of these works and of the present volume cannot fail to assist those who are interested in the practical study of Yoga philosophy.

The word Yoga means Junction, Meeting, Union, Conjunction, Connection, &c., but it is employed here to expound the mode and means systematically employed to bring about the union of the Soul with the Spirit, or the Para Bramha. One who follows and practises this system is called a Yogi.

Though Patanjali was the founder of the school of Yoga Philosophy, still it has been universally admitted that he was not the originator of this system. It is acknowledged on all hands that Shankara, or Mahadeva, was the originator and the first expounder of this knowledge. Patanjali himself in the commencement of his work praises him as the originator of the philosophy. He knows the science in all its branches and bearings. He imparted this knowledge to Dattátraya a great sage and adept in this shastra and Brahmavidyâ (divine science). It is a general belief that this ancient sage still lives and visits the earnest seekers of the true knowledge. He imparted the knowledge of this science to Shukráchárya and other Rishis and has even done so to the Sadhus of modern times. Shukráchárya taught it to Yáguyavalkya and he in his turn, to his pupils. We do not find it stated in any book who had taught the philosophy to Patanjli. Before his time, this knowledge was imparted verbally by preceptors to their pupils. Patanjali was, it seems, the first to reduce it to writing in the form of Aphorisms for the benefit of students. Hence, we presume, it was that he was accepted as the founder of the school.

The Yoga system is divided into two principal parts.—Hatha and Rája Yogas. There are many minor divisions which can be brought under one of these heads. Hatha Yoga was promoted and practised by Matsendra Nath and Goraksh Nath and their followers and by many sects of ascetics in this country. This system deals principally with the physiological part of man with a view to establish his health and train his will. The processes prescribed to arrive at this end are so difficult that only a few resolute souls go through all the stages of its practice, while many have failed and died in the attempt. It is, therefore, strongly denounced by all the philosophers. The most illustrious Shankarâchârya has remarked in his treatise called Aparokshánubhuti that " the system of Hatha Yoga was intended for those whose worldly desires are not pacified or uprooted". He has strongly spoken elsewhere against its practice.

On the other hand the Rája Yogis try to control the mind itself by following the rules laid down by the greatest of adepts. These rules are collectively called साधनचतुष्टय, signifying a collection of four accomplishments. These accomplishments are 1. विवेक (the right knowledge of the real and the unreal), 2. वैराग्य (perfect indifference to enjoyment here and hereafter), 3. शमादि षट् संपत्ति (the six qualifications:—शम is perfect control over the mind which is the seat of emotions and desires; दम is perfect control over the senses; श्रद्धा is implicit faith in one's own Guru and the Shruti; समाधान is concentration of mind in the attainment of spiritual knowledge; उपरति is the renunciation of formalities of religion; तितिक्षा

is forbearance.) 4. मुमुक्षुता is an ardent desire to be free from the bonds forged by *Ahánkara* and *Máya* and to know one's proper "self."

Besides these four accomplishments, the student of Rája Yoga has to acquire four other subsidiary accomplishments. These are श्रवण (the hearing of lectures, the elucidation of the philosophy or the reading of it), मनन (contemplating on what the student has read or heard), निदिध्यासन (the constant thinking of the object in view and the convictions springing therefrom), तत्त्वंपदशोध (trying to realize one self in relation to the Universal Soul).

After mastering these eight accomplishments the student becomes qualified for the reception of further instructions to arrive at the final beatitude or the sumum bonum of his existence.

Buddha and his followers have inculcated ideas and views similar to those of the Raja Yogi or the Vedantin. They say, that the destruction of Skandhas and desires are the ways to Nirván or Moksha. To destroy these is to subdue the mind and its desires by following the eight-fold path that has been prescribed by Buddha and not by undergoing physical mortifications to cultivate the Will, which is the principal factor in all the practices of the Hatha Yogins. The Noble Eightfold path is :—1 Right belief: free from superstition or delusion; 2 Right thought: high and worthy of the intelligent and earnest man; 3 Right speech: Kindly, open, and truthful; 4 Right conduct: peaceful, honest, and pure; 5 Right means of livelihood: bringing hurt or danger to no living thing; 6 Right endeavours: in self-training, and self-control; 7 Right mindfulness: active and watchful mind; 8 Right meditation: earnest thought on the deep mysteries of life. By following these with strict attention and without a moment's loss of time, the followers of Buddha have secured to themselves the highest Nirvàn.

The Bhágwat and some of the Vaishnava Puránas strongly advocate the superiority of Bhakti Yoga, which is also recommended highly in Chapter XII of the Bhagvat-Gita by Shree Krishna.

The leading feature of this is devotion without intermission, and absorbing, ecstatic thought regarding the Deity. The difference between this and Ráj Yoga is that the former is based on pure and rational metaphysics, while the latter is founded on mere faith. In their results the former is by most considered superior to the latter.

In the Shaiva Purânas and the Tântric Works, Yoga, or the bringing about the union of the soul with the spirit, is treated in various ways. The doctrines in some of these works are written in a language so repulsive that we abstain from even mentioning them here. These works advocate the Black Art also and are calculated to do great harm.

The student should very clearly notice that the modern Mesmeric science if exhaustively and experimentally studied is the key to an understanding of ancient Yoga, however practised and by whatever school. Yoga, in its psychological aspect, is self mesmerization. It differs from the practices of the ordinary mesmeric operator, in that the 'subject' in this case is the mystic's own body, instead of another's person. In both cases, there is the development of a current of psychic aura—if the word be permissible—and its direction by an operative will upon a selected receptive object. The Western Mesmeriser throws out his current upon a passive subject, and in that organization provokes the result his mind had conceived and his will commanded. The Yogi develops the same potential aura, but turns it in upon himself. He first, by determined concentration, vanquishes the natural restlessness of the body and supremacy of the physical appetites; reducing the physical self to the condition of a passive 'subject'. Then, only, when his will has fully asserted its power, can he develop within himself those transcendental powers of intelligence which befit him to observe the laws and phenomena of the spiritual world. The 'Siddhis' of Patanjali mark the successive stages of this self-unfolding; the last stage of all being a self-induced extasis in which unlike the extasis of the somnambule which has been developed under a mesmerizer's passes, or the extasis of an impassioned monk or nun, there is not only consciousness but also self-control. The extatic Yogin can return from the highest flight into the supernal spheres by an effort of his will and terminate his 'Samadhi' whenever he likes. But the somnambulic seer or seeress is always in danger of being so transported by his or her radiant visions as to snap the thin cord, which still links him or her to the earthly life.

Some Hindus believe that no one can acquire the Siddhis (psychic powers) of adeptship without passing through the initiatory training of Hatha-Yoga, the course of posturings and gymnastic exercises hereinafter described. But by comparing the ascetic training followed by the Buddhist Arahat with that prescribed by Patanjali a difference will be observed, and yet the Buddhist books, alike of the Northern and Southern churches, relate the performance of so-called 'miracles,' more properly 'phenomena' of the same character, and equally remarkable as those ascribed to the Hindu 'Sadhoos.' The painful postures, and sometimes revolting practices laid down in the Hatha Yoga are, therefore, not indispensable. The living adepts now known to exist eschew them entirely, and yet their powers are as great, it would seem, as are attainable by man. Hatha Yoga may from their point of view, be described as the bigotry of psychic training, bearing almost the same relation to what is essential as the most superstitious rites of exoteric religions do to the spirit or the esoteric part of religion proper. These lower practices of Yoga are, moreover, dangerous unless begun very early in life and practised under the vigilant eye of a master, who is himself profoundly versed in the theory and practice of the subject. Many rash experimenters, being still bound by their carnal natures and so rendered unfit for rapid progress, have been made insane and even driven to suicide. The struggle of the base animal nature against any attempt to curb and subdue it is one, through which only the grandest souls can hope to come out victorious. As but few in any human group are able to provide themselves with these requisites, few become Adepts. And nature herself has wisely so ordered it; for if a majority of men could become adepts, the foundations of society would soon be destroyed and social chaos be upon us. He who feels within himself the spurrings of desire of this higher knowledge will surmount every barrier to its attainment. For the guidance of such, and the information of an enquiring public, the present compilation has been made.

There are expressions running throughout the whole work of Patanjali which no ordinary reader could comprehend without the friendly help of Mesmeric study. For instance, the words ध्रुवे निश्चले * * * कृतसंयमस्य, translated by Dr. Ballantyne as "performs his restraint with regard to the Polar Star" convey no meaning. How could one understand what is implied in such vague words?

But when it is conceived that this really means the concentration of thought upon the point in the heavens occupied by the star, with such intensity that the thinker can transfer his consciousness to that standing-point of observation, then we may easily understand how he could gather within the sweep of his spiritual sight all of our universe that lies between that star and our earth. So as regards the other points of concentration. The Yogin must learn to compress his whole sentient consciousness into a chosen spot, or upon a certain piece of information he desires. Outside that spot or apart from that subject he must, for the moment, feel no existence. In the *Siva Samhita* is a drawing, which represents the successive stages of, so to say, the Yogin's soul-journey around his body in his campaign of self conquest. The author's meaning is that the ascetic must force himself to live in turn, as it were, only at a spot above the eyebrows, or in the brain, or at the root of the throat, in the heart, the Solar plexus, or elsewhere throughout the body. He must select some one spot as his point of departure; when he has perfected concentration there, shift to the next; hence pass to the next, and so keep on until he has made a circuit through six different vital points or seats.

of animal life. At each of these vital centres he fights his fight with his animal nature, dislodges the habitual sovereign, usurps its control by implanting there the authoritative impress of the self-liberating will—the real Self—and so conquers his empire piecemeal. When he has thus gone down the body in front, he passes up the spinal cord to and through the cerebellum into and through the cerebrum, and so on to the original point of departure: or he may reverse the order. When this grand cycle of psychic evolution has been completed he is free and master. Thenceforth neither matter, time nor space can obstruct his quest after the Highest knowledge. He knows Brahma—he *is* Brahma. In a Lahore pamphlet* one of the drawings shows a sphere of silvery light around the Yogin's head. In this are pictured the heavenly orbs, and an outline map of the earth's continents. The meaning of this is that when his self-evolution is perfected, the Yogin can see through the pure Akása (astral light, or ether) all that concerns the orbs of space, as well as all that is transpiring upon our globe. The ancients represented their saints thus with a radiant *nimbus*, and the idea was borrowed from them by Christian painters and sculptors, Whether we observe the dying, whose "clay lamp" of the body, as Robertus de Fluctibus so beautifully expresses it, is almost *shattered*; or the lucid ecstatic of the mesmerists; or the canonized Christian saint to whom "Heaven" shows its effulgence; or the Aryan Agni Hotri priest, who in awe repeats his 'mantra'; or the Magus of Chaldea, who sees the glory of Ormazd in the flame of the altar; or the Buddhist Ráhat, who in his state of Iddhi solves the riddle of Nirvana, we shall always find them in the presence of this radiant, this silvary Light. And whatever the path the seer

* In an interesting yet crude and unscholarly treatise upon the Vedanta, Ràja Yoga by Sabhàpaty Swàmi, the process described is far from the system of Ràja Yoga. From his treatment of the subject, it is clear that it is a part of the Hatha Yoga as it recommends to students the practices of regulating the Prana from one nervous centre to the other by stages till it is finally taken round to the Brahmarandhra, the seat of the soul in the brain. In attempting this, one has many risks and hardships to undergo.

may choose to climb to the crests of Being where this light can touch his brow, he must follow the one close rule of discipline—the subjugation of the meaner man in his composite self by the nobler demi-god.

The leading idea of Patanjali's philosophy is that all things result from the action of spirit upon matter; that the universe arose from the reflection of spirit upon matter in a visible form; as contradistinguished from the atomic theory of the Nyâya and Vyisheshika schools, and that of the Sânkhya, which affirms that matter possesses in itself the power of assuming all manner of forms. But most Indian philosophers agree that matter and that force which moves it (spirit ?) are eternal. None affirms that something can be made out of nothing. Patanjali, in common with other teachers of the East and West, holds that in a world of ever-shifting phenomena arising from a hidden cause, the bodily senses, which themselves are but the instruments of a concealed apprehending consciousness, cannot distinguish the real from the unreal. They are the easy dupes of delusion; and he who trusts to their guidance is like the blind man led by the blind. The truth can only be seen by that which is independent of external appearances—Spirit. "Spirit is omnipresent, unchangeable, everlasting, undivided, and wisdom itself." False ideas "are destroyed by examining that which is not Spirit, and from this examination will result the knowledge of Spirit. Clear knowledge of Spirit arises from Yoga, or abstraction of mind; and this leads to liberation; but not immediately: for discrimination, Wisdom is necessary. An error is removed first, by doubts respecting the reality of our conceptions, and then by more certain knowledge". Dr Ward ably summarises Patanjali's doctrines [View of the Hist. Lit. and Myth. of the Hindus.] The Yogi passes through four principal stages in the course of his psychic development: (a) He learns the rules of Yoga; (b) Acquires perfect knowledge, that is complete emancipation from the delusive influences of the external senses; (c) Employs this knowledge practically, and overcomes the material influence of the primary elements;

(d) Destroys all consciousness of personality and individuality अहंकार (ahankára), and thus frees the soul from matter.

In reviewing all the systems of the Yoga Philosophy, we have come to the conclusion that Patanjali's Yoga Aphorisms are a compromise between Ràj and Hatha Yoga practices. Notwithstanding this, they form a complete system in themselves, and are made simple and easy to comprehend by the various commentators and Vrittikaras. Among these, Shree Veda Vyasa, Bhoraj Raja, Vàchaspati Misra, and Vignyana Bhikshu are the chief.

In concluding this introduction, we strongly advise our readers to peruse the learned and able introduction of Dr. Rajendralala Mitra, L. L. D., C. I. E., of Calcutta, to his translation of the Yoga Aphorisms of Patanjali. He has ably discussed various points of philosophy and compared the use of Yoga shastra with the opinions of the greatest thinkers of modern Europe. He has also thrown light on the chronology of the Author of the Yoga Aphorisms and given his life at length.

In addition to this Introduction, there is reprinted here for the edification of the reader an article on Yoga Vidya, a careful perusal of which is highly essential, since the student cannot grasp the spirit of the philosophy without having a clear knowledge of the soul, its attributes and capacity.

Adyar, August 1885. H. S. OLCOTT, P. T. S.

YOGA VIDYA.

By a F. T. S.

Look where we will around us, in every direction the sources of pure spiritual life appear to be either altogether stagnant, or else trickling feebly in shrunken and turbid streams. In religion, in politics, in the arts, in philosophy, in poetry even—wherever the grandest issues of Humanity are at stake, man's spiritual attitude towards them, is one either of hopeless fatigue and disgust, or fierce anarchical impatience. And this is the more deplorable, because it is accompanied by a feverish materialistic activity. Yes, this age of ours is materialist; and perhaps the saddest and dreariest thing in the ever-increasing materialism of the age, is *the ghostly squeaking and gibbering of helpless lamentation made over it by the theologists, who croak about their old dry wells wherein no spiritual life is left.* Meanwhile society appears to be everywhere busily organizing animalism. [LORD LYTTON—in *Fortnightly Review for* 1871.]

Lord Lytton here paints the spiritual darkness of Kali Yug with realistic fidelity. The reading of this paragraph has suggested the making of an effort to bring back to India, to some extent at least, the ancient light of Aryàvarta. With his Lordship's sympathetic co-operation, much would be possible. Let us begin with an attempt at explaining what is the almost forgotten science of Yogism.

No man can understand the meaning of Patanjali's Aphorisms of the Yoga Philosophy, who does not perfectly comprehend what the soul and body are and their respective powers. The lucubrations of commentators, for the most part, show that when their author is thinking of the one they fancy he means the other. When he describes how the latent psychical senses and capabilities may be brought out of the bodily prison and given free scope, he appears to them to be using metaphorical terms to express an utopy of physical perceptions and powers. The 'organized animalism' of the Nineteenth century, which Lord Lytton stigmatizes, in the paragraph from the *Fortnightly Review* above quoted—would have totally obliterated, perhaps, our capacity to grasp the sublime idea of Yoga, were it not for the glimpses that the discoveries of Mesmer and Reichenbach, and the phenomena of mediumship, have afforded of the nature of the Inner World and the Inner Man. With these helps most of what would be obscure is made plain. These give us a definite appreciation of the sure and great results that the *Yogi* ascetic strives for, and obtains by his self-discipline and privations. For this reason, the Theosophical Society insists that its Fellows, who wish to comprehend alike the hidden meaning of ancient philosophies and the mysteries of our own days, shall first study magnetism, and then enter the 'circle-room' of the spiritualists.

May we not compare the unveiling of the soul's senses of sight, hearing, smell, taste and touch, and the awakening of its will-power, which result from Yog training, with that change which comes to the bodily senses and will, when the child emerges from its fœtal home into the outer world? All the physical faculties it will ever exercise were potentially in the babe before birth, but latent. Given scope and exercise, they became developed in proportion to their innate energies—more in some people than in others. How vastly different they are in *posse* and in *esse*! And yet this contrast affords but a very meagre idea of that between the dormant powers of the soul in the man of matter, and the transcendent reach of these same powers in the full-trained Yogi. Rather compare the shining star with a yellow taper. The eye of the body can at best see only a few miles, and its ear hear but what is spoken near; its feet can carry it but ploddingly along the surface of the ground, a step at a time; and its hands grasp nothing that is more than a yard off. If securely locked in a closet, the body is powerless to effect its deliverance, and can neither see, hear, touch, taste, nor smell what is outside its prison wall. But the unbound soul of the Yogi is limited by neither time nor space; nor obstructed by obstacles; nor prevented from seeing, hearing, feeling or knowing anything it likes, on the instant; no matter how distant or hidden the thing the Yogi, would see, feel, hear or know. The soul has potentially, in short, the qualities of omniscience and omnipotence, and the object of Yoga Vidya is to develop them fully.

We have a great desire that the Yoga Philosophy should be familiarized to students of psychology. It is particularly important that Spiritualists should know of it; for their numbers are so large that they could, by united action, counteract in large degree the 'organized animalism' that Lord Lytton complains of. Give the century a worthy ideal to aspire to, and it would be less animal: teach it what the soul is, and it will worship the body less. As a commencement in this direction, we begin in this number of the THEOSOPHIST, a translation of part of Chapter XV of the eleventh Skandha of *Shrimad Bhagavata.* The authorship of this important Sanskrit work is so disputed as by some to be ascribed to Bopadeva, the celebrated grammarian of Bengal, thus giving it an age of only eight centuries; by others to Vyasa, author of the other Puranas, and so making it of archaic origin. But either will do; our object being only to show modern psychologists that the science of soul was better understood, ages ago, in India than it is to-day by ourselves. Sanskrit literature teems with proofs of this fact, and it will be our pleasure to lay the evidence supplied to us by our Indian brothers before the public. Foremost among such writings stand, of course, Patanjali's own philosophical teachings, and these we will come to later on.

The student of Yoga will observe a great difference in *Siddhis* ('Superhuman faculties,' this is rendered; but not correctly, unless we agree that 'human' shall only mean that which pertains to physical man. 'Psychic faculties' would convey the idea much better: man can do nothing *superhuman*) that are said to be attainable by Yoga. There is one group which exacts a high training of the spiritual powers; and another group which concerns the lower and coarser psychic and mental energies. In the *Shrimad Bhagavata,* Krishna says: "He who is engaged in the performance of Yoga, who has subdued his senses, and who has concentrated his mind in me (Krishna), [all] the Siddhis stand ready to serve."

Then Uddhava asks: "Oh, Achyuta (Infallible One) since thou art the bestower of [all] the Siddhis on the Yogis, pray tell me by what *dhárаná** and how, is a Siddhi attained; and how many Siddhis there are. Bhagván replies: "Those who have transcended the dhàrana and yoga say that there are eighteen Siddhis, eight of which contemplate *me* as the chief object of attainment (or are attainable through me), and the [remaining] ten are derivable from the gunás;"—the commentator explains —from the preponderance of *satva guná*. These eight superior Siddhis are: *Animá, Mahimá, Laghima* [of the body], *Prapti* (attainment by the senses), *Prákáshyama, Ishitá, Vashitá*, and an eighth which enables one to attain his every wish. "These," said Krishna, "are my Siddhis."

The Siddhis of Krishna may be thus defined:

1. *Animá*—the power to atomize "the body;" to make it become smallest of the smallest.

2. *Mahimá*—the power to magnify one's body to any dimensions.

3. *Laghima*—the power to become lightest of the lightest.

These three, the commentator says, relate to "the body;" but he does not enlighten us as to whether the outer or inner —the physical or astral—body is meant. Turning to Bhoja Raja's commentary on Patanjali (Govinda Deva Sástri's translation, in *Pandit*, Vol. V. p. 206), we find Animà explained as "Minuteness—attainment of an atomic form, or the power of becoming as minute as an atom; [by this power the ascetic can enter into a diamond, etc.]"

Garimá—is the obtaining of control over the attraction of gravitation, so that one's body may attain such great heaviness as to weigh tons if one chooses; or acquire such levity as to be like a flake of cotton in lightness.

Let the reader observe that here are two Siddhis (*animá* and

* *Dhàranà.* The intense and perfect concentration of the mind upon one exterior object;—accompanied by complete abstraction from things of the internal world.

mahimá); which can only refer to conditions of the astral body, and a third which may be applicable to either the astral or physical body of the ascetic. Whenever we have such instances coming under notice our first thought must be that *there is no such thing possible as a miracle; whatever happens does so in strict compliance with natural law.* For instance; knowing what we do of the composition and structure of a man's body,—a mass of bioplastic matter—it is unthinkable that he should make it small enough to enter into an atom or a diamond-grain. So, also, that he should illimitably swell it out and stretch it, so as to "occupy as much space as he likes." A living adult man cannot be compressed into a speck. But as to the inner body, or soul, the case is different. By 'soul' we mean, in this instance, the plastic, ethereal inner-self, that which corresponds to the Western idea of a "double,"* and, in the ancient Indian philosophy is known as the मायावीरूप—*máyávi-rupa*—(illusionary form), and as कामरूप—*Káma-rupa*—(WILL-form). These are identical, for the *double* exists in its latent state in every living being, as it is the exact ethereal counterpart of the outer body. The difference in name but indicates the different circumstances under which it is at times made to become objective—that is visible. In the case of mediums, or when, as a result and the unconscious effect of an intense desire which attracts a person's thoughts to a certain place, or prompts him to a certain action, it thus oozes out of its envelope of flesh, it then is called *Màyàvi-rupa* (illusionary form). It made itself visible because compelled to it by the law of the inter-magnetic action, which, when left to itself, acts blindly. But when it is projected by the trained will of an adept, a Yogi, who directs it at his own convenience, then it is designated as *Kámá-rupa*,—WILL-form, or Desire-form; *i. e.* so to say, created, or called forth into objective shape, by the will, and at the desire of its possessor.

---

* The *double* which appears under two aspects at times as a dull non-intelligent form or animate statue, at other times as an intelligent entity. More than any one else, the Spiritualists ought to be aware of the difference.

This "dual-soul," must not be confounded with either *Jiváṭma* (the vital principle resident in inert matter), or, the *Ling-Sharir*. The last named is the subtile, ethereal elements of the *ego* of an organism; inseparately united to the coarser elements of the latter; it never leaves it but at death. While its functionary principle—the *Linga Deha*—is the executive agent, through which it works; the objective formation of *Káma-rupa* being performed by the power of *Yoga bal* (योगबल.)

This "dual-soul" possesses properties peculiar to itself, and as distinctly its own as those of the physical body are peculiar to it. Among these properties are compressibility, the power of passing through the most solid substances, infinite expansibility, and many more that might be enumerated. These are not idle words, but facts derived from the experiences of many Yogis, adepts, ascetics, mystics, mediums, etc., of many different classes, times and countries. We may think, therefore, of the capacity of the *Kama-rupa* to become a mere speck or enlarge itself to enormous dimensions; entering a grain of diamond dust, and the next moment filling every pore of the entire globe for thought is unparticled and illimitably elastic. And, we could apprehend how, when once in the grain or in the globe, our trained *thought* can act there as if it were our own whole *self.* So, too, we may conceive of the astral-body—or *Kama-rupa*, which although material as compared with pure spirit, is yet immaterial in comparison with the dense physical body—having like properties, and thus come to an understanding of the esoteric (secret) meaning of *Animá* and *Mahimá*.

Whole libraries have been written to define what soul is, and yet for our practical purpose, it will suffice to sum up the definition in a word: man's soul is the aggregate of all the above given sub-divisions. This "self" through the *Linga-Deha* is ever conscious during the sleep of the body, and transfers the sense of this inner consciousness into the waking brain; so that the Yogi may, at will, be informed of what is transpiring in the outer world through his physical organs, or in the inner world, through his soul perceptions. While average mortals maintain their perceptions only during the day, the initiated Yogi has an equally real, undimmed, and perfect appreciation of his individual existence at night, even while his body sleeps. He can go even further: he can voluntarily paralyze his vital functions so that his body shall lie like a corpse, the heart still, the lungs collapsed, animal heat transferred to the interior surfaces; the vital machine stopped, as it were, like a clock which waits only the key that rewinds it, to resume its beating. What nature does for the scores of hybernating quadrupeds, reptiles and insects, under the spontaneous action of her established laws, the Yogi effects for his physical body by long practice, and the intense concentration of an undaunted will. And what he can do for himself the magnetizer can do for his cataleptic subject; whose body in the state of *ecstasis*, the highest in the range of mesmeric phenomena, presents all the physical appearances of death, including even *rigor mortis*; while the active vitality of the soul is shown in the descriptions given by the ecstatic, either of distant events, on the earth, or the scenes in which he is taking part in the world of the invisible. The records of a thousand such cases occurring in every part of the world, combine to show (*a*) that the soul has the capacity of a conscious existence separate from the body; (*b*) that it is limited by neither time nor space, it being able to visit and return in an instant from the farthest localities, and to reach such—the tops of mountains, for instance, or the centres of deserts, or the bottoms of rivers or lakes, as the walking man could either not exist in or could only visit with the most tedious exertions and the greatest precautions; (*c*) that it can penetrate closed rooms, rocky walls, iron chests, or glass cases, and see and handle what is within. All these, if it were particled and unyielding, like the physical body, would be impossibilities; and so, seeing what our modern experience has taught us, we can readily comprehend Patanjali's meaning and avoid the absurd conclusions which some of his materialistic and inexperienced commentators have reached. "Hundreds of times" says Professor

Denton, "have I had the evidence that the spirit (meaning 'soul'—the two words are most unhappily and we fear inextricably confounded—*Ed.*) can smell, hear, and see, and has powers of locomotion." Cicero calls the soul *spiritus* (a breathing), as also does Virgil, and both regard it as a subtile matter which might be termed either *aura* (a breeze), or *ignis* (fire), or *æther*. So that here again we are assisted to the conception that *Animá* applies only to a certain portion of the soul —(*psuché*) and not to the body. And, we thus find that this Siddhi is entirely possible for one who has learnt the manifold faculties of the *inner* man, and knows how to apply and utilize the manifold functions of *jivatma, ling-sharir*, and the *máyávi* and *káma-rupa.* Plutarch makes pretty nearly the same division of the functions of the "Soul." The *ling-sharir* he calls *psuché* (physical entity), and teaches that it never leaves the body but at death; *máyávi* and *káma-rupa* answer to his *dæmon*, or spiritual-double, one half of which is *irrational* and called by him *eïdolon*, and the other *rational* and usually termed "blessed god."

But while the physical body may not be atomized or magnified illimitably, *its weight may be voluntarily changed without transcending natural law in the slightest degree.* Hundreds, if not thousands, are living in India to-day who have seen ascetics, while in the state of dhàranà, rise from the ground and sit or float in the air without the slightest support. We doubt if a phenomenon seen by so many reputable persons will be seriously denied. Admitting, then, that this levitation does happen, how shall we explain it? That has already been done in "Isis Unveiled," where the author shows that by simply changing the polarity of his body, so as to make the latter similarly electrified to the spot of ground upon which he stands, the ascetic can cause himself to rise perpendicularly into the air. This is no miracle, but a very simple affair of magnetic polarity. The only mystery is as to the means by which these changes of polarity may be effected. This secret the Yogi learns, and Patanjali's name for the Siddhi is *Garimá*, which includes *Laghimá*. It follows, of course, that he who knows how to polarize his body so as to cause himself to be "light as a flake of cotton" and rise into the air, has only to reverse the process to make his body abnormally heavy. We stick to the surface of the earth because our bodies are of an opposite polarity to the ground on which we stand. Science explains that we are attracted towards the centre of the earth by gravity, and our weight is the measure of the combined attraction of all the particles of our physical body towards the central point at the earth's centre. But if we double the intensity of that attraction we become twice as heavy as we were before; if we quadruple it, four times as heavy; centiple it, one hundred times as heavy. In short, by a mere alteration of our polarity we would be giving our flesh the weight of an equal bulk of stone, iron, lead, mercury, etc. And the Yogi has this secret, or Siddhi, also.

Many Hindus who admit that their sacred books contain accounts of the phenomena of levitation, that is, of walking or floating in the air—affirm that the power has been lost, and that there is none living who can exhibit it, or even the appearance of it, save through the help of jugglery. This false conclusion is assisted by the tendency of Western education, which but reflects the materialism of modern experimental science—so misnamed, for it is but partly experimental and preponderatingly inferential guess-work. Forgetting that the law of gravitation is, after all, but an incomplete hypothesis which holds its ground for the want of a better one,—our young men say that scienee has defined the laws of gravity, hence levitation is an absurdity, and our old books teach nonsense. This would be sufficient if the premiss were not false. Science has but noted the more familiar phenomena of gravity, and knows nothing whatever of its nature, or its variable manifestations under the impulse of the undiscovered primal force. Open any book on any branch of physical science, and the author, if he has any professional reputation to lose, will be detected in the confession of his ignorance of the ultimate cause of natural phenomena. Superficial readers will be deceived by glittering generalizations from partially proved data, but the thoughtful student will ever find the empty void at the bottom. Huxley sums it all up in the self-condemnatory sentence, "we,"—that is *we* scientists, we men who talk so glibly about ancient superstition and ignorance, and would impress Indian youth with the notion that *we* are the very High Priests of nature, the only competent instructors of her mysteries, the key to which we all carry in our vest pockets—"*we know nothing* about the composition of any body whatever, as it is."

But supposing that not one witness could be found in all our India to-day to prove the fact of levitation, would we have to let the case go by default? By no means; for, to say nothing of the unbroken chain of lay testimony that stretches from the earliest historic period to our times, we can take that of eminent Western physicians who have witnessed such levitations in the cases of patients afflicted with certain nervous diseases; —Professor Perty, of Geneva, and Dr. Kerner, of Wurtemberg, among others. If a phenomenon of such a nature takes place in a diseased body, without being regarded as a violation of the "laws of nature," why should it not occur—provided the same conditions, *i. e.*, a reversed polarity, are furnished it—in a body free from disease? This testimony of science secured, we need not hesitate to cull from contemporaneous records the mass of available proof that the bodies of living men can be, and are, floated through the air. Who shall deny it! Science? No, for we have seen that it is attested by some of the most eminent scientific men of our day; and to these we may add Lord Lindsay, President of the Royal Astronomical Society, and one of the Council of the Royal Society itself. One witness of his stamp is enough, and he is on record (London Dialec. Soc. "*Report*," p. 215) as saying that he had seen a certain medium, not only float through the air of a drawing-room, but carry with him the chair upon which he had been sitting, and with it "pushing the pictures out of their places as he passed along the walls." They were far beyond the reach of a person standing on the ground. And he adds the highly important fact, "The light was sufficient to enable me to see clearly." This same medium he saw floated horizontally out of the window in one room of a house, in Victoria Street, London, and again at the window of the adjoining room. "I saw him," says Lord Lindsay, "outside the other window (that is in the next room) floating in the air. *It was eighty-five feet from the ground*. There was no balcony along the windows. * * * I have no theory to explain these things. I have tried to find out how they are done, but the more I studied them, the more satisfied was I that they could not be explained by mechanical trick. I have had the fullest opportunity for investigation." When such a man gives such testimony, we may well lend an attentive ear to the corroborative evidence which has accumulated at different epochs and in many countries.

The case of the levitated 'medium' of the modern Spiritualist affords us an example of a phase of *Laghima* of which no mention is made in the portion of the *Shrimad Bhagavata* under consideration, but may be found in many other manuscripts. We have seen that a Yogi may reverse his corporeal polarity at pleasure, to make himself light as a cotton flake or heavy as lead; and that he acquires this Siddhi by long self-discipline, and the subordination of the general law of matter to the focalized power of spirit. It has also been affirmed that the cataleptic similitude to death, which in India is called *Samadhi*, may be produced in the mesmerised, or magnetized, subject by the magnetizer. We have the report of the late William Gregory, Professor of Chemistty in Edinburgh University, (*Animal Magnetism; or Mesmerism and its Phenomena*, pp. 154, 155) of one of many experiments, at his own house, by Mr. Lewis, a famous negro mesmerizer:

"**Case 5.**—Mr. J. H., a young and healthy man, could be rendered instantly and completely cataleptic by a glance, or a single pass. He could be fixed in any position, however inconvenient, and would remain ten or fifteen minutes in such a posture, that no man in a natural state could have endured it for half a minute. * * * When Mr. L. stood on a chair and tried to draw Mr. H., without contact, from the ground, he gradually rose on tiptoe, making the most violent efforts to rise, till he was fixed by cataleptic rigidity. Mr. Lewis said that, had he been still more elevated above Mr. H. he could have raised him from the floor without contact, and held him thus suspended for a short time, while some spectator should pass his hand under the feet. Although this was not done in my presence, *yet the attraction upwards was so strong that I see no reason to doubt the statement made to me by Mr. Lewis, and by others who saw it, that this experiment has been successfully performed. Whatever be the influence which acts, it would seem capable, when very intense, of overpowering the law of gravity.*"

Let us first clearly comprehend the meaning of the word gravity, and then the inference of Professor Gregory will not seem so extravagant after all. In this phase of *Laghima*, observe that the changed polarity of the human body is effected by the magnetiser's will. We have, therefore, one class of cases where the effect is selfproduced by the conscious will of the Yogi; another where it occurs involuntarily in the subject as the result of an outside will directed upon him. The third class is illustrated in the example of the floating medium which Lord Lindsay attests. Here the *æthrobat*—as air-walkers were called by the Greeks—neither practises Yoga Vidya, nor is visibly depolarized by a living magnetiser, and yet his body also rises from the earth, light as a cotton-flake or thistledown. If this happens, where is the cause; for cause there must be, since miracle is an impossibility? Modern Spiritualists as we are informed vaguely ascribe the fact to the agency of the disembodied spirits of their dead friends, but have given no sufficient explanation of the method employed. One of their most intelligent writers—Miss Blackwell, who won the gold medal of the British N. A. S. for her essay on Spiritualism—attributes it to "jets or currents of magneto-vital force," which sounds vaguely scientific, to say the least. To follow out this branch of the subject would cause too wide a digression for our present purpose. Suffice it that the medium's body is depolarized, or differently polarized, by some force external to him, which we have no warrant for ascribing to the voluntary action of living spectators.

Another branch of this great subject of Laghima is reserud- for our next article. The more it is studied, the more cumve lative is the proof that Patanjali was a master of Psychology.

History affords many proofs that even inanimate objects, such among others, as huge bronze and marble statues, may be differently polarized, and illustrate the condition of *Laghima.* It being an established maxim that it is easy to learn from an enemy, let us first call the Heathen-hating, Pope-adoring bigot Des Mousseaux of France, to the witness-stand. This contemporary champion of Roman Catholicism is a voluminous and sharp writer, but in his eagerness to prove the divinity of his own religion unwittingly gives the most numerous proofs of the superiority of the despised Heathen in psychological science. True, he ascribes every phenomenon to the Devil, but few readers of this journal will be frightened by this poor tattered 'bogey'. In his " Les Hauts Phenomenes de la Magie" he admits that "several thousand" of these animated statues are noticed by unexceptionable witnesses, and bids us stand aghast at these evidences of diabolical interference in the affairs of men. He quotes from Titus Livy the account of the statue of Juno at Veii—the Eutruscan rival of Rome—which miraculously answered the taunting question of a Roman soldier at the sack of the city by Camillus. " Juno", said the soldier, " will it please you to quit the walls of Veii and settle yourself at Rome ?" The statue inclined its head to signify assent, and then audibly replied, "Yes, I will;" whereupon, being lifted upon the shoulders of the conquerors, the huge image " seemed instantly to lose its weight, and rather follow them, as it were, than make itself carried." According to Dionysius of Halicarnassus (*Ant.*, book I, ch. xv.) the household gods (*penates*), carried away from the Troad to Lavinium and placed in a new temple, rose from their pedestals and floated back to their old places, though the temple doors were fast shut; and this happened a second time. In M. Bresseur de Bourbourg's "Histoire de Mexique" (Vol. II, p. 588, and V. III, p. 664) is mentioned a curious building—no less than a prison for gods. Herein were confined by chains and under secure bolts and locks, the tutelar gods of the people conquered by the Mexicans, under the belief that, as long as these images could be prevented from transporting themselves back to their own countries, their several ward-nations would be kept under subjection; which proves that under its local Mexican name Patanjali's Laghima science was generally known to those ancient people of India's antipodes.

Lucian (*de Syria Dea*) describes a scene of which he was an eye-witness in a temple of Apollo. When the god wished to express his will his statue would move on its pedestal; if not immediately taken, upon their shoulders, by the priests, it would sweat, and "come forth into the middle of the room." When being carried, the statue would become preternaturally light in weight, and once Lucian, the sceptic and priest-scoffer, saw it levitated. "I will relate" says he, "another thing also which he did *in my presence.* The priests were bearing him upon their shoulders—he left them below upon the ground while he himself was borne aloft and alone into the air." In the mouth of such an unbeliever and shrewd observer as Lucian is known to have been, this testimony is of great importance.

We have thus purposely drawn upon other than Aryan or other cis-Himalayan sources for the proof we needed of the existence of a Laghima property in nature. Since our Indian youth are having so poor an opinion of their own literature, they may be willing to see the case proved without recourse to it. And doubtless, after running around the circle of foreign authority, and then stooping to consult some humble *shastri* about the contents of the Veda and later home wirtings, they may discover that their own ancestors were not such superstitious fools, after all, but did, in fact, give the Western world its entire patrimony of philosophy and spiritual science. Following out the same policy, let us transfer to these pages from those of the *Quarterly Journal of Science* (February, 1875), a list of æthrobats whom the Roman Catholics have canonized into saints, and which the Editor (Mr. Crookes) takes from the

Bolandists' *Acta*, giving volume and page in each instance. Before doing so, however, we will premise by saying, for the benefit of our Oriental readers, who this Mr. William Crookes is. This gentleman is one of the most eminent living chemists of England, and among the best known throughout the Western world. His attention has for years been largely given to the application of chemical science to the development of the useful arts, and in this direction has done a deal of important and valuable work. He discovered (in 1863) the new metal *Thallium,* and gave to modern science that delicate little instrument, the Radiometer, which measures the force in the heat rays of a beam of light. One of the cleverest of the Fellows of the Royal Society, and Editor of the *Quarterly Journal of Science,* he felt it his bounden duty, in the summer of 1870, to investigate mediumistic phenomena and expose the fraud, if such it should prove to be. Before entering upon the inquiry, he laid down with minute particularity the tests that exact science would demand before accepting the phenomena as manifestations that a new force had declared itself. So sternly exacting did they seem, that the whole scientific body applauded his intention, and prematurely rejoiced over the certain exposure of the 'humbug.' But the end was not to be as expected; the 'new force' beat Mr. Crookes completely, upset all his theories, confounded and shocked the Royal Society, immeasurably strengthened the Spiritualist party, and gave such an impetus to this branch of scientific enquiry as to threaten a total reconstruction of Westren ideas of Force and Matter. Though Mr. Crookes' inquiry first occupied itself with the simple percussive sounds, called 'raps,' it soon widened so as to embrace the visible apparition of 'materialized spirits,' and, later, the question of levitation.

The consideration of this part of the subject led to the appearance of the article from which we will now quote the abovementioned list of æthrobats whom the Roman Catholic church has crowned as 'saints':

Forty levitated Persons, Canonized or Beatified.

Name, Country, and Condition.	Date of Life.	Acta Sanct.	Vol.	Pages.
Andrew Salus, Scythian Slave	880- 946	May.	VI	16*
Luke of Soterium, Greek Monk... ...	890- 946	Feb.	II	85
Stephen I., King of Hungary	978-1038	Sept.	I	541
Ladislaus I., Ditto (his grandson) ...	1041-1096	June.	V	318
Christina, Flemish Nun	1150-1220	July	V	656
St. Dominic, Italian Preacher	1170-1221	Aug.	I	405,573
Lutgard, Belgian Nun	1182-1246	June	III	238
Agnes of Bohemia, Princess	1205-1281	March	I	522
Humiliana of Florence, Widow	1219-1246	May	IV	396
Jutta, Prussian Widow Hermit... ...	1215-1264	May	VII	606
St. Bonaventure, Italian Cardinal ...	1221-1274	July	III	827
St. Thomas Aquinas, Italian Friar ...	1227-1274	March	I	670-1
Ambrose Sansedonius, Italian Priest...	1220-1287	March	III	192
Peter Armengol, Spanish Priest... ...	1238-1304	Sept.	I	334
St. Albert, Sicilian Priest	1240-1306	Aug.	II	236
Princess Margaret of Hungary	1242-1270	Jan.	II	904
Robert of Solentum, Italian Abbot ..	1273-1341	July	IV	503
Agnes of Mt. Politian, Italn. Abbess..	1274 1317	April	II	794
Bartholus of Vado, Italian Hermit...	1309	June	II	1007
Princess Elizabeth of Hungary	1297-1338	May	II	126
Catharine Columbina, Spanish Abbess	1387	July	VII	352
St. Vincent Ferrer, Span. Missionary.	1359-1419	April	I	497
Coleta of Ghent, Flemish Abbess ...	1381-1447	March	I	559,576
Jeremy of Panormo, Sicilian Friar ...	1381-1452	March	I	297
St. Antonine, Archbishop of Florence.	1489-1459	May	I	335
St. Francis of Paola, Missionary ...	1440-1507	April	I	117
Osanna of Mantua, Italian Nun	1450-1505	June	III	703, 705
Bartholomew of Anghiera, Friar ...	1510	March	II	665
Columba of Rieti, Italian Nun	1468-1501	May	V	332*-4,*360*
Thomas, Archbishop of Valencia ...	1487-1555	Sept.	V	832, 969
St. Ignatius Loyola, Sp. Soldier... ...	1491-1556	July	VII	432
Peter of Alcantara, Spanish Friar ...	1499 1562	Oct.	VIII	672, 673, 687
St. Philip Neri, Italian Friar	1515-1595	May	VI	590
Salvator de Hortâ, Spanish Friar ...	1520 1567	March	II	679-80

St. Luis Bertrand, Sp. Missionary ...	1526-1581	Oct.	V	407, 483
St. Theresa, Spanish Abbess	1515-1582	Oct.	VII	399
John á Cruce, Spanish Priest	1542-1591	Oct.	VII	239
J. B. Piscator, Roman Professor ...	1586	June	IV	976
Joseph of Cupertino, Italian Friar ...	1603-1663	Sept.	V	1020-2
Bonaventure of Potenza, Italian Friar.	1651-1711	Oct.	XII	154, 157-9

The compiler, Mr. Crookes, adds the following reflections :

"As the lives of all these are pretty fully recorded, we have the means of drawing several generalisations. It is plain that all displayed the qualities most distinctive of the present "spirit-mediums" and many were accompanied from childhood by some of the same phenomena, though I find nothing resembling the "raps". The herditary nature of their gifts is shown by the Hungarian royal family producing five examples ; and it is also notable, on this head, that out of 40 there should not be one of British or French birth, although some of the most remarkable spent much of their lives in France, and all other Christian races seem represented. A feature absolutely common to the whole 40 is great asceticism. Only four married, and all were in the habit of extreme fasting, "macerating" their bodies either with hair shirts or various irons under their clothes, and many of submitting to bloody flagellations. Again, all, without exception, were ghost-seers, or second-sighted ; and all subject to trances, either with loss of consciousness only, or of its motion and flexibility too, in which case they were often supposed dead; and the last in our list, after lying in state for three days, and being barbarously mutilated by his worshippers for relics, was unquestionably finally buried alive.* Many were levitated only in these unconscious states; others, as Joseph of Cupertino (the greatest æthrobat in all history), both in the trance and ordinary state, and (like Mr. Home) most frequently in the latter : while a very few, as Theresa, seem to have been always conscious when in the air. Several were,

* This appalling story of insane superstition, to be paralleded probably among no non-Catholic people on earth, will be found in *Acta Sanctorum Octobris*, Vol. XII., pp. 158-60.

in certain states, fire-handlers, like Mr. Home. The Princess Margaret was so from the age of ten. Many had what was called the "gift of tongues," that is, were caused (doubtless in an obsessed state) to address audiences of whose language they were ignorant. Thus the Spaniard, Vincent Ferrer, is said to have learnt no language but his own, though he gathered great audiences in France, Germany, England and Ireland. Connected with this, we should note how general a quality of these persons was eloquence. All the men (except the two kings), and most of the women, were great preachers, though few wrote anything, except Bonaventure and Thomas in the thirteenth century, and Theresa in the sixteenth, who were the greatest Catholic writers of their ages. It is also very notable that the list contains the founders of six religious orders—the first special preaching order, Dominicans, the Jesuate Nuns, Minim Friars, Jesuits, Carmelite Nuns, and Oratorians; and all of these, except the second, great and durable.

"The great majority of them, though often seen suspended, were at heights from the ground described only as "a palm," half a cubit, a cubit, and thence up to five or six cubits, or, in a few cases, ells. But the Princess Agnes and the Abbess Coleta were, like Elijah, carried out of sight, or into the clouds and Peter of Alcantara and Joseph of Cupertino to the ceilings of lofty buildings. The times that these and others were watched off the ground often exceeded an hour; and the archbishop of Valencia (1555) was suspended in a trance 12 hours, so that not only all the inmates of his palace and clergy, but innumerable lay citizens, went to see the marvel. On recovery with the missal he had been reading in his hand, he merely remarked he had lost the place.* In this and all cases the

* This prelate, the annual income of whose see was 18,000 ducats, had no sooner settled in his palace than he got rid of all luxurious furniture, and made it a hospital or poor-house; himself often sleeping on straw, if beds ran short for the paupers. Charles V. had named another person for this see, but the secretary to whom he was dictating mistook the name, and taking another paper said, "I imagined your Majesty to have said Thomas of Villanova, but the error will soon be rectified." The Emperor said, "By no means: the mistake was providential; let it stand."

subjects were either praying at the time, or speaking or listening to a particular religious topic that, in each case, is recorded to have generally affected that person either with trance or levitation. We have seen that Apollonius vanished on declaiming his favourite verse of Homers. So the topic of the Incarnation would cause Peter of Alcantara to utter a frightful cry, and shoot through the air "*ut sclopeto emissus videretur;*" that ot Mary's birth would have a like effect on Joseph of Cupertino; and Theresa, after obtaining by prayer the cessation of her early levitations, was yet obliged to avoid hearing John à Cruce on the Trinity, finding that this topic would cause both him and her to be raised with their chairs from the floor. A contemporary painting of them in the position, beside the grating where it occurred, has been engraved in the volume above cited. Joseph of Cupertino, on entering any church having a Madonna or his patron, St. Francis, as an altarpiece, would be borne straight thereto, crying, "My dear mother!" or "My father!" and remain with his arms and robe so among the candles as to alarm all with the danger of his catching fire; but always flying back to the spot whence he had risen. Others were raised up to images or pictures, as the Abbess Agnes in early girlhood, often before a crucifix, "in tantum eam arripuit amor Sponsi sui, quód relictà tam altê fuit corpus suum purissimum sublevatum in aère, quód ipsi imagini, supra altare in eminenti loco positæ, se pari situ conjunxit; ubi osculans et amplexans, visa est super Dilectum suum innixa."

"Of invisible transfer to a distance, the only subjects seem to have been Columba of Rietti, said to have been carried from her mother's house in that town to the nunnery that afterwards received her at Spoleto, 20 miles distant; and the river transits of Peter of Alcantara. The lives of Joseph of Cupertino, indeed, allege that the rare miracle of "geminatio corporis," or bodily presence in two distant places the same day, was twice vouchsafed to him while dwelling at Rome—once to assist at the death-bed of a named old man of his native village, whom he had promised to attend if possible; and again at the death of his mother. It is also related of the great Spanish æthrobat that, while the business of a Jubilee detained him at Madrid (1556-9), a lady, Elvira de Caravajal, in Estremadura, declared her resolve to have no other confessor till Father Peter might be within reach; and the same day he presented himself at her castle announcing that he had been brought expressly from Madrid, and that she ought not to choose confessors so distant. There is doubtless plenty of exaggeration, and many stories of this kind must be apocryphal, but the notable fact is that they are told only of the same persons as the fully attested levitations and other phenomena parallel to the modern so-called Spiritism."

The student of Patanjali will remark two facts in connection with these air-walkers,—*they were all ascetics*, and not only were all but four unmarried, and, presumably, chaste, but inflicted upon their bodies the extreme rigors of maceration, that is to say that same stern repression of the physical appetites and desire which is common among our Indian Yogis and Sannyasis. Though they knew not the fact, they were in reality practising the extremest austerities of the Yoga system. Another fact will not fail to be observed, viz., that the thaumaturgic power was in several cases hereditary. We of the East know how often it happens that this abundance of psychical power passes down the generations in certain families—that, in short, there are 'born magicians' as certainly as there are born poets, painters, or sculptors. If we may credit the records of Western Spiritualism the quality of 'mediumship' is also known to run in families. Neither of these examples of heredity will surprise any student of either physiology or psychology, for the annals of the race are full of proof that the child is but the evolution of his double line of ancestors, with, in individual cases, a tendency to 'breed back' to some one relative on either paternal or maternal side. Among the most interesting of English medical writers upon this subject is Dr. Charles Elam, of London. Though not a professed psycholgist, he has collected in his "A Physician's Problems" some most valuable data for the student of that science, supplementing them with judicious and intelligent criticism. "The various races of men," he says, (*Op. cit.* p. 33.) "have characteristics quite as distinctly marked ... But *races consist of individuals*: it is clear therefore, that to a certain extent individuals have the power of *transmitting their own specific psychical nature.*" M. Giron, a great physiologist, remarks that "acquired capacities are transmitted by generation, and this transmission is more certain and perfect in proportion as the cultivation has extended over more generations." Sir H. Holland, Esquirol, Dr. Virey, Montaigue, Riecken, Baethius, among moderns, and Hippocraetes, Homer, Horace, Juvenal, among ancients, are a few of the great authorities who have noticed the constant assertion of this law of nature. Herodotus, the 'Father of History' to Western people, who knew nothing of our Indian literature, mentions the heritage of caste, of profession, and of moral and intellectual qualities. He speaks of Evenius as possessing the power of divination and transmitting it, *as a natural consequence*, to his son, Deiphonus. Men of Eastern birth may, in considering these facts, the more readily understand why so many more great psychologists and philosophers have flourished in this part of the world than in the West, where the rugged conditions of life, especially the climate, food, and the common use of stimulating beverages, have so largely tended to the development of the animal, at the expense of the spiritual, nature, ever since the exodus of people from the warm Eastern climes to settle in those countries. The love of mystical study, and the tendency to practice ascetism are inherent in our blood, and absorbed through our mothers' milk. Generations after generations of white men pass away without producing a single adept of the Secret Science, while it would be hard to find a parallel to this in India—even in these degenerate days, when our cleverest young scholars are worshipping Wertern idols, and it almost seems as if the very recollection of Yoga and the Yogis were dying out of the popular mind.

(*Summary of Patanjali's Sutra by*) *Mr. J. C. Thomson.*

In the first Chapter of Patanjali's Sutras, contemplation is described as two fold :—First संप्रज्ञात, the first exercise of contemplation, in which reason still works; but the object of which is to destroy the consciousness of one's individual existence, and to bring the mind to that state, in which it is entirely oblivious of the reality of all external matter, and is convinced that the soul is actually connected and united with the Supreme One. The object towards which this contemplation is directed is either nature, comprising the whole universe or one's own soul. It is then divided into the following four stages :—

1 As to the distinction between the name of a thing and the thing named. The internal repetition of the name accompained by conception of the thing named until at last all distinction is lost between the name and the thing named; so that when the Yogin, ar practiser of Yoga, internally pronounces the word ईश्वर, or Deity, the name of the Supreme Being, he may have the form of that Being vividly pictured on his mind.

11 Losing by constant practice all distinction of form, time and place; so that he may, and eventually does believe himself to be any thing at any time and anywhere.

111 The constant association of nature प्रकृति, and spirit पुरुष until he imagines the latter only to exist in everything loses the sense of the existence of matter generally and of his own body in particular, and thus becomes mentally bodiless विदेहि.

IV A stage in which his own individual existence अहंकार appears to be a mere reflection on his sensibility मनस and the Supreme Being alone is manifest.

Second, असंप्रज्ञात contemplation, in which reason is lost sight of ; a complete restraint of the action of thought; the last stage of mental abstraction; in which even the reflection of his individual existence is lost sight of, and he is mentally one with the Supreme Being.

These are the stages of contemplation which lead to final emancipation. The first steps towards entering on these stages are three:—

I. The abandonment of all worldly interests, hopes, desires, love or hate; by means of which the Yogin, or devotee, overcomes the five obstacles to Yoga, viz. pain, grief, trembling, asthmatic breathing, and sighing.

II. प्राणायाम-A peculiar exercise, which consists in restraining the breath, sometimes performed by closing the right nostril with the thumb, while breath is inhaled through the left, then closing both, and at length opening the right nostril in order to exhale, and so on. During this exercise, his thoughts should be fixed on the localities of the organs of sense, such as the tip of the nose, the point of the tongue, the drum of the ear, &c. &c. until he identifies these with the Supreme Being. Again, he should place his thoughts on external visible objects such as the Sun, the Moon, Fire, &c., or within his own heart, or at the bottom of his throat or at the centre of his skull. The heart is the supposed seat of the soul, and its supposed passage at death is through the coronal artery passing through the throat to the centre of the skull, and thence on a beam of the Sun, to the Moon, through Fire up to the Sun and so on to the Supreme Being. By fixing his thoughts on these localities, he imagines that his soul is actually taking this final journey, and is thus mentally emancipated.

III. In muttering the names and attributes of the Deity. He should so completely associate them with the Being they indicate, that he at last finds himself mentally in the presence of that Being.

In the second Chapter it is shown that these exercises prepare the Yogin for perfect knowledge (विज्ञान), which is further acquired by the following eight stages of Yoga:—

1st. यम, or self-government, is of five kinds:

a. Freedom from any wish to injure others.

b. Truth in reference to words and thoughts.

c. Freedom from appropriation of others' property in thought, word or deed.

d. The subjection of one's members, in order to overcome desire.

e. Renunciation of all indulgences of pleasure.

2nd. नियम, or self-restraint, is of five kinds:—

a. Purity of mind and body.

b. Cheerfulness under all circumstances.

c. Religious austerity.

d. Repetition of incantation.

e. The association of all Religious ceremonies with the Supreme Being.

3rd. आसन, The ascetic posture admits of 84 varieties, each more uncomfortable than the last, in which the Yogin must by degrees become quite easy.

4th. प्राणायाम, Restraint of the breath, already described.

5th. प्रत्याहार, Complete control over the senses and organs. Exclusive Meditation on the Supreme Being, and the withdrawal of the senses from all external objects, compared in the भगवद्गीता to the tortoise gathering its limbs together under its shell.

These exercises are continued in the third Chapter, which afterwards treats of the transcendental powers (विभूति) aquired by them.

6th. धारणा, Steady immoveble abstraction.

7th. ध्यान, Exclusive meditation of the Supreme Being.

8th. समाधि, Continual concentration of thought, by means of which all external objects, and even one's own individuality are forgotten, and the mind fixed completely and immoveably on the One Being.

These last three exercises constitute संयम (*Sanyama*) or perfect concentration; and when the Yogi has arrived at perfection in them, he obtains innumerable superhuman powers, of which the following 25 are enumerated:—

1st. Knowledge of the past, present and future things.

2nd. By fixing his mind on words, knowledge of universal sciences.

3rd. By the same on the lines in his hands, knowledge of his former states of existence.

4th. On the hearts of others, knowledge of their thoughts.

5th. On his own person, invisibility of form.

6th. On his own actions, knowledge of their future consequences.

7th. On compassion and sympathy, a feeling of beneficence to all beings.

8th. On strength, perfect strength.

9th. On the Sun, the power, like it, of viewing all things.

10th. On the Moon, knowledge of astronomy.

11th. On the Polar star, knowledge of the constellations.

12th. On the heart and stomach, knowledge of anatomy.

13th. On the bottom of the throat, freedom from hunger and thirst.

14th. On the nerve in the throat, called कूर्मा, (*Kurmi*) rigidity of posture.

15th. On the universality of मनस, (*Manas*) knowledge of all invisible objects.

16th. On the seat of the mind, knowledge of the thoughts, past, present and future, of himself and others.

17th. On the state of a Yogi when emancipated, knowledge and sight of the spirit unassociated with matter.

In the last Chaptar the कैवल्य (*Kaivalya*) or state of emancipation even during life is described. This is the जिवन्मुक्ति (*Jivan Mukti*) of which we have already spoken. It is the highest state of Yoga before the soul is actually re-absorded into the Supreme Being. The body still exists, and of course the soul exists within it, but its connection with it is supposed to be entirely broken, and the soul can consequently quit and re-enter the body, and wander about where and as it lists. In this condition it is supposed to attain the remaining eight transcendental powers विभूती (*Vibhûti*):—

18th. The power of entering a living or dead body and causing it to act as if it were its own.

19th. Extreme lightness.

20th. Resplendent brilliancy.

21st. The power of hearing sound, however distant, even from the other worlds.

22nd. Of transforming himself into each or all of the five elements.

23rd. Of passing and penetrating anywhere.

24th. Of changing the course of Nature.

25th. Of final liberation.

These last are variously given, and the following names will spare us the trouble, and the reader the tedium, of examining these variations. अणिमा (*Animâ*) "extreme minuteness;" लघिमा (*Laghimá*) "lightness;" प्राप्ति (*Prápti*) "attainment of any object;" प्राकाम्य (*Prákámya*) "fulfilment of every wish;" महिमा (*Mahimá*) "size;" ईशिता (*Isitá*) "supremacy;" वशिता (*Vasita*), "power (over nature);" कामावशिता. (*Kámávasita*) "attainment of every wish."

The Yogi thus passes through four principal stages—

1st. He learns the rules of Yoga.

2nd. He acquires perfect knowledge.

3rd. He employs this knowledge practically, and overcomes the material influence of the primary elements.

4th. He destroys all consciousness of personality and individuality अहंकार (*Ahankára*), and the soul thus becomes free from matter.

Such are the details given by Ward and Windischmann of Patanjali's doctrines * * * If we arrogate for the सांख्य (*Sankhya*), the honor of having systematized philosophical theories at an age when Greece could boast of nothing more advanced than a Lycurgus, or of anticipating by some three and twenty centuries the denial of a void in the enlightened West, we may at least call पातञ्जली (*Pátanjali*) the Mesmer, and more than the Mesmer of India. Sufficient praise be it to the mystic old Bráhman to have inferred amid darkness and ignorance, the *Vast powers of the mind and the will, and to have claimed for the soul the noble capability of making the body and even external matter its slave.*

(LIFE OF PATANJALI.)

The Rudra Jamala the Vrihannandikeshwara and the Padma-purana, supply some information respecting this sage to whom the Patanjali school of philosophy owes its origin, and who wrote a work on the civil and canon law. He is said to have been born in Illavrita Varsha, where his father Angira and his mother Sati resided, and that immediately on his birth he made known things past, persent and future. He married Lolupa, whom he found on the north of Sumeru, in the hollow of a "Vata" tree, and is said to have lived as a mendicant to a great age. Being insulted by the inhabitants of Bhotabhàndàra, while engaged in religious austerities, he reduced them to ashes by fire from his mouth.

He taught that the Divine Spirit and the soul of man were distinct; that the former was free from passion, but not the latter; that God was possessed of form, or was to be seen by the Yogis; that he is placable, glorious, the creator, preserver, and the destroyer of all things; that the universe first arose from his will or command, and that he infused into the system a power of perpetual progression; that the truth of things was discoverable by the senses, by experience, comparison and revelation; that some material things were unchangeable, and others changeable: and that the latter pass through six changes, such as birth, increase, &c., that every thing arose from five elements, fire, water &c ; that knowledge is of five sorts, certain, uncertain, &c ; that there are five kinds of men: those who are governed by their passions, the wrathful, the benevolent, the pious and those who are free from worldly attachments: that emancipation is to be obtained by Yoga, that is by perfect abstraction of mind.

LIST OF ERRATA.

Page.	Line.	Errata.	Corrections.
xxiii	1	Reserud	Reserved.
,,	2	Cumvelative	Cumulative.
xxiv	29	Wirtings	Writings.
xxv	18	Seience	Science.
xxvii	34	Parelleded	Paralleled.
xxix	8	Ot	Of.
xxxi	35	Wertern	Western.
xxxv	35	Re-absorded	Re-absorbed.
		Book I.	
1	12	Vernerable	Venerable.
3	9	Follws	Follows.
,,	20	lntern	Internal.
7	15	Knowldge	Knowledge.
12	15	,,	,,
18	6	Penomenal	Phenomenal.
20	26	Ahh	Aph.
22	11	Mecditotion	Meditation.
26	6	Undersirable	Undesirable.
29	25	Repectively	Respectively.
41	6	Avishistalina	Avishistalinga.
,,	9	Alina	Alinga,
47	7	Whsch	Which.
		Book II.	
71	13	Is lation	Isolation.
72	19	Sh—od	Should.
83	2	Abscnse	Absence.
		Book III.	
129	10	Distruction	Destruction.
129	34	O	Q.
138	27	Perceving	Perceiving.
		Book IV.	
142	29	Husbanman	Husbandman.
157	8	Pecipient	Percipient.
162	19	Dificient	Deficient.
164	13	Unintellignt	Unintelligent.
166	15	tne	the.
167	6	Passessed	Possessed.
		Appendix.	
183	3	Fram	From.
189	15	Rielgion	Religion.
191	17	Deligently	Diligently.
194	36	qe	Be.
196	12	Beathing	Breathing.
201	1	Propells	Propels.
211	18	Extolls	Extols.
214	19	Deliverence	Deliverance.

THE

SÁNKHYA

OR

YOGA APHORISMS

OF

PATANJALI.

INTRODUCTION.

a. Salutation to Ganésa! May that union of the twin-persons of Shiva and his spouse,—by the recollection of which one enjoys emancipation, hard as it is to attain,—produce for you all blessings!*

b. From such passages of the scripture as this—viz.—"NA'CHIKETA having received this science [viz. the Vedánta] declared to him by Yama, and all the rules of the *yoga*, and having arrived at the Supreme Soul, became passionless and immortal:—whosoever else also thus knows the Supreme Spirit, &c.,"—it is inferred that the rules of the *yoga* ought to be understood and practised by those who are desirous of emancipation. Therefore, the vernerable PATANJALI, being about to exhibit the rules of the *yoga*, in order to gain the attention of his disciples, states as follows the doctrines of that science.†

---

* श्री गणेशायनमः। देहार्द्धयोगश्शिवयोस्स श्रेयांसि तनोतु वः। दुष्प्रापमपि यत्स्मृत्या जनः कैवल्यमश्नुते॥

† मृत्युप्रोक्तां नाचिकेतो ऽथ लब्ध्वा विद्यामेतां योग विधिञ्चकृत्स्नं॥ ब्रह्मप्राप्तो विरजो ऽभूद्विमृत्युरन्यो ऽप्येवंयो वेदाध्यात्ममेवेत्यादिश्रुतिषु मुमुक्षूणां योगविधिरनुष्ठेयत्वेन श्रेयतयावगम्यते ऽतोयोगविधिमुपादिदिक्षुर्भगवान् पतञ्जलिश्शिष्यावधानाय तच्छास्त्रारम्भं प्रतिजानीते॥

अथातो योगानुशासनम् ॥ १ ॥

The subject proposed.

Aph. 1.—Now, then, the exposition of *yoga* or Concentration [is to be made].

a. The expression 'Now, then,' intimates [that] a [distinct] topic [here commences]; and it serves as a benediction* [—the particle *atha* being regarded an auspicious one].

b. The word *yoga,* from the root *yuj* 'to keep the mind fixed in abstract meditation,' means such a restraining of the exercise of the mind, or Concentration.†

c. An 'exposition' is that whereby something is expounded, or declared, through its characteristic marks, its nature, &c. An 'exposition of the *yoga,*'—[such is the meaning of the compound word *yogánúsáshana.*] This [—viz, the expounding of the nature, &c., of Concentration—] is to be understood to be the topic even to the end of this Institute‡ [of PATANJALI'S].

d. But what *is* Concentration *(yoga)*? To this he replies §—

योगश्चित्तवृत्तिनिरोधः ॥ २ ॥

Concentration defined.

Aph 2.—Concentration (*yoga*) is the hindering of the modifications of the thinking principle.

a. That is to say,—Concentration is the hindering, or the preventing, of the modifications—to be described hereafter [see § 5] —of the Mind or internal organ [—to which modifications the internal organ is liable when allowed to come into contact with objects, as will be explained further on—]; and this 'hindering' is a super-sensual species of effort which is the cause of the destruction of these modifications.||

---

* अथशब्दोऽधिकारद्योतको मङ्गलार्थश्च ॥

† युक्तिर्योगस्समाधानं । युज समाधौ ॥

‡ अनुशिष्यते व्याख्यायते लक्षणस्वरूपादिभिर्येन तदनुशासनं योगस्यानुशासनं योगानुशासनम् । तदाशास्त्रपरिसमाप्तेरधिकृतं बोद्धव्यम् ॥

§ को योग इत्यत आह ॥

|| चित्तस्यान्तःकरणस्य वक्ष्यमाणा या वृत्तयस्तासां निरोधो निवर्त्तनं योग इत्यर्थः । निवर्त्तनञ्चातीन्द्रियः प्रयत्नविशेषोवृत्तिविलयहेतुरिति ॥

b. But then [a doubt may here occur]. It is a tenet [—see Nyáya Aphorisms No. 31—] both of the *Sánkhya* and the *Yoga* that the soul just consists of the knowledge which has as its objects the modifications [in question—the two being united] like fire and the wood [or fuel of the fire]:—on the destruction of the modifications, then, the Soul too should be annihilated, as the fire is in the absence of the fuel :—and therefore, at the time of Concentration, what is the soul concerned about? With reference to this he declares as follws:*—

तदा द्रष्टुः स्वरूपे ऽवस्थानम् ॥ ३ ॥

Condition of the soul during concentration.

Aph. 3.—Then [i. e. at the time of Concentration] it [the Soul] abides in the form of the spectator [without a spectacle.]

a. 'Then';—i. e. at that time.†

b. 'In the form of the spectator;—i. e. of soul [—see *Tattwa-samása* §31—], in the form of Thought simply [without any object thought of]. 'Its state is' :—such is the force of the term *avasthánam*‡ [rendered 'it abides,' &c.]

c. And so the definition [of Concentration] is this, that concentration is the hindering of the modifications of the internal organ, thy which [prevention of its being modified] is the cause of the abiding in the form of soul simply.§

d. What then is the form of this [Soul] when in a state other than that of Concentration? To this he replies:||—

वृत्तिसारूप्यमितरत्र ॥ ४ ॥

Condition of the soul at other times.

Aph. 4.—At other times [than that of Concentration] it [the soul] is in the same form as the modifications [of the internal organ—§ 2. *b.* and 5.]

---

* ननु वृत्तिविषयकबोधस्वरूप एव पुरुषः काष्ठाग्निवदिति सांख्ययोगयोः सिद्धान्तो वृत्तिविलये पुरुषोऽपि नश्येत्काष्ठापायेऽग्निवत्ततश्च योगकाले कः पुरुषार्थः इत्याकाङ्क्षायामाह ॥

† तदा तस्मिन् काले ॥

‡ द्रष्टुः पुरुषस्य स्वरूपे । चिन्मात्रस्वरूपे । अवस्थानं । स्थितिर्भवति ॥

§ तथाच द्रष्टुः स्वरूपावस्थितिहेतुश्चित्तवृत्तिनिरोधो योग इति लक्षणम् ॥

|| व्युत्थानदशायां तस्य किं स्वरूपमित्यत आह ॥

a. 'At other times;'—i. e. at another time than that of Concentration. The 'modifications' are those that are to be described [see § 5]. To be 'in the same form' as these—means to consist of these. The meaning [of the whole] is that when the internal organ [or Mind], through the senses, is affected [or modified] by the form of some object, the soul also [viewing the object through its organ the Mind] is as it were altered into that form, as the moon [reflected] in the moving ripples of the water, looks as if that orb itself were moving*.

b. Well, then:—it was stated that the modifications [of the internal organ] are to be hindered. Of how many kinds, then, are these [modifications], or what are they like? To this he replies:†—

वृत्तयः पञ्चतय्यः क्लिष्टा अक्लिष्टाः ॥ ५ ॥

The modifications of the thinking principle, how many and what like.

Aph. 5.—The Modifications [of the internal organ] are of five kinds, [and they are either] painful or not painful.

a. 'Modifications';—i. e. various altered states of the internal organ. 'Of five kinds,' or of five sorts. 'Painful';—i. e. invaded by vexations which will be defined in the sequel. 'Not painful';—i. e. the reverse thereof.‡

b. Which are those five Modifications? With reference to this, he states:§—

प्रमाणविपर्ययविकल्पनिद्रास्मृतयः ॥ ६ ॥

---

* इतरत्र योगादन्यस्मिन्काले । वृत्तयो वक्ष्यमाणलक्षणाः । ताभिस्सारूप्यं तद्रूपत्वं । अयमर्थश्चित्ते इन्द्रियद्वारा विषयाकारेण परिणते सति पुरुषस्तदाकार इव परिभाव्यते यथा जलतरङ्गेषु चलत्सु चन्द्रश्चलन्निव भवति तद्वदिति ॥

† ननु वृत्तयो निरोद्धव्या इत्युक्तं । ताः पुनः कियत्प्रकाराः कीदृश्यो वेत्याकाङ्क्षायामाह ॥

‡ वृत्तयश्चित्तपरिणामविशेषाः । पञ्चतय्यः पञ्चप्रकाराः । क्लिष्टाः क्लेशैर्वक्ष्यमाणलक्षणैराक्रान्ताः अक्लिष्टास्तद्विपरीताः ॥

§ कास्ताः पञ्च वृत्तय इत्याकाङ्क्षायामाह ॥

These Modifications specified.

Aph. 6.—[The modifications of the internal organ are] evidence [or right notion], misconception, fancy, sleep, and memory.

a. [All this is] clear.*

b. He defines these [modifications] in their order.†

प्रत्यक्षानुमानागमाः प्रमाणानि ॥ ७ ॥

Right notions.

Aph. 7.—The evidences [§6.] are Perception, Inference, and Testimony.

a. Here [—it will be observed—] without stating the definition of the several kinds of evidence, this being so familiarly known, he has only divided them. [Lest, however, the reader should require the information, we may remark, in passing, that] the evidence called Perception is that modification of the internal organ which takes the form of assurance in respect of some object not previously apprehended. Inference is the modification of the internal organ produced from a correct notion of a general proposition, &c. [—respecting objects previously apprehended—as explained in the works of the Nyáya]. And the evidence called Testimony is [what produces] that modification of the internal organ which arises from the words of one worthy‡ [to be received as an authority].

b. Having thus spoken of the modification of the internal organ which consists in evidence [—or, as we should rather say—which consists in the correct state of cognition resulting from good evidence—], he mentions that which is in the shape of misconception.§

विपर्ययो मिथ्याज्ञानमतद्रूपप्रतिष्ठम् ॥८॥

---

* स्पष्टम् ॥

† आसां क्रमेण लक्षणान्याह ॥

‡ अत्रातिप्रसिद्धत्वात् प्रमाणानां लक्षणमनुक्त्वैव विभागः कृतः । तत्रानधिगतार्थनिश्चयरूपा चित्तवृत्तिः प्रत्यक्षं प्रमाणं । व्याप्त्यादिप्रमाणन्या वृत्तिरनुमानं । योग्यशब्दजन्यः वृत्तिश्च शब्दः प्रमाणमिति ॥

§ एवं प्रमाणरूपां वृत्तिं व्याख्याय विपर्ययरूपामाह ॥

Misconception what.

Aph. 8—Misconception is a wrong notion, not staying in the [proper] form of that [in respect whereof the misconception is entertained].

a. [That is to say—] misconception is a notion arising, in respect of something that is *not* so and so, that it *is* so and so; as, in the case of mother o'pearl, the notion of silver. 'Not staying in the [proper] form of that';—that is to say, which does not abide in that form which is the form of that thing [in respect of which the notion is entertained],—which amounts to its not *revealing* the form [or real nature] which belongs to the thing.*

b. [To illustrate this language of our author, we may here state the theory of Understanding which he adopts, as we find it laid down in the *Vedánta Paribháshá.* The internal organ is there compared to water, in respect of its readiness to adapt itself to the form of whatever mould it may enter. "As the water of a reservoir, having issued from an aperture, having entered, by a channel, the basins [or beds with raised edges formed in the fields that require irrigation—] becomes four-cornered or otherwise shaped just like them; so the manifesting internal organ [or Mind,] having gone, through the sight or other channel, to where there is an object, for instance a jar, becomes modified by the form of the jar or other object. It is this altered state [of the internal organ] that is called its modification."† This 'manifesting internal organ,' whilst it is regarded as moulding itself upon the object, is regarded as at the same time manifesting it—or revealing it as a mirror does. To a considerable extent this theory of the Understanding is analogous to the theory of vision entertained by those who

---

* अतथाभूतेऽर्थे तथोत्पद्यमानं ज्ञानं विपर्ययः । यथा शुक्तिकायां रजतज्ञानं अतद्रूपप्रतिष्ठामिति । तस्यार्थस्य यद्रूपं न तस्मिन् रूपे प्रतिष्ठते तस्यार्थस्य यद्रूपं न तत्प्रति भासयतीति यावत् ॥

† यथा तडागोदकं छिद्रान्निर्गत्य कुल्यात्मना केदारान् प्रविश्य तद्वदेव चतुष्कोणाद्याकारं भवति तथा तैजसमन्तःकरणमपि चक्षुरादिद्वारा घटादिविषयदेशं गत्वा घटादि विषयाकारेण परिणमते । स एव परिणामो वृत्तिरित्युच्यते ॥ वेद॰ परि॰॥

regard the retina as reflecting to the intelligent principle those visible forms of which the retina itself is uncognisant; whilst the intelligent principle itself is cognisant of things visible only inasmuch as they are reflected to it by the retina. ['The modifications' are akin to Locke's 'ideas']

c. Doubt also—for example whether the object be a man or a post—is a wrong notion [§8], inasmuch as the real nature of the object is not thereby revealed.*

d. In order to declare what modification [of the internal organ] is fancy—he says as follows:—†

शब्दज्ञानानुपाती वस्तुशून्यो विकल्पः ॥ ९ ॥

Fanciful notions defined. *Aph.* 9.—A fancy is [a notion] devoid of a thing [in reality corresponding thereto], following upon knowledge [conveyed] by words.

a. 'Knowldge produced [or conveyed] by words:'— [such is the sense of the compound] *'sabda-dnyán,* the habit whereof is to follow this [verbal information],' and that is what is so named [viz. fancy]. The meaning is— that a fancy is a conception, without a thing‡ [corresponding to it].

b. Examples of this are such notions as 'The head of *Ráhu,*' and 'The soul's Thinking,'—and 'Something like the horns of a hare,' &c. Even after [discovering] the absurdity [involved in such notions], people yet deal with verbal knowledge [as if it were strictly receivable] in such senses, [—and it depends upon circumstances whether any serious error would result from this or not.]§

c. [As a hare has no horn, the notion of a hare's horn is a fanciful one, 'devoid of a thing *in rerum natura* corresponding

---

* संशयोऽप्यतद्रूपप्रतिष्ठत्वान्मिथ्याज्ञानं यथा स्थाणुर्वापुरुषो वेति ॥

† विकल्पवृत्तिं व्याख्यातुमाह ।

‡ शब्दजनितं ज्ञानं शब्दज्ञानं । तदनुपातितुं शीलं यस्य स तथोक्तः । वस्तुशून्यः प्रत्ययो विकल्प इत्यर्थः ॥

§ अस्योदाहरणानि । राहोश्शिरः । पुरुषस्य चैतन्यम् । शशशृङ्गतुल्यमित्यादि ज्ञानानि । बोधोत्तरमप्येतादृशज्ञानैश्शब्दज्ञानरूपो व्यवहारः क्रियत इति ।

to the notion.' A person hearing the expression 'The head of *Ráhú'* naturally proceeds to fancy that there is a *Ràhu* to whom this head belongs;—but *Ràhu* is *all* head—being a bodiless monster who is held to cause eclipses by swallowing the sun and the moon, which emerge from obscuration when they come to the end of his dissevered gullet. The notion, therefore, raised by the expression 'The head of *Ráhu,*' that there is any more of him besides the head, is a fancy—equally with that of the hare's horn—'devoid of a thing corresponding to the notion.' So again, a person hearing the expression 'The soul's Thinking,' naturally proceeds to fancy that there is some Soul to whom this Thinking belongs,—whereas the Soul is nothing besides the Thinking. Although, according to the commentator, such expressions are liable to suggest fancies that have nothing in reality corresponding to them, yet the employment of the expressions does not necessarily mislead, if we carefully bear in mind what is the real state of the case. Much on the same principle people in Europe continue to speak of the sun's rising and setting, though, holding the heliocentric theory, they do not really fancy that the sun either rises or sets].

d. In order to declare what is sleep, he says*—

अभावप्रत्ययालम्बना वृत्तिर्निद्रा ॥ १० ॥

Definition of sound sleep.

Aph. 10.—Sleep is that modification [of the internal organ] which depends on the conception of nothing.

a. Of that modification [of the internal organ] the ground is the conception of nothing; this is what is so called† [—viz. sleep].

b. This may be [also] stated as follows:—Sleep is that modification [of the internal organ] which takes place on the quitting of all objects, through [the quality of] Darkness getting everywhere the upper hand‡ [—to the exclusion of the other two

* निद्रां व्याख्यातुमाह । † अभावप्रत्यय आलम्बनं यस्या वृत्तेस्सा तथोक्ता ॥

‡ एतदुक्तं भवति । या सन्ततमुद्रिक्तत्वात्तमसस्समस्त विषयपरित्यागेन प्रवर्त्तते वृत्तिस्सा निद्रेति ॥

qualities, which,—see Lecture on the Sankhya§ 96,—are held to be constituents of the phenomenal universe].

c. And the fact that this [dreamless sleep] *is* a modification [of the internal organ, and not a mere blank,] is proved by our seeing that one recollects [on arising from profound and dreamless sleep] that 'I slept pleasantly:'—and there could not be a *recollection* if there had not been a state of consciousness* [to furnish the matter of the recollection. *Conf.* Lecture on the Vedánta§ 33].

d. In order to describe memory, he says†—

अनुभूतविषयासम्प्रमोषः स्मृतिः ॥ ११ ॥

Memory defined. *Aph.* 11.—Memory is the not letting go of an object that one has been aware of.

a. [That is to say]—memory [or recollection] is the not letting go—or, by means of the self-reproductive quality [of the Soul—see *Tarka Sangraha* p 55]—the arising, in the understanding, of that which has been cognised through evidence‡ [of the senses, for example see § 7].

Waking, sleeping, and dreaming. *b.* Of these [modifications of the internal organ, the three following, viz.] right notion [§ 7. *a.*] misconception [§ 8.] and fancy [§ 9.] are *waking* states. When just these [impressions—in the absence of the objects or of what gave rise to them] are sensible, through the force [or vividness] of the impression, then there is *dream*. But [dreamless] sleep [§ 10] is without any object cognised. And Recollection may take its rise either in a right notion, in a misconception, in a fancy, or in [dreamless] sleep§ [—see§ 10 *c.*]

---

* अस्याश्च सुखमहमस्वाप्समिति स्मृतिदर्शनात् स्मृतेश्चानुभवव्यतिरेकेनानुपपत्तेर्वृत्तित्वम् ॥ † स्मृतिं व्याख्यातुमाह ॥

‡ प्रमाणेनानुभूतस्य विषयस्ययो-यनसम्प्रमोषः संस्कारद्वारेण बुद्धावुपारोहः सा स्मृतिः ॥

§ तत्र प्रमाणविपर्य्ययविकल्पा जाग्रदवस्थाः । त एव यदानुभवबलात्प्रत्यक्षायमाणास्तदा स्वप्नः निद्रात्वसंवेद्यमानविषया । स्मृतिश्च प्रमाणविपर्य्ययविकल्पनिद्रानिमित्ता ॥

c. Having thus described the modifications [of the internal organ], in order to explain the prevention of these [§ 2. *a.*] with the means thereof, he says*—

अभ्यासवैराग्याभ्यां तन्निरोधः ॥ १२ ॥

Exercise and dispassion the means of repelling the transient.

Aph. 12. The hindering of these [modifications of the internal organ—§ 2—is to be effected] by means of exercise and dispassion.

a. ' Exercise and dispassion ' will be defined [in § 13 and 15]. By these [viz. exercise and dispassion], the repelling of those modifications of the internal organ which [modifications, at different times] have the form of revealing, energising, and obstructing,—*this* is the ' hindering'—[which is to be striven after, and which is tantamount to] the resting [of these modifications], in a potential shape, in their cause, viz: in the internal organ† [without taking an actual shape as products of the internal organ modified.]

b. Of the two [viz. exercise and dispassion, §12,] it is from ' dispassion,' which originates in our discerning the perniciousness of the objective, that aversion thereto arises. And, by ' exercise,' confirmed steadfastness [in the indifference towards all objects] is produced. So, by these two, the internal organ is hindered from undergoing modification.‡

d. In order to describe 'exercise' [§12] he says.§—

---

* एवं वृत्तीव्याख्याय सोपायं निरोधं व्याख्यातुमाह ॥

† अभ्यासवैराग्ये वक्ष्यमाणलक्षणे । ताभ्यां तासां प्रकाश प्रवृत्तिनियमरूपाणां चित्तवृत्तीनां यत्प्रतिहननं स निरोधः । स्वकारण एव चित्ते शक्तिरूपतयावस्थानम् ॥

‡ तत्र विषयदोषदर्शनजेन वैराग्येण तद्वैमुख्यमुत्पाद्यते । अभ्यासेनच दृढं स्थैर्यमुत्पाद्यते । इत्याभ्यां भवति चित्तवृत्ति निरोधः ॥

§ अभ्यासं व्याख्यातुमाह ॥

तत्रस्थितौयत्नोऽभ्यासः ॥ १३ ॥

Exercise defined. *Aph.* 13.—'Exercise' is the [repeated] effort that it [—viz. the internal organ—] shall remain in its [unmodified] state.

a. The condition of the internal organ, when free from modification, existing only in its own [unmodified] form, is what we mean by its [unmodified] state. And what we mean by 'exercise' is the effort, or endeavour, again and again to reduce the internal organ to such a condition* [of freedom from modification].

b. He next mentions a special character of this same† [exercise or persevering effort].

स तु दीर्घकालनैरन्तर्यसत्कारसेवितोदृढभूमिः ॥ १४ ॥

Aph. 14—But this [exercise—§ 13—] is a firm position observed out of regard [for the end in view, and perseveringly adhered to] for a long time unintermittingly.

a. That is to say:—it [—exercise—] is a firm ground [or state of steadfastness],—to be firm [we may remark in passing] is to be steadfast,—this [state of steadfastness] being assiduously attended to, during a long time unintermittingly, out of the excess of regard‡ [which one entertains for the end to be gained.]

b. He now mentions the definition of 'dispassion'§ [§ 12]

दृष्टानुश्रविकविषयवितृष्णस्यवशीकारसंज्ञावैराग्यम् ॥ १५ ॥

Dispassion defined. *Aph.* 15. Dispassion is the consciousness of having overcome one's desires,—[this consciousness being that] of him who thirsts after neither the objects that are seen [on earth] nor those that are heard of [in scripture].

---

* वृत्तिरहितस्य चित्तस्य स्वरूपनिष्ठः परिणामः स्थितिः । तस्यां यत्नः उत्साहः पुनः पुनस्तथात्वेन चेतसि विनिवेशनमभ्यासः इत्युच्यते ॥

† तस्यैव विशेषमाह ॥

‡ बहुकालं नैरन्तर्येणादरातिशयेन सेव्यमानो दृढभूमिःस्थिरो भवति दार्ढ्याय प्रभवतीत्यर्थः ॥

§ वैराग्यस्य लक्षणमाह ॥

a. Object is of two kinds—'seen' *(drishta)* and 'heard of' *(ànus'ravika)*. One 'seen' is one apprehended here [on earth] —such as a Sound [or other object of sense]. One 'heard of' means one in the world of the gods or elsewhere [where it cannot be seen by us]. The *Veda* is called *anus'rava* because it is [not first *read* by the young student, but is] listened to (*sruyate*) from the mouth of the preceptor [—and heard *after*, or consequently on, the teacher's utterance,—as the prefix *anu* implies]. What [object] comes [to our knowledge] therefrom [i. e. from the Veda] is what we mean by one 'heard of* *ânu-sravika.*)

b. What is called 'dispassion' is the reflection that "These [objects—whether of this world or of the one beyond—§ 15. *a.* —] are *my* subjects; I am not *their* slave."—This 'consciousness of having overcome' is entertained by him who, from discerning the insipidity of the results of both of those [classes of objects] has dismissed all eagerness about them.†

c. He next mentions a peculiar aspect of this same‡ [i. e., of 'dispassion.']

तत्परं पुरुषख्यातेर्गुणवैतृष्ण्यम् ॥ १६ ॥

Dispassion carried the length of indifference to all objects.

Aph. 16—This [viz. 'dispassion,'] carried to the utmost is indifference regarding the 'qualities' [i. e. every thing else than Soul], and this indifference arises from a knowldge of Soul [as distinguished from the qualities.'] [See Lecture on the *Sànkhya* §49.]

a. 'This:'—i. e. 'dispassion,' 'carried to the utmost:'—i. e. elevated [to its utmost]. The first [degree of 'dispassion,'— see§ 15—] has regard to [ordinary] *objects*;—but the second [§16], has regard to the 'qualities' [from which, according to

---

* द्विविधो विषयो दृष्ट आनुश्रविकश्च । दृष्ट इहैवोपलभ्यमानश्शब्दादिः देवलोकादावानुश्रविकः । अनुश्रूयते गुरुमुखादित्यनुश्रवो वेदस्तत आगत आनुश्रविकः ॥

† तयोर्द्वयोरपि परिणामविरसत्वदर्शनाद्विगतगर्द्धस्य यावशीकारसंज्ञा ममैते वश्या नाहमेतेषां वश्य इति यो ऽयं विमर्शस्तद्वैराग्यमुच्यते ॥

‡ तस्यैव विशेषमाह ॥

the Sánkhya, ordinary objects arise]. This arises only from familiarity with the distinction between the 'qualities' and Soul [—or the objective and subjective]. From its extreme conduciveness to abstract meditation* it ranks above the dispassion which has regard only to the grosser objects.

b. Having thus stated the nature of concentration *(Yoga)*, he [next] mentions the difference between the nature of [meditation, which is of two kinds—viz.] that 'in which there is distinct recognition,' *(samprajnata)* and that 'in which distinct recognition is lost,'† *(a-samprajnata)*

वितर्कविचारानन्दास्मितानुगमात्सम्प्रज्ञात: ॥ १७ ॥

Meditation, with an object.

Aph. 17.—[Meditation—of the kind called] that 'in which there is distinct recognition [arises, in its fourfold shape,] from the attendance of (1) 'argumentation' *(vitarka)*, (2) deliberation' *(vichara)*, (3) 'beatitude' *(ananda*, and (4) 'egoism' *(asmita)*.

a. The word 'Meditation' is required to supply the ellipsis in the aphorism.‡

b. Meditation 'in which there is distinct recognition' *(samprajnata)* is a kind of 'pondering' *(bhavana)* whereby the nature of that which is to be pondered is known thoroughly and well—apart from either doubt or error. This meditation 'in which there is distinct recognition' excludes every modification of the mind [or every idea—see§8. *b*] other than what is to be pondered :—it is, in short, meditation with its *seed*§ [i. e. with the object, in the effort to apprehend which exclusively the meditation originates].

---

* तद्वैराग्यं परमुत्कृष्टं । प्रथमं वैराग्यं विषयविषयं द्वितीयन्तु गुणविषयमुत्पन्न गुणपुरुषविवेकख्यातेरेव भवति निरोधसमाधेरत्यन्तानुकूलत्वात् ॥

† एवं योगस्य स्वरूपमुक्त्वा सम्प्रज्ञातासम्प्रज्ञातरूपभेदमाह ॥

‡ समाधिरिति शेषः ।

§ सम्यक् संशयविपर्ययरहितत्वेन प्रज्ञायते प्रकर्षेणज्ञायते भाव्यस्यस्वरुपं येन स सम्प्रज्ञातः समाधिर्भावनाविशेषः । ध्येयाति रिक्तसकलवृत्तिनिरोधसम्प्रज्ञातस्सबीजसमाधिरितियावत् ॥

c. This [meditation 'in which there is distinct recognition'—(17—], through its division into the 'argumentative' &c., is of four kinds, viz. (1) the 'argumentative,' (2) the 'deliberative,' (3) the 'beatific,' and (4) the 'egoistic.'*

d. As for 'Pondering' [§17. *b.*], this means the taking into the mind again and again, to the exclusion of all other objects, that which is to be pondered. And that which is [a suitable object] to be pondered is of two kinds, being either the Lord *(Ishwara)* or the twenty-five principles [—see *Tattwa-samasa* §37—]. These [twenty-five principles] also are of two kinds, through their distinction as senselss and not senseless. Twenty-four [of the principles, including Earth, &c.] are senseless :—that which is not senseless is Soul.†

e. Among these [objects suitable for being pondered —§17*d.*—] when, having taken as the object the Senses and the Elements which are gross [in comparison with the Subtile Elements next to be spoken of], pondering is engaged in, in the shape of the investigation as to which is antecedent and which is consequent [—i. e. whether the Senses generate the Elements or the Elements generate the senses—] then the Meditation is [technically said to be] argumentative' *(savitarka.)*‡

f. When, having taken as the object something subtile, as the Subtile Elements and the Internal Organ, pondering is engaged in, in so far as regards the *where* and the *when* thereof,—then it [—the pondering—] is [technically said to be] deliberative' (*savichàra*).§

---

* स सवितर्कादिभेदाच्चतुर्विधःसवितर्कस्सविचारसानन्द स्सास्मितश्च ।

† भावना तावत् । भाव्यस्य विषयान्तरपरिहारेण चेतसि पुनःपुनर्निवेशनं । भाव्यश्च द्विधा ईश्वरस्तत्वानिच । तान्यपि द्विविधानि जडाजडभेदात् जडानि चतुर्विंशातिरजडः पुरुषः ।

‡ तत्र यदा महाभूतेन्द्रियाणि स्थूलानि विषयत्वेनादाय पूर्वापरानुसन्धानेन भावना प्रवर्त्तते तदा सवितर्कस्समाधिः ॥

§ तन्मात्रान्तःकरणलक्षणं सूक्ष्मं विषयमालम्ब्य तस्य देशकालधर्म्मावच्छेदेन यदा भावना प्रवर्त्तते तदा सविचारः ॥

g. But when the 'pure element' (*sattwa*—see *Sànkhya Lecture* §50) of the Internal Organ, commingled with somewhat of [the two other elements,—viz.] 'passion' and 'darkness' [—*Sànkhya Lecture* §51 and 52], is pondered, then the meditation is [technically termed] 'beatific' (*sananda*—§17 *c.*), because the 'pure element' then pondered, which consists in the manifestation of joy [*Sànkhya Lecture* §50], is predominant —inasmuch as the intellectual faculty is then [—i. e. in this particular case of pondering—] a secondary matter.*

h. After that [pondering of the 'pure element' commingled with the two others—§ 17. *g.*—], the meditation which is engaged in, having, as that on which it rests, the clear 'pure' element' unaffected by even a little of 'passion' or 'darkness' is called 'egoistic' meditation [§ 17. *c*], because, here, personal] existence only remains, since the intellectual faculty becomes now predominant inasmuch as the 'pure element' which is to be apprehended [as the object of the meditation] is here disregarded† [as the mere stepping stone to higher things].

i. Among these [four kinds of 'meditation, where there is distinct recognition' of an object,—§ 17 *c.*], the first, the 'argumentative' meditation[§ 17. *e.*] includes all [that belongs to] the four. The second, the 'deliberative,' leaves out the 'argumentation' [of the preceding] :—the third, the 'beatific,' leaves out the deliberation [of the second]:—the fourth, consisting in mere self-consciousness, leaves out that [beatitude which belongs to the third] :—and all these [four] are meditations with something to rest upon‡ [as the object pondered ;—the soul of the

---

* यदा तु रजस्तमोलेशानुविद्धमन्तःकरणसत्वं भाव्यते तदा गुणभावाच्चिच्छक्तेस्सुखप्रकाशमयस्य सत्वस्य भाव्यमानस्योद्रेकात्सानन्दस्समाधिर्भवति॥

† ततः परं रजस्तमोलेशानभिभूतं शुद्धं सत्वमालम्बनी कृत्य या प्रवर्त्तते भावना तस्यां ग्राह्यस्य सत्वस्य न्यग्भावात् चिच्छक्तेरुद्रेकात्सत्तामात्रावशेषत्वेन समाधिस्सास्मित इत्युच्यते ।

‡ तत्र प्रथमश्चतुष्टयानुगतस्समाधिस्सवितर्कः । द्वितीयो वितर्कविकलस्सविचारः तृतीयो विचारविकलस्सानन्दः । चतुर्थस्तद्विकलो ऽस्मितामात्र इति सर्वे एते सालम्बना स्समाधय इति ॥

ascetic, like the body of the young swimmer, requiring supports to begin with, which are successively laid aside as power and confidence are gained by practice].

j. He next tells what is meant by that [meditation] 'in which distinct recognition is lost'* [§ 16. *b.*—the practised ascetic having parted with every vestige of object, as the practised swimmer with his last cork or bladder].

विरामप्रत्ययाभ्यासपूर्व्वस्संकारशेषो ऽन्यः ॥ १८ ॥

Meditation without an object.

Aph. 18.—The one [kind of meditation just described] is preceded by the exercise of thought in the shape of repose;—the other [—independent of any fresh antecedent—] is in the shape of the self reproduction [of thought, after the departure of all objects].

a. By 'repose' *(virama)* we mean that whereby one is rested —the abandonment of all anxiety about argumentation, &c. [§17.]. Well—'thought' in the shape of this 'repose' is what we mean by the compound expression *virama-pratyaya;*—and what we mean by the 'exercise' *(abhyasa)* of this, is the reiteratedly dwelling mentally thereon, and constantly rejecting with a negative [as a delusion and an unreality] whatever 'modification' [or idea,—see§ 5.—] springs up there [to interfere with it];—such is 'the exercise of thought in the shape of repose.' This [as remarked in the first half of the aphorism] produces meditation 'in which there is distinct recognition'† [§17 :—and we have now to consider that kind of meditation which differs from this].

b. The other [kind of meditaion] has nothing left but the self-reproduction of thought. It is different from that [above described]; that is to say, it is [as contradistinguished from

---

* असम्प्रज्ञातमाह ॥

† विरम्यते अनेनेति विरामः। वितर्कादिचिन्तापरित्यागः। विरामश्चासौ प्रत्ययश्च विरामप्रत्ययः।तस्याभ्यासः पौनः पुन्येन चेतसि निवेशनं तत्र याकाचिद्वृत्तिरुल्लसति तस्यां नेतिनेतीति नैरन्तर्येण पर्युदसनं विरामप्रत्ययाभ्यासः। तत्पूर्वकोऽसम्प्रज्ञातसमाधिः।

meditation 'in which there is distinct recognition,'] that 'in which distinct recognition is lost.' Here there is nothing to be thought of or accurately apprehended [—as it was necessary that there should be in the former process—] ;—it is meditation *without* a seed* [—i. e. without any object—see § 17 *b.*—in any effort to confine one's self to the apprehension of which the meditation has been entered upon].

c. Well, having thus stated the [two] distinctions [§18] in the nature of Concentration [§2], and having compendiously mentioned its methods, the author proceeds to speak of these methods more fully, first premising some account of the spurious semblance of concentration.†

भवप्रत्ययो विदेहप्रकृतिलयानाम् ॥ १९ ॥

Spurious semblances of abstract Meditation.

Aph. 19.—Of [the meditative state attained to by the two classes of aspirants, technically called] 'the unembodied and resolved into Nature,' *the world* is the cause.

a. By 'the unembodied and resolved into Nature' we mean to speak of [those technically called] 'the unembodied' [as one set], and 'the resolved into Nature' [as another set.] Of these the Meditation is caused by *the world,*—that is to say, it is such that the cause, or instrumental agency on which it depends, is the world—the creation—[—the phenomenal—beyond which the vision of these extends not to the discrimination of pure Spirit, and the uncreated energy Nature].‡

b. The meaning is this—that, only while the world is manifest, are these men participators in such [inadequate] meditation [as we have described]. And this is a mere false semblance

---

* संस्कारशेषोऽन्यः तद्विलक्षणः । असम्प्रज्ञात इत्यर्थः । नत्वत्र किञ्चिद्वेद्यं सम्प्रज्ञायत इत्यसम्प्रज्ञातो निर्बीजसमाधिः ।

† तदेवं योगस्य स्वरूपभेदं संक्षेपेणोपायश्चाभिधाय विस्तरेणोपायं योगाभासप्रदर्शनपूर्वकं वक्तुमुपक्रमते ।

‡ विदेहाश्च प्रकृतिलयाश्च विदेहप्रकृतिलयाः। तेषां समाधिर्भवप्रत्ययः भवस्संसार एव प्रत्ययः कारणं यस्य तादृशो भवतीत्यर्थः ।

meditation, because these do not discern the ultimate Reality. Hence, by him who desires emancipation, effort is to be made for [attaining to] the knowledge of the ultimate Reality, and for pondering *that** [instead of the lower things pondered by those of narrower ken, whose vision cannot pierce the penomenal, and discriminate the spectator Soul, and the *natura naturans*].

c. And, of the persons spoken of in the aphorism, those who having their energies directed to 'beatific' meditation [§ 17. *g.*] do not discern any other Reality, in the shape of Nature or Soul, these are they who are meant by the term the 'unembodied, (*videha*), because their body and their self-consciousness are departed [—but they are not *further* advanced towards emancipation]. And those who [going just one step further] are content with the 'egoistic' meditation [§ 17. *h.*] but do not discern the Supreme Soul, and whose intellect has been resolved into [the *natura naturans* which is] its cause, these are they who are called the 'resolved into Nature† (*prakritilaya*)—[See *Sánkhya Lecture*, § 15 and 54].

d. But of others than those‡ [whose inadequate style of meditation has been stated in aphorism 19, the meditation is as stated in the aphorism here following].

श्रद्धावीर्यस्मृतिसमाधिप्रज्ञापूर्वक इतरेषाम् ॥ २० ॥

The genuine order of abstract Meditation.

Aph. 20.—[In the practice] of others this [Meditation] is preceded by Faith, Energy, Memory, Meditation, and Discernment.

a. "Of others"—i. e. of *yogís* other than [those called] the 'unembodied' [§19 *c.*] and the 'resolved into nature'§[§19. *c.*]

---

* अयमर्थः । आविर्भूतमात्र एव संसारे तंथाविधसामाधिभाजो भवन्ति । तेषां परतत्वादर्शनातयोगाभासोऽयं । अतः परतत्वज्ञाने तद्भावनायाश्च मुक्तिकामेन यत्नो विधेय इति ।

† अत्रच ये सानन्दसमाधौ बद्धधृतयस्तत्वान्तरं प्रधानपुरुषं न पश्यन्ति ते विगतदेहाहङ्कारत्वाद्विदेहशब्दवाच्या. । येच सास्मितसमाधो कृतपरितोषाः परं परमात्मानं न पश्यन्ति येषाश्च चेतस्स्वकारणे लयमुपगतं ते प्रकृतिलया इत्युच्यन्ते ॥

‡ तदन्येषान्तु ॥

§ इतरेषां । विदेहप्रकृतिलयव्यतिरिक्तानां योगिनां ॥

b. "Preceded by Faith, &c." To complete the sense, we must supply the word 'Meditation.' 'Preceded by Faith, &c.,'—that is to say—the means antecedent [and conducive] to which are Faith, &c. And these, 'Faith &c.,' acting in the relation of means to an end, constitute the means [or appliances] for Meditation 'in which there is distinct recognition'* [—§ 17.].

Faith defined. *c.* Among these [antecedents enumerated in the Aphorism], 'Faith' *(shraddhá)* means a mental approval of Concentration† [as a worthy and possible aim].

Energy. *d.* 'Energy' (*virya*) means perseverance.‡

Memory. *e.* 'Memory' [or Recollection'—*smriti*] has already been explained,§[—see§11].

Meditation. *f.* 'Meditation' (*samádhi*) means intentness on a single point.||

Discernment. *g.* 'Discernment' (*prajná*) means thorough discrimination of that which is to be known.$

Reason for this order of statement. *h.* Among these [antecedents,—to account for the order of statement adopted in the aphorism, we may remark, that]—of him who has 'Faith' there arises 'Energy,'— he becomes persevering in meditation ;—and to one thus persevering the 'Memory' of past subjects springs up; and his mind becomes absorbed in 'Meditation' in consequence of the recollection thereof; and he whose mind is absorbed in meditation arrives at a thorough 'Discernment' of the matter pondered.¶'

---

* श्रद्धादिपूर्वकः ॥ श्रद्धादयः पूर्वे उपाया यस्य स श्रद्धादि पूर्वकस्समाधिरिति शेषः । तेच श्रद्धादय उपायोपेयभावेन प्रवर्त्तमानाः सम्प्रज्ञातस्य समाधेरुपायतां प्रतिपद्यन्ते । † तत्र श्रद्धा योगविषये चेतसः प्रसादः ।

‡ वीर्यमुत्साहः । § स्मृतिर्व्याख्याता । ॥ समाधिरेकाग्रता ।

$ प्रज्ञा ज्ञातव्यप्रविवेकः ।

¶ तत्र श्रद्धावतो वीर्यं जायते योगविषये उत्साहवान् भवति सोत्साहस्यच पाश्चात्यासु भूमिषु स्मृतिरुपजायते तत्स्मरणाच्चेतस्समाधीयते समाहितचित्तश्च भाव्यं सम्यग्विजानाति ।

i. Such are [according to those whose practice is recorded in §20.] the means of that Meditation 'in which there is distinct recognition' [§ 17]. The [still higher step—] Meditation 'in which distinct recognition is lost' [§ 18.] is arrived at through diligent practice [§ 13] of this ['in which there *is* distinct recognition' of some object pondered], and through extreme 'Dispassion'* [§ 16].

j. He next mentions the subdivisions of *Yogís,* adopting the above-mentioned means, according to the difference of method adopted by them.†

तीव्रसंवेगानामासन्नः ॥ २१ ॥

Ascetics divisible according to their method of procedure.

Aph. 21.—[The attainment of the state of abstract Meditation is] speedy in the case of the hotly impetuous.

a. To complete the aphorism, the words 'The attainment of the state of abstact Meditation' require to be supplied.‡

b. By impetuosity, (*samvega*) is meant a more energetic, self-reproducing impulse, which is a cause of action. Those persons in whose 'transcendent' methods [§22.] this [impetuosity] is violent, are close upon the attainment of abstract meditation and the fruits of meditation;—that is to say, this is in their case, rapidly brought about.§

c. Who are those 'hotly impetuous' [§21]? To this he replies.||

मृदुमध्याधिमात्रत्वात्ततोऽपि विशेषः ॥ २२ ॥

Ahh. 22.—Through the 'mild,' the medium,' and the transcendent' [nature of the methods adopted] there is thence also a distinction [among the ascetics who adopt the methods].

---

* त एते सम्प्रज्ञातसमाधेरुपायाः। तस्याभ्यासात्पराच्च वैराग्याद्भवत्यसम्प्रज्ञातः॥

† उक्तोपायवतां योगिनामुपायभेदाद्भेदानाह ॥

‡ समाधिलाभ इति शेषः ।

§ संवेगः क्रियाहेतुर्दृढतरस्संस्कारः सः तीव्रो येषामधिमात्रोपायानां तेषामासन्नस्समाधिलाभस्समाधिफलञ्चासन्नं भवति शीघ्रमेव निष्पद्यत इत्यर्थः ॥

|| के ते तीव्रसंवेगा इत्यत आह ॥

a. Through the diversity of these various methods, viz. the 'mild' &c., there is a distinction of those who employ the methods. The divisions of method are the 'mild' (*mridu*), the 'medium' (*madhya*), and the 'transcendent' (*adhimátra*). These are severally threefold from their being severally subdivided into the 'mildly impetuous,' the 'middlingly impetuous,' and the 'transcendently impetuous.' And in accordance with this division there are nine classes of followers of the *Yoga*. Thus—there is the 'mild method'—[the follower of which may be] the 'mildly impetuous,' the 'middlingly impetuous,' or the transcendently impetuous.' Then there is the 'medium method'—the follower of which may be the 'mildly impetuous,' the 'middlingly impetuous,' or the 'transcendently impetuous.' And there is the 'transcendent method'—[the follower of which may be] the 'mildly impetuous,' the 'middlingly impetuous,' or the 'transcendently impetuous.' And great endeavours ought to be made after the 'transcendent method' and after warm impetuosity [in following out the same]. So much for the declaration of the distinctions* [among the followers of the *Yoga*].

The nine divisions of ascetics.

b. By 'mildness' [as we learn from Bhávágaņes'á] is here meant 'smallness'. The meaning of 'middlingness' is the familiar one. By 'transcendentness' is meant the exceeding of all measure,—excessiveness, in short.†

c. Now he mentions a method which differs from these methods in being an easy one.‡

---

* तेभ्यः उपायेभ्यो मृद्वादिभेदभिन्नेभ्य उपायवतां विशेषो भवति । मृदुमध्योऽधिमात्रं इत्युपायभेदाः । ते प्रत्येकं मृदुसंवेगमध्यसंवेगतीव्रसंवेगभेदात्त्रिविधाः। तद्भेदेनच नव योगिनो भवन्ति । मृदूपायः । मृदुसंवेगो मध्यसंवेगः तीव्रसंवेगश्च । मध्योपायः । मृदुसंवेगो मध्यसंवेगः तीव्रसंवेगश्च । अधिमात्रोपायः । मृदुसंवेगो मध्यसंवेगः तीव्रसंवेगश्च । अधिमात्रोपाये तीव्रेच संवेगे महान् यत्नः कर्त्तव्य इति भेदोपदेशः ॥

† मृदुत्वमल्पता । मध्यत्वं प्रसिद्धम् । अधिमात्रत्वमति मात्रत्वमतिशयितत्वमिति यावत् ॥ इति भावागणेशः ॥

‡ इदानीमेतदुपायविलक्षणं सुगममुपायान्तरमाह ॥

ईश्वरप्रणिधानाद्वा ॥ २३ ॥

The devotional method.

Aph. 23—Or by profound devotedness towards the Lord, [the ascetic may attain to the state of abstract Meditation].

a. By "the Lord" (*Ishwara*) we mean what will be defined [in §24]. By "profound devotedness" towards Him, we mean a kind of devoted attachment, a peculiar serving of Him, the consigning of all one's actions to Him. The person [under the influence we speak of] desiring no fruit [of his actions] in the shape of enjoyment of sense-objects, or the like, makes over all his actions to Him, the pre-eminent guide. This 'profound devotedness' is a pre-eminent means of abstract Mecditation and of the attainment of its fruits.*

The devotional method has reference to the Lord.

b. It has been just stated that abstract Meditation may be attained through profound devotedness towards *the Lord.* With reference to this, he now proceeds to declare, in order, the nature, [§24], the proofs [§25], the pre-eminence [§26], and the name [§27], of the Lord, the order of His worship [§28], and the fruit thereof† [§29].

क्लेशकर्मविपाकाशयैरपरामृष्टपुरुषविशेष ईश्वरः ॥ २४ ॥

The term 'Lord' defined.

Aph. 24.—The Lord is a particular Spirit (*Purusha*) untouched by troubles, works fruits, or deserts.

a. 'Troubles'—i. e. things that distress,—such as ignorance &., which will be spoken of [in the 2nd section]. 'Works'—i. e. [actions involving] merit or demerit. 'Fruits'—i. e. what ripen out of works, as birth, life, or whatever is experienced [by mortals as the consequences of their actions]. By' deserts'

---

* ईश्वरो वक्ष्यमाणलक्षणः । प्रणिधानं तत्र भक्तिविशेषो विशिष्टमुपासनं सर्वक्रियाणामपि तत्रार्पणं विषयसुखादिकं फलमनिच्छन् सर्वाः क्रियास्तस्मिन् परमगुरावर्पयति तत्प्रणिधानं समाधेस्तत्फललाभस्यच प्रकृष्ट उपायः ॥

† ईश्वरस्य प्रणिधानात्समाधिलाभ इत्युक्तं । तत्रेश्वरस्य स्वरूपं प्रमाणं प्रभावं वाचकमुपासनाक्रमं तत्फलञ्च क्रमेण वक्तुमाह ॥

are meant those self-continuant conditions, or tendencies [—leading to their inevitable consequences—], which take the name of *ásaya* [—from the root *si* ' to sleep,—] because they rest on the tablets of the mind until their fruit shall have ripened. [The Lord, to whom no such things are attributable. is declared to be] 'Untouched' by these—i. e. not affected by them during any of the three times, [—past, present, or future].*

b. A 'particular Spirit,'—i. e one who is different from other spirits;—such is the force of the term here rendered ' particular.'†

The Lord upholds all things by His mere will.

c. 'The Lord' *(Ishwara)*—i. e. [—from the root *sí* ' to possess power'—] who is accustomed to rule,—who is able to uphold the world by his mere will. Such is the nature of ' the Lord.'‡

d. Having thus stated the nature of the Lord, he now [§23. *b.*] states the proofs§ [that such a Being exists].

तत्र निरतिशयं सर्वज्ञबीजम् ॥ २५ ॥

Proof that there is such a Being as the Lord.

Aph. 25.—In Him does the germ of the omniscient become infinite.

a. 'In Him'—i. e. in that divine Being. The germ of omniscience is the less or more of the knowledge of the past, the future, &c. This is the germ; because like a germ it is the root [of what springs from it]. This [knowledge which in others is less or more] in Him, is infinite, or reaches its extreme limit. [And it is held to be a fair inference that Knowledge reaches the limit of Omniscience *somewhere*], for, properties that are capable of degrees, such as Parvitude and Magni-

---

* क्लिश्यन्तीति क्लेशाः अविद्यादयो वक्ष्यमाणाः । कर्म धर्माधर्मौ । विपाकाः कर्मफलानि जन्मायुर्भोगाः । आफलविपाकात् चित्तभूमौ शेरत इत्याशयाः वासनाख्याः संस्काराः । तैरपरामृष्टः त्रिष्वपि कालेषु न संस्पृष्टः

† पुरुषविशेषः । अन्येभ्यः पुरुषेभ्यो विशिष्यत इति विशेषः ।

‡ ईश्वरः । ईशनशीलः । इच्छामात्रेण सकलजगदुद्धरणक्षमः इति स्वरूपमीश्वरस्येति ॥ § एवमीश्वरस्य स्वरूपमभिधाय प्रमाणमाह ॥

tude, are [in particular instances] seen to have reached their extreme limits,—Parvitude, for example, in an Atom, and pre-eminent Magnitude in the Ether. So too Knowledge and the like, properties of the intellect, are seen admitting of degrees. They reach their extreme limit *somewhere*, and He in whom they are infinite is the Lord.*

b. Having thus declared the nature of the Lord, and the proof that such a Being exists, he next [§23. *b.*] declares His pre-eminence.†

स एष पूर्वेषामपि गुरुः कालेनानवच्छेदात् ॥ २६ ॥

The pre-eminence of the Lord.

Aph. 26.—He is the preceptor even of the first, for he is not limited by time.

a. 'Of the first;'—that is to say, even of the earliest [of created beings], such as Brahmá, &c, He [the Lord] is the preceptor, or instructor; for He is not bounded by time, since He is without beginning,—and *these*, on the other hand, *are* limited by time because they *had* a beginning.‡

b. Having thus declared the pre-eminence [of the Lord], he declares His name [§23. *b.*], with a view to its employment in devotion.§

तस्य वाचकः प्रणवः ॥ २७ ॥

The mystical name of the Lord.

Aph. 27. His name is Glory.

a. 'His,'—i. e. of the Lord as thus defined [§24], the name,

---

* तत्र । तस्मिन् भगवति । सर्वज्ञत्वस्य यद्बीजं अतीतानागतादिग्रहणस्याल्पत्वं महत्त्वंच मूलत्वात् बीजमिव बीजंतत्तत्र निरतिशयं काष्ठांप्राप्तं । दृष्टाह्यल्पत्वमहत्त्वादीनां धर्माणां सातिशयानां काष्ठाप्राप्तिर्यथा परमाणावल्पत्वस्य आकाशेच परममहत्वस्य । एवं ज्ञानादयोऽपि चित्तधर्मा स्तारतम्येन परिदृश्यमानाः क्वचिन्निरतिशयतामासादयन्ति यत्रचैते निरतिशयास्स ईश्वरः इति ॥

† एवमीश्वरस्य स्वरूपं प्रमाणञ्चाभिधाय प्रभावमाह ॥

‡ पूर्वेषां । आद्यानां ब्रह्मादीनामपि स गुरुरुपदेष्टा यतस्स कालेननावच्छिद्यते अनादित्वात् । तेषां पुनरादिमत्त्वादस्ति कालेनावच्छेदः ॥

§ एवं प्रभावमुक्त्वोपासनोपयोगाय वाचकमाह ॥

or appellation, is 'Glory' *(pranava)* [which is the technical term employed in speaking of the mystical name]' *Om.*'*

a. 'And of the two [—i. e. of the Lord and this name, or as 'denoted and denoter,' is eternal. It is conventionally *declared,*—but not *made* by any one. Just in like manner as the actual relation between a father and his son is *declared* [and not *created*] by some one who says "This is that one's father, and that is this one's son."†

c. He next speaks of worship‡ [—§23. *b.*]

तज्जपस्तदर्थभावनम् ॥ २८ ॥

How the name of the Lord is to be used in worship.

Aph. 28.—Its repetition [should be made and also] reflection on its signification.

a. 'Its'—i. e. of this mystical name, consisting of three and a half prosodial moments [viz: $(a=2)+(u=1)+(m=\frac{1}{2}) = (om=3\frac{1}{2})$], the repetition, or proper pronunciation; and reflection on, or re-iterated mental attention to, its signification—viz: the Lord,—is a means of concentrating the thoughts; therefore it is here stated that the follower of the *Yoga* ought to repeat the mystical name and to reflect upon its import, with a view to the effecting of abstract Meditation.§

b. He next mentions the fruits [§23. *b.*] of such worship.§

ततःप्रत्यक्चेतनाधिगमोऽप्यन्तरायाभावश्च ॥ २९ ॥

Aph. 29.—Thence comes the knowledge of the rightly intelligent [Spirit]' and the absence of obstacles.

a. 'The rightly intelligent [Spirit]'—i. e. the Spirit possess-

---

‡ इत्थमुक्तस्वरूपस्य तस्येश्वरस्य वाचकोऽभिधायकः प्रणव ओङ्कारः ।

* तयोश्च वाच्यवाचकभावलक्षणस्सम्बन्धोनित्यः । सङ्केतेन प्रकाश्यते नतु केनचित्क्रियते । यथा पितृपुत्रयोर्विद्यमानस्सम्बन्धोऽस्यायं पितास्यायं पुत्र इति केनचित्प्रकाश्यते॥ † उपासनामाह ॥

‡ तस्य सार्द्धत्रिमात्रस्य प्रणवस्य जपो यथावदुच्चारणं तद्वाच्यस्येश्वरस्य भावनं पुनःपुनश्चेतसि निवेशनं एकाग्रताया उपायोऽतस्समाधिसिद्धये योगिना प्रणवो जप्यस्तदर्थश्च भावनीय इत्युक्तं भवति ॥ § उपासनायाः फलमाह ॥

ed of knowledge,—He being an intelligence who rightly knows, —i. e. who knows in an opposite, or inverse way, [as contradistinguished from mortals, whose understanding—as explained under § 5.—is supposed to flow out and become modified by objects. Such a process of gaining knowledge, being regarded as undersirable in the case of mortals, is not to be imagined to belong to the Lord, who is therefore said to know in some opposite way]. There accrues to him [the ascetic] a knowledge, a complete apprehension, of Him,* [through the practice recommended in § 23].

b. The obstacles [to the attainment of the end in view] will be mentioned. The absence of these means the exclusion of their power.†

c. Now, which are those *obstacles?* This being a point in doubt, he proceeds to remark as follows.‡

व्याधिस्त्यानसंशयप्रमादालस्याविरतिभ्रान्तिदर्शनालब्ध
भूमिकत्वानवस्थितत्वानि चित्तविक्षेपास्ते ऽन्तरायाः ३०

The obstacles of the ascetic.

Aph. 30.—Sickness, languor, doubt, carelessness, laziness, addiction to objects [of sense], erroneous perception, failure to attain any stage [of abstraction], and instability [in the state when attained],—these distractions of the mind are obstacles [in the way of the ascetic].

a. These nine, prevailing through the power of the passionate and dark qualities [—the two which are opposed to the element of pure or good in the phenomenal world—] become distractions of the mind :—that is to say, the mind is distracted by these which are opposed to the mind's concentrating itself on any point.§

---

* प्रतीपं विपरीतं अञ्चति विजानातीति प्रत्यक् । स चासौचेतनश्चेति प्रत्यक्चेतनो विद्वान् पुरुषः । तस्य अधिगमो ज्ञानं स्वरूपतोऽस्य भवति ।

† अन्तराया वक्ष्यमाणास्तेषामभावः शक्तिप्रतिबन्धो भवति ॥

‡ अथ के तेऽन्तराया इत्याशङ्कायामाह ॥

§ नवैते रजस्तमोवशात् प्रवर्त्तमानाश्चित्तस्य विक्षेपा भवन्ति । तैरेकाग्रताविरोधिभिश्चित्तं विक्षिप्यत इत्यर्थः ॥

Sickness. *b.* Among these, 'Sickness,' is a fever, or the like, caused by disorder of the humours.*

Languor. *c.* 'Languor' is the mind's inactivity.†

Doubt. *d.* 'Doubt' is a [sort of] notion that leans to both alternatives. As, for example, [where one hesitates] "Is the *Yoga* practicable [e. g. for me the doubter], or is it not?"‡

Carelessness. *e.* 'Carelessness' is a habit of inattention,—a listlessness about the effecting of abstract meditation.§

Laziness. *f.* 'Laziness' is a heaviness of the body and mind, which causes a want of exertion in the department of abstract meditation.||

Addiction to objects. *g.* 'Addiction to objects, (*avirati*) is a greediness consisting in attachment of the mind to objects of senses.$

Erroneous perception. *h.* Erroneous perception' is a mistaken notion [§8. *a.*] such as the notion that the thing is silver when it is mother o'pearl.₩

Failure to attain any stage of abstraction. *i.* By 'failure to attain any stage' we mean the failing, for some reson or another, to attain to, or arrive at, the state of abstract meditation.¶

Instability. *j.* 'Instability' is, even when the state of abstract meditation has been reached, the mind is not continuing steadily therein.**

---

* तत्र व्याधिर्धातुवैषम्यनिमित्तो ज्वरादिः ॥

† स्त्यानमकर्मण्यता चित्तस्य ॥

‡ उभयकोट्यालम्बनं विज्ञानं संशयः । योगस्साध्यस्स्याद्वानवेति ॥

§ प्रमादोऽननुष्ठानशीलिता समाधिसाधने औदासीन्यम् ॥

|| आलस्यं कायचित्तयोर्गुरुत्वं योगविषये प्रवृत्यभावहेतुः ॥

$ अविरतिश्चित्तस्य विषयसम्प्रयोगात्मा गर्द्धः ॥

₩ भ्रान्तिदर्शनं शुक्तिकायां रजतत्ववद्विपर्ययज्ञानम् ॥

¶ अलब्धभूमिकत्वं कुतश्चिन्निमित्तात्समाधिभूमेरलाभअसम्प्राप्तिः ॥

** अनवस्थितत्वं लब्धायामपि समाधिभूमौ चित्तस्यतुतत्राप्रतिष्ठा ॥

k. These [§30.] are called 'obstacles' because, as they present themselves, they oppose concentration or meditation.*

l. In order to declare other obstacles also, which cause distraction of mind, he says†:—

दुःखदौर्मनस्याङ्गमेजयत्व श्वासविक्षेपसहभुवः ॥ ३१ ॥

Aph. 31.— Grief, Distress, Trembling, and Sighing, are accompaniments of the distractions.

a. When, from whatever cause, distractions [such as enumerated in § 30.] have arisen, then these, viz. Grief, &c. [§ 31.] come on.‡

Grief. *b.* Among, these [§31.] 'Grief' is a modification of mind, resulting from [other] mental affections and characterised by annoyance, in consequence of which annoyance sentient creatures exert themselves for its removal.§

Distress. *c.* 'Distress' is a tremulousness of mind, arising either from external or internal causes.||

Trembling. *d.* 'Trembling' (*angamejayatwa*) is a shaking of the whole body which prevents steadiness either in prescribed postures or in mind.$

Sighing. *e.* 'Sighing' (*shwása*) is an excessive entrance of air into the body. An excessive expiration of air from the body, is what is meant by *prashwása.*❦

f. These [§31.], prevailing along with the distractions [enumerated in§ 30.], are to be excluded by means of 'exercise'

---

* एते समाधेरेकाग्रताया यथायोगं प्रतिपक्षत्वादन्तराया इत्युच्यन्ते ॥

† चित्तविक्षेपकारकानन्यानप्यन्तरायान् प्रतिपादयितुमाह ॥

‡ कुतश्चिन्निमित्तादुत्पन्नेषु विक्षेपेषु एते दुःखादयः प्रवर्तन्ते

§ तत्र दुःखं चित्तस्य राजस परिणामो बाधनालक्षणो यद्बाधात् प्राणिनस्तदुपघाताय प्रवर्त्तन्ते ॥

|| दौर्मनस्यं बाह्याभ्यन्तरैः कारणैर्मनसश्चाञ्चल्यम् ॥

$ अङ्गमेजयत्वं सर्वाङ्गिनो वेपथुरासनमनस्थैर्यबाधकः ॥

❦ श्वासो देहान्तर्वायोराधिकः प्रवेशः । प्रश्वासो देहाद्वायोरधिकनिर्गमः ॥

[§ 13.] and 'dispassion' [§ 15.] as aforesaid; and therefore it is that they are mentioned here.*

h. He now mentions another method for the prevention of the obstacles [§ 30.] together with their supervenients [§ 31].†

तत्प्रतिषेधार्थमेकतत्त्वाभ्यासः ॥ ३२ ॥

Means of combating distractions. *Aph.* 32—For the prevention thereof let one truth be dwelt upon.

a. For the prevention, or hindrance, of these distractions, one should dwell upon, or again and again confine the attention, to one truth,—some accepted truth,—by force of which, when concentration on one point has taken place, the distractions subside.‡

b. He next states another method, premising some mention of purifying processes which conduce to the perfecting of the mind.§

मैत्रीकरुणामुदितोपेक्षाणां सुखदुःखपुण्यापुण्यविषयाणां भावनातश्चित्त-
प्रसादनम् ॥ ३३ ॥

Aph. 33.—Through the practising of benevolence, tenderness, complacency, and disregard towards objects [i. e. persons who are respectively in possession] of happiness, grief, virtue, and vice, the mind becomes purified.

Amiable habits recommended.

a. 'Benevolence' is good-heartedness; 'tenderness' is compassion; 'complacency' is sympathetic joy; 'disregard' is indifference. He should exercise these, repectively, towards the happy, the grieved, the virtuous, and the vicious. That is to

---

* त एते विक्षेपैस्सह प्रवर्त्तमाना यथोदिताभ्यासवैराग्याभ्यां निरोद्धव्या इत्येषामुपदेशम् ।   † सोपद्रवविक्षेपप्रतिषेधार्थमुपायान्तरमाह ॥

‡ तेषां विक्षेपाणां प्रतिषेधार्थं निषेधार्थमेकस्मिन् कस्मिंश्चिदभिमते तत्त्वे अभ्यासश्चेतसः पुनःपुनर्निवेशनं कुर्य्यात् यद्बलात् प्रत्युदितायामेकाग्रतायां विक्षेपाः प्रशममुपयान्ति ।

§ इदानीं चित्तसंस्कारापादकपरिकर्मकथनपूर्वकमुपायान्तरमाह ॥

say, when people are happy, he should show benevolence, saying, "Blessings on their joy!",—and not [show] envy. When people are grieved, he should show tenderness, saying 'By what means, verily can they be freed from their grief?,'—'and not [show] a disposition to stand aloof. And when people are virtuous, he should exhibit complacency, by sympathetically rejoicing in their virtue,—and not [show] aversion by saying, "What!—are these forsooth *virtuous*?" And in regard to the vicious he should practise simply indifference, showing neither sympathy nor aversion.*

b. In the aphorism, by the words, 'happiness' 'grief', &c. are denoted those to whom these belong. So, in this manner, by the purifying influences of friendliness, &c, the mind being rendered cheerful, the production of abstract meditation takes place readily.†

c. This purifying process is an external one [and not an intimate portion of the *Yoga* itself]. As, in arithmetic, in effecting the calculations of questions of Alligation, &c. the operations of Addition &c., are valuable [not so much in themselves, but] as aids in effecting the *important* matter, so by exercising benevolence, &c, which are [moods of mind] opposed to aversion and covetousness, the mind, in which composure has [thereby] been produced, becomes fitted for meditation —that 'in which there is distinct recognition of an object' [§ 17.], &c. Covetousness and aversion are the very chief raisers of distractions :—if therefore these be radically extirpated, then,

---

* मैत्री सौहार्दं । करुणा कृपा । मुदिता हर्षः । उपेक्षा औदासीन्यं । एता यथाक्रमं सुखितेषु दुःखितेषु पुण्यवत्सु अपुण्यवत्सु च विभावयेत् । तथाहि । सुखितेषु साध्वेषां सुखित्वमिति मैत्रीं कुर्य्यान्नत्वीर्ष्याम् । दुःखितेषु कथन्नामैषां दुःखविमुक्तिः स्यादिति कृपामेव कुर्य्यान्न ताटस्थ्यं पुण्यवत्सु च पुण्यानुमोदनेन हर्षं कुर्य्यान्नतु किमेते पुण्यवन्त इति द्वेषं । अपुण्यवत्सु चौदासीन्यमेव भावयेन्नानुमोदनं न द्वेषम् ॥

† सूत्रे सुखदुःखादिशब्दैस्तद्वन्तः प्रतिपादिताः । तदेवं मैत्र्यादिपरिकर्म्मणा चित्ते प्रसीदति सुखेन समाधेराविर्भावो भवति ॥

through its composure [and freedom from distraction], the mind the more readily becomes concentrated on one point.*

d. He mentions another expedient.†

प्रच्छर्दनविधारणाभ्यां वा प्राणस्य ॥ ३४ ॥

Another expedient for combating distraction.

Aph. 34.—[Or, he may combat distractions] by forcibly expelling and by restraining the breath.

Regulation of the breath.

a. The 'expelling' of the breath is the vomiting or emitting it [by a slow but complete expiration]. The 'restraining' it, is the stopping it [by shutting the mouth and closing both nostrils with the fingers of the right hand]. And this, we mean to say, takes place after *inhalation* [—though mentioned in the aphorism as if immediately following *expiration*—], because, after expelling the breath, it is impossible to *restrain* it without [having made a previous] inhalation. Thus, then, the regulation of the breath [*prànàyàma*], being of three descriptions according to the distinction of 'expiration' *(rechaka)*, 'inspiration' *(pùraka)*, and 'restraining' *(kumbhaka)*, causes steadiness of the mind, and its concentration in a single direction.‡

b. He states another means of steadiness.§

विषयवती वा प्रवृत्तिरुत्पन्ना स्थितिनिबन्धनी ॥ ३५ ॥

---

* परिकर्मैतद्बाह्यं कर्म । यथा गणिते मिश्रकादिव्यवहारगणितनिष्पत्तये सङ्कलितादिकर्मोपकारकत्वेन प्रधानकर्मनिष्पत्तये प्रभवति एवं द्वेषरागादिप्रतिपक्षभूतमैत्र्यादिभावनया समुत्पादितप्रसादं चित्तं सम्प्रज्ञातादिसमाधियोग्यं सम्पद्यते । रागद्वेषावेव मुख्यतया विक्षेपमुत्पादयतः । तौ चेत्समूलमुन्मूलितौ स्यातां तदा प्रसन्नत्वान्मनसो भवत्येवैकाग्रता ॥

† उपायान्तरमाह ॥

‡ प्राणस्य प्रच्छर्दनं वमनं रेचनमिति यावत् । विधारणं कुम्भकं । तच्चार्थात् पूरकानन्तरं। रेचकोत्तरं पूरकं विना विधारणासम्भवात्। तदेवं रेचकपूरककुम्भकभेदेन त्रिविधः प्राणायामश्चित्तस्य स्थितिमेकाग्रतां निबध्नाति ॥

§ स्थितिनिबन्धान्तरमाह ॥

Another expedient. *Aph.* 35.—Or a sensuous immediate cognition, being produced, may serve as a cause of the steadiness [of the mind].

a. To complete the sentence, we must supply 'of the mind.'*

b. Objects of sense are odour, savour, colour, touch, and sound. Wherever these exist as fruits, that case of perception, or especially immediate cognition, is sensuous:—and this, when it is excited, causes fixation of the mind.†

Mystical sense-perception. *c.* To explain:—in the case of him who fixes his mind on the tip of his nose, there arises a perception of celestial odour. [If he fix his mind] on the tip of the tongue, in like manner, there is a perception of savour; on the fore-part of the palate, a perception of colour; on the middle of the tongue, a perception of the touch; on the root of tongue, a perception of the sound. Thus, then, through this or that organ, the perception arising of this or that celestial sense-object becomes a cause of the mind's concentration in one direction.‡

d. He mentions another expedient of the like description.§

विशोका वा ज्योतिष्मती ॥ ३६ ॥

Another expedient. *Aph.* 36.—Or a luminous [immediate cognition, being produced,] free from sorrow, [may serve as a cause of the steadiness of the mind.]

a. To complete the aphorism, we must supply 'an immediate cognition, being produced, may serve as a cause of the steadiness of the mind.'||

---

* मनस इति वाक्यशेषः ॥

† विषया गन्धरसरूपस्पर्शशब्दास्ते विद्यन्ते फलत्वेन यस्यां सा विषयवती प्रवृत्तिः प्रकृष्टा साक्षात्काररूपा वृत्तिः । साचोत्पन्ना मनसस्स्थैर्य्यं करोति ॥

‡ तथाहि । नासाग्रे चित्तं धारयतो दिव्यगन्धसंविदुपजायते । तादृश्येव जिव्हाग्रे रससंवित् । ताल्वग्रे रूपसंवित् । जिव्हामध्ये स्पर्शसंवित् । जिव्हामूले शब्दसंवित् । तदेवं तत्तदिन्द्रियद्वारेण तस्मिन् तस्मिन् दिव्ये विषये जायमाना संवित्चित्तस्यैकाग्रताया हेतुर्भवति ॥ § एवंविधमेवोपायान्तरमाह ॥

|| प्रवृत्तिरुत्पन्ना चित्तस्य स्थितिनिबन्धिनीति वाक्यशेषः

b. Here, by the word 'lumen' (*jyotis*) is meant the light that consists of the Pure element [out of the three elementary qualities that constitute the phenomenal]. A luminous immediate cognition [§ 35. *b.*] is that in which this [Pure element] is excellent, abundant, exceeding.*

c. 'Free from sorrow,'—that is to say, that cause of the steadiness of the mind in respect of which [agency] all sorrow, which [—see *Sánkhya Lecture,* § 61.—] is a modification of the Passionate [or *foul* element of the phenomenal universe], is removed by virtue of the exercise of the 'beatific'† [degree of meditation—§ 17. *g.*,—where the ascetic, not yet liberated from the phenomenal, is nearly freed from the two coarser of its three chains].

Dwelling on the inner light of the heart.

d. The meaning is this, that, on the disappearance of all 'modifications' [§ 5.] through the beholding of perfect knowledge, steadiness takes place in the mind of him who, in the midst of the lotus-cup of his heart, broods on the Pure element of thought [spread out in the heart] like the milky ocean when its waves are stilled.‡

e. By means of exhibiting another expedient, he declares an object [worthy of being meditated] in the meditation 'in which there is distinct recognition of an object.'§—[§ 17].

वीतरागविषयं वा चित्तम् ॥ ३७ ॥

Dwelling on admirable examples.

Aph. 37.—Or the thought, taking as its

---

* अत्र ज्योतिःशब्देन सात्त्विकःप्रकाश उच्यते । सप्रशस्तो भूयानतिशयवांश्च विद्यते यस्याः सा ज्योतिष्मती प्रवृत्तिः ॥

† विशोका विगतस्सुखमयसत्त्वाभ्यासबलात् शोको रजः परिणामरूपो यस्याः सा चेतसः स्थितिनिबन्धिनी ॥

‡ अयमर्थः । हृत्पद्मपुटमध्ये प्रशान्तकल्लोलक्षीरोदधिप्रख्यं चित्तसत्त्वं संभावयतः प्रज्ञालोकात् सर्ववृत्तिक्षये चेतसः स्थैर्यमुत्पद्यत इति ॥

§ उपायान्तरप्रदर्शनद्वारेण सम्प्रज्ञातसमाधेर्विषयं दर्शयति ॥

object some one devoid of passion, [may find what will serve as a cause of the steadiness of the mind].*

a. To complete the aphorism we must supply' may [find what will] serve as a cause of the steadiness of the mind.'*

b. 'Devoid of passion,' i. e., who has abandoned all desire for objects of sense,—like Sanaka and others. [The mind, we repeat, may be steadied by the expedients previously mentioned,] or the thoughts of the Yogi, directed to *this* [—i. e. to one devoid of passion as Sanaka was—],becomes fixed ;—that is to say, the unimpassioned thought becomes more firmly steady through reflecting on one whose thoughts are devoid of passion.†

c. He mentions another expedient of this description.‡

स्वप्ननिद्राज्ञानालम्बनं वा ॥ ३८ ॥

Recourse had to dreaming and sleeping.

Aph. 38.—Or the dwelling on knowledge [that presents itself] in dream, or in sleep, [may serve as a cause of the steadiness of the mind].

Dreaming defined.

a. 'Dream' is that wherein the soul is affected through the mind alone, when the modifications of the external organs of sense have departed.§

b. 'Sleep' has already been defined‖[—see § 10].

c. [We say, then, that] knowledge dependent on dream, or dependent on sleep, when dwelt upon, causes steadiness of mind,$—[there being in either case nothing to distract the attention].

d. Since [different] men have different tastes ; on whatever thing the Yogi places his faith, by meditating on that same

* मनसः स्थितिनिबन्धनम्भवतीति वाक्यशेषः ॥

† वीतरागः परित्यक्तविषयाभिलाषस्सनकादिः । तद्विषयकं वा योगिचित्तं निबद्धं भवति विरक्तचित्तस्य भावनया विरक्तं चित्तं दृढस्थितये भवतीत्यर्थः ॥

‡ एवंविधमुपायान्तरमाह ।

§ प्रत्यस्तमितबाह्येन्द्रियवृत्तेः मनोमात्रेणैव यत्र भोक्तृत्व मात्मनः स स्वप्नः ॥

‖ निद्रा उक्तलक्षणा ॥

$ स्वप्नालम्बनं निद्रालम्बनं वा ज्ञानमालम्ब्यमानं चेतसः स्थितिं करोति ॥

thing he may attain what he wants [—viz. steadiness of mind]:—in order to declare this, he states as follows.*

यथाभिमतध्यानाद्वा ॥ ३९ ॥

Anything you please may be dwelt upon to steady the mind.

Aph. 39.—Or [the steadying of the mind may be effected] by pondering anything that one approves.

a. [That is to say]; the mind becomes steadied when any object that one prefers is pondered,—whether external, as the Moon or the like, or internal, as a congeries of arteries or the like.†

The fruit of meditation. *b.* Having thus exhibited the means [of accomplishing meditation], in order to exhibit the fruits, he proceeds to remark.‡

परमाणुपरममहत्त्वान्तो ऽस्य वशीकारः ॥ ४० ॥

To apprehend the infinitely small or great.

Aph. 40.—His mastery extends to the atomic and to the infinite.

a. The ascetic effecting, by these methods, steadiness of mind, obtains, through meditation on subtile objects, unresisted mastery as far as the Atoms;—that is to say, his mind, in [dealing with] subtile objects, even as far as the Atoms [which elude the cognizance of ordinary perspicacity], is nowhere baffled. In like manner no mental obstacle arises anywhere to him meditating the gross, even to the extent of infinite magnitude,—as the Ether, for example;—but everywhere he is uncontrolled,—such is the meaning.§

---

* नानारुचित्वात्प्राणिनां यस्मिन् कस्मिंश्चिद्वस्तुनि योगिनः श्रद्धा भवति तस्य ध्यानेनापि भक्तीष्टसिद्धिरिति प्रतिपादयितुमाह ॥

† यथाभिमते वस्तुनि बाह्ये चन्द्रादावाभ्यन्तरे नाडीचक्रादौ वा भाव्यमाने चेतः स्थिरंभवति ॥ ‡ एवमुपायान् प्रदर्श्य फलप्रदर्शनार्थमाह ॥

§ एभिरुपायैश्चित्तस्थैर्यम्भावयतो योगिनः सूक्ष्मविषयभावनाद्वारेण परमाण्वन्तो वशीकारो ऽप्रतिघातरूपो जायते क्वचित् परमाणुपर्यन्ते सूक्ष्मविषये अस्य मनो न प्रतिहन्यत इत्यर्थः । एवं स्थूलमाकाशादिपरममहत्त्वपर्यन्तम्भावयतो न क्वचिच्चेतसः प्रतिघात उत्पद्यते किन्तु सर्वत्र स्वातन्त्र्यम्भवतीत्यर्थः ॥

b. Of the mind thus by these methods rectified, what is the aspect [or actual condition]? To this he replies.*

क्षीणवृत्तेरभिजातस्येव मणेर्ग्रहीतृग्रहणग्राह्येषु तत्स्थ
तदञ्जनतासमापत्तिः ॥ ४१ ॥

The state of the mind properly intent on a single object.

Aph. 41.—To that [mind whose 'modifications' [—all save that there remains some one object of meditation—]have disappeared, there occurs, as [occurs] to a noble gem [—e. g. rock-crystal, when brought into conjunction with a coloured substance—], when intent on any one out of these—viz.—the perceiver, the perception, and the perceivable,—a tinging thereby.

a. That is to say—to that [mind] whose 'modifications' [§ 5.] have disappeared, which has repelled all modifications *except* that which has to be pondered,—which has accomplished that concentration 'in which there is distinct recognition'†[of a single object to the exclusion of all others,—§ 17.].

b. 'Out of [the three viz.] the perceiver, the perception, and the perceivable'—i. e. Soul, the organs of sense, and the [five] elements.‡

c. 'To it [—the thought—] intent on any one [of these §41, *b.*—]there occurs a tinging thereby.' By 'being intent thereon' we mean attending to that alone. 'A tinging thereby,'—i. e. the [thought's] coming to consist thereof [by taking the colour or character of the object as its own] ;—the coming to be of the same description ;—that is to say, it [—the thought—] becomes modified into the aspect of that § [which is thought upon].

d. He mentions an illustration. To the noble—i. e. pure [transparent and colourless]—gem, such a gem as rock-crystal or the like, there occurs this or that colour in consequence of its

---

* एवमेभिरुपायैसंस्कृतस्य चेतसः कीदृशं रूपम्भवतीत्याह ॥

† क्षीणा वृत्तयो यस्य तस्य निरुद्धध्येयातिरिक्तवृत्तेः सम्पन्नसम्प्रज्ञातयोगस्येत्यर्थः ॥ ‡ ग्रहीतृग्रहणग्राह्येषु पुरुषेन्द्रियभूतेषु ॥

§ तत्स्थतदञ्जनतासमापत्तिः । तत्स्थत्वं तदेकाग्रता । तदञ्जनता तन्मयत्वं । तथाविधा समापत्तिः तद्रूपपरिणामो भवतीत्यर्थः ।

being the receptacle of this or that colour, [—as when the red or other colour of flowers has place within a crystal vase—]. In like manner, to the stainless pure element of thought [§ 36. *d.*] there occurs the hue of this or that, through the adjacent hue of this or that thing which is meditated upon.*

e. 'The perceived, the perception, and the perceiver'—such is the inverse order in which these are to be understood [—instead of the order adopted in the aphorism—], because it is on 'the perceived' [—the external or objective—] that meditation is first fixed,† [—see § 17.*e.* &c].

f. He now states [in three aphorisms] a fourfold division of the abovementioned [§ 41] change ‡ [of the mind into the likeness of what it ponders].

शब्दार्थज्ञानविकल्पैस्सङ्कीर्णा सवितर्का ॥ ४२ ॥

The first stage of the mind properly intent.

Aph. 42.—This [change of the mind into the likeness of what is pondered—§ 41—], when mixed up of the fancy of the 'word,' the 'meaning,' and the 'knowledge,' is [technically termed] the 'argumentative.'

a. A 'Word,' is what is apprehended by the organ of hearing, or [in the technical language of the grammarians] a manifestation§ (*sphota*).

b. The 'Meaning' i. e. the thing meant by a sound or word is a genus [—such as 'cow,' 'horse,'—] &c,,|| [see *Sáhitya Darpana* § 12].

c. 'Knowledge,' is a modification of the understanding [—see § 5 and 6—] where the quality of Purity prevails$ [—to the suppression of the elements of Passion and Darkness,—see§17*g.*]

---

* दृष्टान्तमाह । अभिजातस्य निर्मलस्य मणेः स्फटिकादिमणेः तत्तद्रूपाश्रयवशात् तत्तद्रूपापत्तिः । एवं निर्मलस्य चित्तसत्वस्य तत्तद्भावनीयवस्तूपरागात् तत्तद्रूपापत्तिः ।

† ग्राह्यग्रहणग्रहीतृष्विति व्यत्यासेन योजनीयं यतः प्रथमं ग्राह्यनिष्ठ एव समाधिरिति ॥ ‡ इदानीमुक्ताया एव समापत्तेश्चतुर्विधभेदमाह ॥

§ श्रोत्रेन्द्रियग्राह्यः स्फोटो वा शब्दः ॥ अर्थो जात्यादिः

$ ज्ञानं सत्वप्रधाना बुद्धिवृत्तिः ।

d. A 'Fancy' has been already defined* [in *Aph.* 9].

e. 'Mixed up of these'—i. e. in which the three—viz. the 'Word,' &c., [§ 42],—by mutually commingling, appear in an [ambiguous and] fanciful shape,—in the shape [at once] of the *word* 'cow,' [for example], the *thing* 'cow,' and the *notion* 'cow,'—this is what is called [technically] 'the argumentative' (*savitarka*) change† [of the mind reflecting a mixed object of thought—while the attention is divided among the sound, the thing signified, and the knowledge of the thing.]

f. He now mentions that 'non-argumentative' [affection of the mind] which is the opposite of the one just defined‡ [§42].

स्मृतिपरिशुद्धौ स्वरूपशून्येवार्थमात्रनिर्भासा निर्वितर्का ॥ ४३ ॥

The second stage of the mind properly intent.

Aph. 43.—On the clearing off of the memory [of the word and the sense attached to it by convention], the [mental] display only of the thing itself as if of something indefinite [and no longer referred to any term—no longer regarded as being what is meant by the word 'cow,' or what is meant by the word 'horse,' &c.—], this [affection of the mind which no longer reflects a mixed object of thought—§ 42—] is that which is called [technically] the 'non-argumentative.'

a. 'Of the memory'—i. e., of the memory of the convention as to the sense of the word. 'The clearing off'—i. e., the departure. When this takes place, the change [of the mind] when it reveals the thing itself alone, as if devoid of any character [which would suggest a term as applicable to it],—when it [the mind in its changed state—§ 41—] is employed about the object to be pondered alone [without regard to its having any name], and thus clear of 'fancy' [—nothing being pondered but

---

* विकल्प उक्तलक्षणः ।

† तैस्सङ्कीर्णा । यस्यामेते शब्दादयः परस्पराध्यासेन विकल्परूपेण त्रयः प्रतिभासन्ते गौरिति शब्दो गौरित्यर्थो गौरिति ज्ञानमित्यनेनाकारेण सा सवितर्का समापत्तिरित्युच्यते ।

‡ उक्तलक्षणविपरीतां निर्वितर्कामाह ।

the actual thing itself—], is what is called the 'non-argumentative' [affection of the mind]; such is the meaning.*

b. In order to declare another division, he says :†—

एतयैव सविचारानिर्विचाराच सूक्ष्मविषयाव्याख्याता ॥ ४४ ॥

The third and fourth stages of the mind properly intent.

Aph. 44.—Just by this [mental affection under the two aspects explained in Aphorisms 42 and 43], that which is [technically termed] 'deliberative' (*sa-vichára*), and [that termed] 'non-deliberative' (*nirvichára*), where the object [pondered,—instead of being gross as in these two preceding cases—] is 'subtile,' has been [sufficiently] explained; [—the distinction between this pair, out of the four referred to at § 41 *f.*, being the same as that between the other pair].

a. Just by this mental affection, in the shape of the 'argumentative' [§ 42] and the 'non-argumentative' [§43], where the object is a 'gross' one [as contradistinguished from the 'subtile' objects,—see § 44 *b.*—], the pair of mental affections also, in the shape of the 'deliberative' and the 'non-deliberative,' where the object is 'subtile,' has been explained.‡

b. What sort [of mental affection] is that where the object is *subtile*? That [mental affection] is so called, the object whereof, such as the 'subtile elements' or the 'organs' [§17. *f.*] is subtile. By this [mention that the object, in the case of the latter pair,—§44, *a.*,—as 'subtile'] it is declared that in the former [pair] the object is 'gross,'—for [in truth] it is on the gross elements that it [—the former pair §42—43—] is dependent. That is [called] the 'deliberative' [§44] in which the 'subtile object' appears whether as the object of a question as to the name, the meaning, and the notion [§42], or

---

* स्मृतेः । शब्दार्थसङ्केतस्मृतेः । परिशुद्धिरपगमस्तस्यांसत्यां स्वरूपशू येव अर्थमात्रनिर्भासा ध्येयार्थमात्रावगाहिनी विकल्पशून्या समापत्तिर्निर्वितर्कसंज्ञेत्यर्थः ।

† भेदान्तरं प्रतिपादयितुमाह ॥

‡ एतयैव सवितर्कनिर्वितर्करूपया स्थूलविषयकसमापत्त्या सूक्ष्मविषयापि सविचारनिर्विचाररूपसमापत्तिद्वयी व्याख्याता ।

apart from any such question, but yet as qualified by the characters of space and time, &c. That [on the other hand] is [called] the 'non-deliberative' [§44], in which the 'subtile object,' in the shape of the Subtile Elements or the Organs, independently of the properties of space and time, &c., is presented simply as the thing itself. It is of this [pair of mental modifications] alone that the objects are 'subtile'* [—and not of the other pair,—see §44. *a.*]

c. In reply to the question how far [the term] 'where the object is subtile' [§44] [extends], he says:—†

सूक्ष्मविषयत्वञ्चालिङ्गपर्यवसानम् ॥ ४५ ॥

The limit of analysis. *Aph.* 45—And 'the having a subtile object' ends with the Indissoluble.

a. This fact that has been mentioned of the 'deliberative' and the 'non-deliberative' mental affections [§44], that their object is a 'subtile' one [§44. *b.*], ends with the Indissoluble,—meaning, by the 'Indissoluble,' Nature, [that primordial principle—see Sánkhya Lecture §7—] which is nowhere resolved [into anything underlying it],—or which [to take another etymological explanation] declares or suggests nothing. It is at this point that 'the having a subtile object' ceases‡ [—seeing that, beyond this, there exists nothing more subtile lying further back.]

b. To explain:—in the modification of the Qualities there arise four divisions—(1) that which has a diversified character,

---

* कीदृशी सूक्ष्मविषया । सूक्ष्मस्तन्मात्रेन्द्रियादिर्विषयायस्यास्सो तथोक्ता । एतेन पूर्वस्या स्थूलविषयत्वं प्रतिपादितम्भवति सा हि महाभूतालम्बना । शब्दार्थज्ञानविकल्पाविषयत्वेन तद्रहितत्वेनच देशकालधर्माद्यवच्छिन्नः सूक्ष्मोऽर्थः प्रतिभाति यस्यां सा सविचारा । देशकालधर्मादिरहितो धर्मिमात्रतया सूक्ष्मोऽर्थस्तन्मात्रेन्द्रियरूपः प्रतिभातियस्यां सा निर्विचारेत्यर्थः । अस्या एव सूक्ष्मविषयाः ।

† किम्पर्यन्तस्सूक्ष्मविषय इत्याह ।

‡ सविचारनिर्विचारयोस्समापत्योर्यत्सूक्ष्मविषयत्वमुक्तंतदालिङ्गपर्यवसानं । न क्वचिल्लीयते न वा किञ्चिल्लिङ्गयातिगमयतीत्यालिङ्गं प्रधानं । तत्पर्यन्तं सूक्ष्मविषयत्वमिति ।

(2) that which has an undiversified character, (3) that which merely has a character, and (4) that which has not a character. [By] 'that which has a diversified character' (*vishishta-linga*) [is meant] the [gross] elements [Sánkhya Lecture §33]. [By] 'that which has an undiversified character' (*avishishta-lina*) is meant the subtile elements and the organs [S. L. §25]. [By] 'that which merely has a character, (*linga-mátra*) is meant Intellect [S. L. §8]. [By] 'that which has not a characteristic attribute' (*alina*) is meant the First Principle [S. L. §7] beyond which there is nothing subtile* [underlying or originating it.]

c. He next mentions, as the topic presents itself, the motive for [valuing] these mental affections [or tinges, §41.]†

ता एव सबीजस्समाधिः ॥ ४६ ॥

What the aforesaid mental affections constitute.

Aph. 46.—These themselves constitute 'Meditation with its *seed*' [§17. *b.*]

a. 'These themselves,' i. e. the mental affections above described. Meditation 'in which there is distinct recognition' [§17 *b.*] is called [meditation] 'with its seed'—i. e. that which is with a seed or with something to rest upon—because all these [varieties of mental affection which we have been treating of] have something to rest upon‡ [—which—see §17. *i.*—must eventually be deserted.]

b. Now he states the fruit of the 'non-deliberative' [mental affection], seeing that, of the other mental affections, this 'non-deliberative' one [§44] is the fruit.§

---

* तथाहि । गुणानां परिणामे चत्वारि पर्वाणि विशिष्टलिङ्गमविशिष्टलिङ्गं लिङ्गमात्रमलिङ्गञ्चेति । विशिष्टलिङ्गं भूतानि । अविशिष्टलिङ्गं तन्मात्रेन्द्रियाणि । लिङ्गमात्रं बुद्धिः अलिङ्गं प्रधानमिति नातः परं सूक्ष्ममस्तीत्युक्तं भवति ।

† एतासां समापत्तीनां प्रकृते प्रयोजनमाह ॥

‡ ता एवोक्तलक्षणास्समापत्तयः । सह बीजेन आलम्बनेन वर्तत इति सबीजः सम्प्रज्ञातः समाधिरुच्यते सर्वासां सालम्बनत्वात् ॥

§ अथेतरासां समापत्तीनां निर्विचारफलकत्वाभिधित्सयाऽस्याः फलमाह ॥

निर्विचारवैशारद्येऽध्यात्मप्रसादः ॥ ४७ ॥

The fruit of this. *Aph.* 47.—When wisdom has come, through the 'non-deliberative' [mental affection], there is spiritual clearness.

a. What we mean by 'non-deliberative' has been already explained* [—§44.]

b. 'Wisdom' here stands for 'purity.'†

c. In comparison with the 'argumentative' [mental affection], when the object is a gross one, the 'non-argumentative' is the superior. In respect of that too the 'deliberative,' whose object is a subtile one, [is the superior]. In respect of this again the 'non-deliberative' [where the object is subtile, is the superior]. And when, in virtue of pre-eminent practice of this there has arisen wisdom, or purity, then there is spiritual clearness. By 'spiritual' we mean what resides in the soul, or in the understanding. Such clearness [viz. spiritual clearness] arises [from the 'non-deliberative' mental affection with a subtile object]. And it is just this spiritual clearness which we mean by the firm steadfastness‡ [attained on the removal of distractions—§32].

d. [Well],—this having been attained, what next? To this he replies.§

ऋतम्भरा तत्र प्रज्ञा ॥ ४८ ॥

From spiritual clearness comes right knowledge. *Aph.* 48.—In that case there is 'knowledge which holds to the truth.

a. By 'knowledge which holds to the true' we mean that knowledge which is never overshadowed by error,—which holds to the truth—i. e. to the real.||

---

* व्याख्यातं निर्विचारत्वम् ॥ † वैशारद्यं नैर्मल्यम् ॥

‡ सवितर्कां स्थूलविषयामपेक्ष्य निर्वितर्कायाः प्राधान्यं । ततोऽपि सूक्ष्मविषयायाः सविचारायाः । ततोऽपि निर्विचारायाः । तस्यास्तु प्रकृष्टाभ्यासवशाद्वैशारद्ये नैर्मल्ये सति अध्यात्मप्रसादः । आत्मनि बुद्धौ वर्त्तत इत्यध्यात्मं । तादृशः प्रसादस्समुपजायते । एतदेव चित्तस्य वैशारद्यं यत् स्थितौ दार्ढ्यमिति ॥

§ तस्मिन् सति किम्भवतीत्याह ॥

|| ऋतं सत्यं बिभर्ति कदाचिदपि न विपर्ययेणाच्छाद्यते सा ऋतम्भरा प्रज्ञा ॥

b. 'In that case'—i. e. when *spiritual clearness* has been attained, this [true knowledge] takes place.*

c. And, through this rightly intelligent view, regarding everything as it really is, the *Yogi* attains to pre-eminent Concentration† [§2].

d. He now states the distinction of this from other [forms of] correct knowledge.‡

श्रुतानुमानप्रज्ञाभ्यामन्यविषयाविशेषार्थत्वात् ॥ ४९ ॥

This knowledge differs from ordinary knowledge.

Aph. 49.—[This kind of knowledge differs] from the knowledge due to testimony and inference because the object of these two is not particulars but generals.

a. By 'testimony' we mean scriptural information. By 'inference' we mean what has been already defined [at §7 *a.*] The knowledge which arises from these two [sources of knowledge] has generals [and not individuals] as its object ; for neither testimony nor a [logical] sign [*tekunpiov*] is able, like a sense-organ, to convey a knowledge of particularities§ [meaning thereby the ultimate and no further explicable distinctions that exist between individuals generically similar and numerically different].

b. On the other hand this meditative knowledge—that associated with the clearness which comes through the 'non-deliberative' [mental affection—§47] differs from these two kinds of knowledge [§49 *a.*], in its having individualities as its object ;—that is to say, [it differs from them] because its object is the individual 'subtile element' or the individual Soul itself.‖

---

* तत्र । अध्यात्मप्रसादे सति भवतीत्यर्थः ।

† तस्माच्च प्रज्ञालोकात्सर्वं यथावत्पश्यन् योगी प्रकृष्टं योगं प्राप्नोति ॥

‡ अस्याः प्रज्ञान्तराद्वैलक्षण्यमाह ॥

§ श्रुतमागमज्ञानम् । अनुमानमुक्तलक्षणम् । ताभ्यां या जायते प्रज्ञा सा-सामान्यविषया । नहि शब्दलिङ्गयोरिन्द्रियवद्विशेषप्रतिपत्तौ सामर्थ्यं ॥

‖ इयं पुनर्निर्विचारवैशारद्यसमुपेता समाधिप्रज्ञा ताभ्यां प्रज्ञाभ्यां विलक्षणा विशेषविषयत्वात् । विशेषः भूतसूक्ष्मगतः पुरुषगतो वा विषयो यस्य तत्वादित्यर्थः ॥

[And so this knowledge, since its object is the particular, has an object other than that which belongs to testimony or inference.]

c. Moreover, when this has been attained, one can discern with one's ordinary organs even minute things, hidden or very far off.*

d. He states the [especial] fruit of this correct knowledge.†

तज्जस्संस्कारोऽन्यसंस्कारप्रतिबन्धी ॥ ५० ॥

One train of thought with one object, is to put an end to all other trains.

Aph. 50.—The train [of self-reproductive thought] resulting from this puts a stop to other trains.

a. The [self-reproductive] continuous flow [of thought—§18] produced by this [meditative] knowledge [§49] prevents other trains, whether they arise during relaxation or concentration;—that is to say, it makes them incapable of producing their effects. It is for this reason that it is directed that one should addict himself to this kind of knowledge alone.‡

b. Having thus described Meditation where there is distinct recognition [of an object §17], in order to declare that in which the distinct recognition is dropped [§17. *j*.], he says:—§

तस्यापि निरोधे सर्वनिरोधान्निर्बीजस्समाधिः ॥ ५१ ॥

Aph. 51.—On the removal of this also, since there is removal of all [the mental modifications], the Meditation is 'without a seed.'

Finally this last train of thought is to drop its object.

a. On the removal, i. e. on the dissolution, of this also,—i. e. of the meditation where there is distinct recognition of an object [§17],—when all the modifications of the mind [§5] have been resolved into their causes [or sources—as a jar, when broken, is resolved into the earth which it was made of—], so

* किंचास्यां सूक्ष्मव्यवहितविप्रकृष्टस्य वस्तुनो लोकप्रत्यक्षेण ग्रहणमस्तीति ॥

† अस्याः प्रज्ञायाः फलमाह ॥

‡ तया प्रज्ञया जनितो यस्संस्कारस्सोऽन्यान्व्युत्थानजान् समाधिजांश्च संस्कारान्प्रतिबध्नाति स्वकार्यकरणाक्षमान्करोतीत्यर्थः । अतस्तामेव प्रज्ञामभ्यसेदित्युक्तं भवति

§ एवं सम्प्रज्ञातसमाधिमभिधायासम्प्रज्ञातं वक्तुमाह ॥

that there arises merely a continuous train [of thought self reproductive], thereupon, as there is nothing but negation. 'This is not.' This is not—meditation appears with relinquishment of the seed [§17 *b.*]; on which taking place, the soul is said to abide in its own nature pure—alone—emancipated.*

Recapitulation. *b.* Well then [—to recapitulate briefly—], having set forth the definition [§ 2] of concentration' which is the subject of the work [§ 1], the explanation of the terms 'Modification of the mind' [§ 5] and the 'Prevention' thereof [§ 12], the definition of 'Exercise' [§ 13] and 'Dispassion' [§ 15] and having thus stated the nature of and the difference between these two expedients; then having stated the division of Concentration, into principal and secondary, by distinguishing it as 'Meditation in which there is distinct recognition' [§ 17] and that 'in which distinct recognition is lost [§ 18];' then having exhibited diffusively [§ 20—22] the expedients [for attaining to concentration], after premising an exposure of the 'Spurious semblance of concentration,' [§ 19]; then, with a view to exhibiting an *easy* method, having determined the nature of the Lord [§ 23—24], the proof of His existence [§ 25], His pre-eminence [§ 26], His name [§ 27], the order of His worship [§ 28] and the fruits thereof [§ 29]; then having described the distractions of the mind [§ 30] and their supervenients, grief &c. [§ 31], and diffusively, the means of combating these—viz. the dwelling upon some one truth [§ 32], the practice of benevolence &c. [§ 33], the regulation of the breath [§ 34], and other such means—viz. 'sensuous immediate cognitions &c.' [§ 35—39]—as are conducive to Meditation with or without distinct recognition of an object; having declared the mental affections [§ 41], with an eye to the winding up, with their definitions [§ 42-44], their fruits [§ 46-48] and their object

---

* तस्यापि सम्प्रज्ञातस्यापि निरोधे प्रविलये सति सर्वासां चित्तवृत्तीनां स्वकारणे प्रविलयाद्या या संस्कारमात्रा वृत्ति रुदेति तस्यां नेति नेतिकेवलं पर्युदसनान्निर्बीजस्समाधिराविर्भवति यस्मिन् सति पुरुषः स्वरूपनिष्ठश्शुद्धः केवलो मुक्त इत्युच्यत इति ॥

[§ 49]; then by finally summing up, in regard to the Meditation with distinct recognition and that without distinct recognition of an object,—in words to the effect that Meditation without a seed is preceded by that which has a seed § 51, the chapter on Concentration has been expounded* [by Pantanjali.]

c. Thus is completed the First Book—that on Meditation—of the commentary, composed by the illustrious great king and governor, King Bhojaraja, on the Aphorisms of Patanjali's System of the Yoga.†

Remarks.

d. The commentator, it will be observed [—see Introduction, *b.*—,] justifies Patanjali's undertaking to expound the *Yoga*, by citing a passage from the Veda [—the Nachiketa Upanishad—] recommendatory of the *Yoga*. The *Yoga*, therefore, under that name, was recognised antecedently to Patanjali, and is not to be regarded as an invention of his.

e. The term *Yoga*, we were told [§ 2], implies the hindering of the modifications of the thinking principle. All the six Hindu systems, five of which we have already partially examined, agree in regarding the distinction between Subject and Object as the most momentous of facts, and the emancipation of the former from all entanglement with the latter as the one desirable end. In their treatment of the Objective the systems

---

* तदत्राधिकृतस्य योगस्य लक्षणं चित्तवृत्तिनिरोधपदानां व्याख्यानं अभ्यासवैराग्यलक्षणं तस्योपायद्वयस्य स्वरूपं भेदञ्चाभिधाय, सम्प्रज्ञातासम्प्रज्ञातभेदेन योगस्य मुख्यामुख्यभेदमुक्त्वा, योगाभ्यासप्रदर्शनपूर्वकान् विस्तरेणोपायान् प्रदर्श्य, सुगमोपायप्रदर्शनपरतयेश्वरस्य स्वरूपप्रमाणप्रभाववाचकोपासनाक्रमतत्फलानि निर्णीय, चित्तस्य विक्षेपान् तत्सहभुवश्च दुःखादीन् विस्तरेण च तत्प्रतिषेधोपायनेकतत्त्वाभ्यासमैत्र्यादीन् प्राणायामादीन् सम्प्रज्ञातासम्प्रज्ञातपूर्वाङ्गभूतविषयवतीप्रवृत्तिरित्यादीनाख्यायोपसंहारद्वारेण समापत्तीस्सलक्षणाःसफलाःस्वस्वविषयसहिताश्चोक्त्वा, सम्प्रज्ञातासम्प्रज्ञातयोरुपसंहारमभिधाय सबीजपूर्वको निर्बीजस्समाधिरिति व्याख्यातो योगपादः

† इति श्रीमहाराजाधिराजश्रीभोजराजदेवविरचितायां पातञ्जलयोगशास्त्रसूत्रवृत्तौ प्रथमः समाधिपादः समाप्तः ॥

differ, at least in appearance, more widely than in their treatment of the Subjective. The Vedanta denies reality—or most grudgingly allows any thing of reality—to the Objective. The Nyaya accords to it a reality co-ordinate with that of the Subject, giving impartially the name of Substance to both. The Sankhya steers a middle course between these two. It treats the Objective as an aggregate of *qualities*, whsch exist as *such* but not as substances. In this respect, the Sankhya comes even nearer than the Vedanta to Bishop Berkeley. The *Yoga*, as far as we have seen, concurs with the Sankhya on this point. While the systems thus differ in regard to the Objective or Material, they all agree, on the other hand, in regarding the Subject *(atman)*—call it Soul, or Spirit,—as a self-dependant reality. The only dispute here is, whether Soul, or Spirit, is one or manifold. The Vedanta holds that it is one ; the other systems, so far as we have yet seen, that it is manifold. It is to be observed that nowhere in any of the systems does the notion of a *created* spirit present itself. The Vedanta availing itself of a sufficiently loose analogy, speaks of one Soul pervading all bodies as one thread might pervade a necklace of golden, silver and earthen, beads; while the Sankhya urges the objection that if Soul were but one, then all would be happy when one is happy, all would die, when one died, and so on, which is contrary to experience, [Sánkhya Lecture §48 and 45]. But, whether Soul be one or manifold, every one of the systems holds it to be self-dependant. Soul is the *substance*—beneath which there stands nothing;—and the pity, in the estimation of Hindu philosophy, is, that anything should stand *above* it,—any more than beneath it. It ought to stand alone—apart from everything phenomenal.

f. In order to repel the transient or phenomenal, according to the *Yoga* [§12] we must have recourse to exercise and dispassion, or asceticism and mortification.

g. By means of ascetic exercises and the mortification of all desires, the mind is supposed to attain to a state of undisturbed Meditation [§17], where some one single object is pondered, to the exclusion of all others. But as the practised swimmer parts with his last cork or bladder, so the soul of the ascetic must in due course part with every object, and at length meditate without any object at all [§18]. To effect this being a matter of difficulty, devotion to *the Lord* [§23] is recommended as a comparatively easy method. In admitting the existence of a Divine Being (*Ishwar*) in whom the good qualities belonging to man reach their limit, the Yoga, hence named the *seshwara sankhya* differs from the Sànkhya of Kapila, which is known as *nirishwara.*

h. As the ascetic is exposed to obstacles, these are discussed by Patanjali [§30—31], and means for combating them are indicated [§32—39].

i. When all obstacles have been thus removed, the mind is supposed to be as free from all contamination of the phenomenal as the pure crystal is free from the red colour which *seems* to belong to it while a rose is seen athwart it.

END OF BOOK I.

THE

SANKHYA

OR

YOGA APHORISMS

OF

PATANJALI.

BOOK II.

a. May that three-eyed Lord of the World, by whom were shown the several means for securing the riches of Concentration (*yoga*), attainable with great difficulty, be [adjuvant] for the attainment of what is desired !*

b. Thus then having declared, in the First Book, the Concentration, along with its means, of him whose mind is abstracted [from all objects];—how, preceded by the practice of means, does the concentration of him whose mind is *not* abstrcted, advance to accomplishment. [Since this question presents itself—] in order to set forth the practice of what is instrumental thereto, he declares the practical [part of] Concentration.†

---

* ते ते दुष्प्रापयोगर्द्धिसिद्धये येन दर्शिताः॥ उपायास्स जगन्नाथस्त्र्यक्षोऽस्तु प्रार्थिताप्तये॥

† तदेवं प्रथमे पादे समाहितचित्तस्य सोपायं योगमभिधाय व्युत्थितचित्तस्य कथमुपायाभ्यासपूर्वको योगस्साध्यतामुपयातीति तत्साधनानुष्ठानप्रतिपादनाय क्रियायोगमाह ॥

तपः स्वाध्यायेश्वरप्रणिधानानि क्रियायोगः ॥ १ ॥

Practices conducive to Concentration.

Aph. 1.—The practical [part of] Concentration is mortification *(tapas)*, muttering *(swádhyáya)*, and resignation *(pranidhána)* to the Lord.

a. The penances and fastings enjoined in another Institute [—viz. the *Dharma-shástra*—], are what is meant by 'mortification.' 'Muttering' is the muttered repetition of formulæ preceded by the mystic name of the deity [B. I. § 27]. 'Resignation to the Lord' is the consigning to Him, the Supremely Venerable, without regard to fruit, all one's works. These are what are called the practical [part of] Concentration *(kriyá-yoga)*.*

b. For what purpose is this?—He replies.†—

समाधिभावनार्थः क्लेशतनूकरणार्थश्च ॥ २ ॥

The purpose of such practices.

Aph. 2.—It is for the purpose of establishing meditation and for the purpose of extenuating afflictions.

a. The 'afflictions' *(klesha)* will be mentioned [under § 3], The 'extenuating' of them, is to oppose their producing their effects. 'Meditation' is what has been already defined [B. I. § 20, *f*]. The 'establishing' of it, is the repeatedly taking into one's thoughts [the thing to be meditated upon]. That the purpose, or motive, of which is this, is what is so called [—i. e. is what is spoken of in the aphorism].‡

b. That is to say,—these, viz, penance, &c., being practised, rendering inert the 'Ignorance' and the other afflictions [§ 3] that assail the mind, sustain the part of subservients to Medi-

---

* तपः शास्त्रान्तरोपदिष्टं कृच्छ्रंचान्द्रायणादि । स्वाध्यायः प्रणवपूर्वाणां मन्त्राणां जपः । ईश्वरप्रणिधानं सर्वक्रियाणां तस्मिन् परमगुरौ फलनिरपेक्षतया समर्पणम् । एतानि क्रियायोग इत्युच्यते ॥

† स किमर्थ इत्यत आह ॥

‡ क्लेशाः वक्ष्यमाणास्तेषां तनूकरणं स्वकार्यकरणप्रतिबन्धः । समाधिरुक्तलक्षणः । तस्य भावना पुनःपुनश्चेतसि निवेशनम् । सोऽर्थः प्रयोजनं यस्य सतथोक्तः ॥

tation. Therefore it is to the practical [part of] Concentration that the *Yogi* should first direct his attention.*

c, 'For the purpose of extenuating affliction,'—this has been stated [in § 2];—what are here meant by afflictions? He replies †

अविद्यास्मितारागद्वेषाभिनिवेशाः क्लेशाः ॥ ३ ॥

Afflictions to be alleviated by such practices.

Aph. 3.—The afflictions are Ignorance, Egoism, Desire, Aversion, and Tenacity [of mundane existence].

a. And the 'afflictions,'—Ignorance and the rest,—the definitions of which will be stated [in the sequel], are five; and these, giving rise to distress, the characteristic of which is its being obstructive [to what we miserable mortals wish], are called 'afflictions,' because they, operating in the mind, consolidate that modification of the [three] Qualities which is recognised as mundane existence‡ [—the state of existence which it is the aim of the Yogi to eschew].

b. Although these are all equal in respect of being afflictions, yet, in order to declare that 'Ignorance' *(avidyá)*, from its being the root, is the principal one, he says.§

अविद्या क्षेत्रमुत्तरेषां प्रसुप्ततनुविच्छिन्नोदाराणाम् ॥ ४ ॥

The source of the afflictions.

Aph. 4.—Ignorance is the field of the others, whether they be dormant, extenuated, intercepted, or simple.

a. 'Ignorance' means delusion; the notion, in short, that

---

* एतदुक्तम्भवति । एते तपः प्रभृतयो ऽभ्यस्यमानाश्चित्तगतानविद्यादीन् क्लेशान् शिथिलीकुर्वन्तः समाधेरुपकारकतां भजन्ते । तस्मात् प्रथमतः क्रियायोगावधारणपरेण योगिना भवितव्यमिति ॥

† क्लेशतनूकरणार्थं इत्युक्तं । तेऽत्र के क्लेशा इत्यत आह ॥

‡ क्लेशाश्चाविद्यादयो वक्ष्यमाणलक्षणाः पञ्च । ते बाधनालक्षणं परितापमुपजनयन्तः क्लेशशब्दवाच्या भवन्ति । ते हि चेतसि प्रवर्त्तमानाः संसारलक्षणं गुणपरिणामं द्रढयन्ति ॥

§ सत्यपि सर्वेषां तुल्ये क्लेशत्वे मूलभूतत्वादविद्यायाः प्राधान्यं प्रतिपादयितुमाह॥

what is *not* Soul *is* Soul. This is the 'field,'—the place of origin, of the others, viz., 'Egoism,' &c., which are severally fourfold through the division into 'dormant, &c. Therefore, where Ignorance, in the shape of a mistaken notion [that what is not soul is soul], becomes inoperative, there the springing up of the 'afflictions' is not seen; but, since, where this mistaken notion really exists, they *are* seen to spring up, it is quite settled that it is Ignorance that is the source.*

b. 'The dormant, extenuated, intercepted, and simple':—among these, those 'afflictions' are called 'dormant,' which, deposited in the mind, do not give rise to their effects for want of something to wake them up;—as in the state of childhood;—for the child's 'afflictions,' though present in the shape of mental deposits, are not developed for want of something to assist in awakening them.†

c. Those ['afflictions'] are the 'extenuated,' which through one's meditating something that is opposed to each severally, their power of producing their effect having been rendered inert, abiding in the mind as a species of mental deposit, are incapable of giving rise to their effects without an ample apparatus [of auxiliaries];—for example [such are the 'afflictions'] of the ascetic *Yogi*.‡

d. Those ['afflictions'] are the 'intercepted,' which abide with their power overpowered by some strong 'affliction,'—as

---

* अविद्या मोहः । अनात्मन्यात्माभिमान इति यावत् । सा क्षेत्रं प्रसवभूमिरुत्तरेषामस्मितादीनां प्रत्येकं प्रसुप्तादिभेदेन चतुर्विधानां । अतो यत्राविद्या विपर्ययज्ञानरूपा शिथिलीभवति तत्र क्लेशानां अस्मितादीनां नोद्भवो दृश्यते विपर्ययज्ञानसद्भावे च तेषामुद्भवदर्शनात् स्थितमेव मूलत्वमविद्यायाः ॥

† प्रसुप्ततनुविच्छिन्नोदाराणामिति । तत्र ये क्लेशाश्चित्तभूमौ स्थिताः प्रबोधकाभावे स्वकार्यं नारभन्ते ते प्रसुप्ता इत्युच्यते । यथा बाल्यावस्थायां । बालस्य हि वासनारूपेण स्थिता अपि क्लेशाः प्रबोधकसहकार्यभावेन न व्यज्यन्ते ॥

‡ ते तनवः ये स्वस्वप्रतिपक्षभावनया शिथिलीकृतकार्यसम्पादनशक्तयो वासनाविशेषतया चेतस्यवस्थिताः प्रभूतां सामग्रीमन्तरेण न स्वकार्यमारब्धुं क्षमाः ॥ यथा अभ्यासवतो योगिनः ॥

desire [is overpowered and 'intercepted'] when there is the condition of aversion, or aversion when there is the condition of [an overpowering] desire;—for those two, mutually opposite cannot simultaneously co-exist.*

e. Those ['afflictions'] are the 'simple,' which operate their several effects when the things with which they co-operate are beside them;—[such are,] for example, things adverse to Concentration at all times during the state of non-abstraction.†

f. 'Ignorance,' though standing moreover as the *root* of these four kinds [of 'afflictions'] severally, is recognized as [also] *attending* them; for nowhere is there found the nature of 'afflictions' having the character of being irrespective of the attendance of error; and when that, being a falsity, is removed by right knowledge, these ['afflictions,'] like burnt seeds, never spring up again; hence it is ascertained that Ignorance is their cause and Ignorance is their attendant. Therefore they all partake of the name of Ignorance; and, since all the 'afflictions' cause distraction of mind, the *Yogi* must cut these off at the very outset.‡

g. He defines 'Ignorance.'§

अनित्याशुचिदुःखानात्मसु नित्यशुचिसुखात्मख्यातिरविद्या ॥ ५ ॥

---

* ते विच्छिन्नाः ये केनचिद्बलवता क्लेशेनाभिभूतशक्तयस्तिष्ठन्ति । यथा द्वेषावस्थायां रागो रागावस्थायां वा द्वेषः । न ह्यनयोः परस्परविरुद्धयोर्युगपत् सम्भवोऽस्ति ॥

† ते उदाराः ये प्राप्तसहकारिसन्निधयः स्वं स्वं कार्यमभिनिर्वर्तयन्ति । यथा सर्वदैव योगपरिपन्थिनो व्युत्थानदशायाम् ॥

‡ एषां प्रत्येकं चतुर्विधानामपि मूलभूतत्वेन स्थिताप्यविद्या अन्वयित्वेन प्रतीयते । नहि क्वचिदपि क्लेशानां विपर्ययान्वयनिरपेक्षरूपाणां स्वरूपमुपलभ्यते । तस्याश्च मिथ्याभूतायां अविद्यायां सम्यक् ज्ञानेन निवर्त्तितायां दग्धबीजकल्पानामेषां न क्वचित्प्ररोहो ऽस्तीति अविद्यानिमित्तत्वमविद्यान्वयश्चैषां निश्चीयते । अतः सर्वे ऽप्यविद्याव्यपदेशभाजः सर्वेषाञ्च क्लेशानां चित्तविक्षेपकारित्वात् योगिना प्रथममेव तदुच्छेदे यत्नः कर्त्तव्य इति ॥

§ अविद्याया लक्षणमाह ॥

Ignorance defined. *Aph.* 5.—Ignorance (*avidyá*) is the notion that the uneternal, the impure, evil, and what is not soul, is [severally] eternal, pure, joy, and soul.

a. The definition of ignorance in general is this,—that, ignorance is the notion that what is *not* this *is* this. The declaration of the varieties of that same [is made in the aphorism]. The notion that there is eternalness in things uneternal, such as water-jars, is called 'Ignorance.' So too the notion that things impure, such as the body, are pure; and the notion that the objects which are evil are joy; and the notion that the body, which is not the soul, is the soul, [—as when a bumpkin fancies that his eye *sees*, or a phrenologist that his brain *thinks*—]. This explains the mistake of vice for vitue, and of the useless for the useful.*

b. In order to define 'Egoism,' he says.†

दृग्दर्शनशक्त्योरेकात्मतैवास्मिता ॥ ६ ॥

'Egoism' defined. *Aph.* 6.—Egoism (*asmitá*) is the identifying of the power that sees with the power of seeing.

a. The 'power that sees' is Soul. The power of 'seeing' is a modification of a Quality of 'Purity' [—see Sánkhya Aphorism, B. I. §62,] unobstructed by 'Passion' and 'Darkness,' in the shape of the internal organ [or mind.] What is called 'Egoism' is the notion that these two things, entirely different as being the experienced and the experiencer—the unintelligent and the *not* unintelligent,—are one and the same. For example,—Nature, though really neither agent nor experiencer fancies "*I* am agent,—*I* am experiencer":—this blunder is the

---

* अतस्मिन् तत्प्रतिभासो ऽविद्येत्यविद्यायाः सामान्यलक्षणं । तस्या एव भेदप्रतिपादनं । अनित्येषु घटादिषु नित्यत्वाभिमानो ऽविद्येत्युच्यते । एवमशुचिषु कायादिषु शुचित्वाभिमानो दुःखेषुच विषयेषु सुखत्वाभिमानोऽनात्मनि शरीरे आत्मत्वाभिमानः । एतेन अपुण्ये पुण्यभ्रमो ऽनर्थेचार्थभ्रमो व्याख्यातः ॥

† अस्मितां लक्षयितुमाह ॥

affliction' called 'Egoism.'*

b. He states the definition of 'Desire' (*rága*).†

सुखानुशयी रागः ॥ ७ ॥

Desire defined. *Aph.* 7.—Desire is what dwells on pleasure.

a. 'Dwells on pleasure'—i. e. reposes on [—or is the affection of the mind when the thought rests on—] joy. This 'affection,' named 'Desire,' is a longing, in the shape of a thirst, for the means of enjoyment, preceded by [—or, in other words, consequent on] the remembrance of enjoyment, on the part of him who has known joy.‡

b. He states the definition of 'Aversion' (*dwesha*).§

दुःखानुशयी द्वेषः ॥ ८ ॥

Aversion defined. *Aph.* 8.—Aversion is what dwells on pain.

a. 'Pain' is what has been already defined [—B. I. §31. *b*.]. Of him who has known it, disliking what things occasion it, in consequence of his remembrance of it, the feeling of disapproval is the 'affliction' called 'aversion.'||

b. He states what is 'tenacity of life'$ (*abhinivésha*).

स्वरसवाही विदुषो ऽपि तन्वनुबन्धो ऽभिनिवेशः ॥ ९ ॥

The clinging to mundane existence. *Aph.* 9.—Continuant through its self-reproductive property, even on the part of

---

* दृक्शक्तिः पुरुषः । दर्शनशक्ति रजस्तमोभ्यामनभिभूतः सात्त्विकः परिणामो ऽन्तःकरणरूपः । तयोर्भोग्यभोक्तृत्वेन जडाजडत्वेन चात्यन्तं भिन्नयोरेकताभिमानो ऽस्मितेत्युच्यते । यथा । प्रकृतिर्वस्तुतः कर्तृत्वभोक्तृत्वरहितापि कर्त्र्यहं भोक्त्र्यहमित्यभिमन्यते सो ऽयमस्मिताख्यो विपर्यासः क्लेशः ॥

† रागस्य लक्षणमाह ॥

‡ सुखमनुशेते इति सुखानुशयी । सुखज्ञस्य सुखानुस्मृतिपूर्वकः सुखसाधनेषु तृष्णारूपो गर्धो रागसंज्ञः क्लेशः ॥

§ द्वेषस्य लक्षणमाह ॥

|| दुःखमुक्तलक्षणं । तदभिज्ञस्य तदनुस्मृतिपूर्वकः तत्साधनेषु अनभिलषतो यो ऽयं निन्दात्मकः स द्वेषलक्षणः क्लेशः ॥

$ अभिनिवेशमाह ॥

the wise, attachment to the body is 'Tenacity of life'.

a. Continuant 'through its self-reproductive property;'—that is to say, it flows on by reason of its own nature, just by reason of its being self-continuant. The 'affliction' called 'tenacity of life' is what prevails in the case of every one, from the worm up to Brahmà, without any concomitant cause [in addition to its own self-continuant property], in the shape of the constant clinging [which expresses itself in such terms as], "May I not be separated from the body and things sensible, &c.,"—this springing up in the shape of dread, through the force of the impression from the experience of the pain of a death that took place in a previous life.*

b. Since thus, then, non-abstraction is made up of the 'afflictions,' the 'afflictions' are at the outset to be removed by the practice of intentness on a single point;—such is the import.†

c. And not without their being known can these be romoved; therefore, having, with a view to the knowledge of them, declared their name, source, division, and characteristic, he now states the division of the methods for the removal of these bipartitely gross and subtile:‡

ते प्रतिप्रसवहेयाः सूक्ष्माः ॥ १० ॥

The Subtile afflictions how to be evaded.

Aph. 10.—These, when subtile, are to be evaded by an antagonistic production.

a. These subtile 'afflictions,' which, abiding in the form of mental deposits, do not occasion any change, in the shape of a

---

* स्वस्य रसेन संस्कारेणैव वहतीति स्वरसवाही । पूर्वजन्मानुभूतमरणदुःखानुभववासनाबलात् भयरूपः समुपजायमानः शरीरविषयादिभिर्मम वियोगो मा भूदित्यन्वहमनुबन्धरूपः सर्वस्यैवाकृमेर्ब्रह्मपर्यन्तं निमित्तं विना प्रवर्तमानो ऽभिनिवेशाख्यः क्लेशः ॥

† तदेवं व्युत्थानस्य क्लेशात्मकत्वात् एकाग्रताभ्यासेन प्रथमं क्लेशाः परिहर्तव्या इत्याशयः ॥

‡ नचाज्ञातानां तेषां परिहारः शक्यः कर्तुमिति तज्ज्ञानाय तेषामुद्देशं क्षेत्रं विभागं लक्षणमभिधाय स्थूलसूक्ष्मभेदाभिन्नानां तेषां प्रहाणोपायविभागमाह ॥

'modification' [—see B. I. § 5,—stored in the mind, like Locke's 'ideas' while not objects of attention—], these are 'to be evaded,' to be avoided, 'by an antagonistic production' by an alteration adverse to them. When the understanding, with its deposits, having done its work, lapses into its cause, viz., egoism, then how should these ['afflictions,'] being deprived of their root, possibly continue ?*

b. He now mentions the method for the removal of the 'gross' ones.†

ध्यानहेयास्तद्वृत्तयः ॥ ११ ॥

The gross 'afflictions' how to be got rid of.

Aph. 11.—Their 'modifications' [—when the 'afflictions' modify the mind by pressing themselves upon the attention—] are to be got rid of by meditation.

a. The 'modifications,' in the shape of pleasure, pain, or indifference, which consist of these 'afflictions' that have set in operation their effects,—*these* are 'to be got rid of,' to be quitted, by means of meditation, i. e., by intentness of the mind on a single point;—such is the meaning.‡

b. These 'from their being gross,' can be removed by the mere practice of what purifies the mind [—see B. I. § 33, *c*—], as the coarse, gross dirt on clothes and the like is removed by mere washing; but that subtile [impurity] which is in them can be removed only by such [more recondite] expedients as bleaching, &c.§

---

* ते सूक्ष्माः क्लेशाः ये वासनारूपेणावस्थिता न वृत्तिरूपं परिणाममारभन्ते ते प्रतिप्रसवेन प्रतिलोमपरिणामेन हेयास्त्यक्तव्याः । स्वकारणास्मितायां कृतार्थं सवासनं चित्तंयदा प्रविष्टं भवति तदा कुतस्तेषां निर्मूलानां सम्भवः ॥

† स्थूलानां हानोपायमाह ॥

‡ तेषां क्लेशानामारब्धकार्याणां याः सुखदुःखमोहात्मिकाः वृत्तयः ताः ध्यानेन चित्तैकाग्रतालक्षणेन हेयाः हातव्या इत्यर्थः ॥

§ चित्तपरि कर्माभ्यासमात्रेणैव स्थूलत्वात्तासां निवृत्तिर्भवति यथा वस्त्रादौ घनः स्थूलो मलः प्रक्षालनमात्रेणैव निवर्त्तते यस्तु तत्र सूक्ष्मः स तैस्तैरुपायैरुत्तापनप्रभृतिभिरेव निवर्त्तयितुं शक्यते ॥

c. Having thus mentioned what the 'afflictions' are, he remarks as follows, with the view of mentioning the stock of works* [that stands at each man's credit or discredit].

क्लेशमूलः कर्माशयो दृष्टादृष्टजन्मवेदनीयः ॥ १२ ॥

One's merits and demerits.

Aph. 12.—The stock of works, whose root is the 'afflictions,' is what is to be had fruition of in this visible state, or in that unseen.

a. By 'the stock of works' the nature of this [that he is speaking of] is set forth, for works exist only in the shape of mental deposits. †

b. By 'whose root is the afflictions' the *cause* is set forth, since the 'afflictions' alone are the cause of acts.‡

c. By 'what is to be had fruition of in this visible state, or in that unseen,' the fruit is declared. What is to be experienced in this present state, is 'what is to be had fruition of in this visible state'. What is to be experienced in another life, is 'what is to be had fruition of in that unseen.'§

d. Thus some meritorious acts, such as the worship of the gods, peformed with excessive impetuosity [—see B. I.§21, *b*—], bestow, even in this life, fruit in the shape of rank, years, and enjoyment,—as distinguished rank [—that of a demigod —], &c., accrued, even in this life, to Nandishwara, through the force of his worship of the divine Maheshwara. So to others, as Vishwamitra [—who, according to the *Rámáyana,* from being a *Kshattriya* was raised to the rank of a *Bráhman*—], through the efficacy of penance, rank and long life [have accrued]. To others [has accrued change of] rank only,—as the change to another rank, &c., of those doing wicked acts with hot impetuosity, such as Nahusha [who was changed to a snake]. and Urvasi [—the nymph who was punished] by her meta-

---

* एवं क्लेशानां तत्त्वमभिधाय कर्माशयस्याभिधातुमाह ॥

† कर्माशयः इत्यनेन तस्य स्वरूपमभिहितं यतो वासनारूपाण्येव कर्माणि ॥

‡ क्लेशमूलः इत्यनेन कारणमभिहितं यतः कर्मणां क्लेशा एवनिमित्त म् ॥

§ दृष्टादृष्टजन्मवेदनीयः इत्यनेन फलमुक्तम् । अस्मिन्नेव जन्मनि अनुभवनीयो दृष्टजन्मवेदनीयः । जन्मान्तरानुभवनीयो ऽदृष्टजन्मवेदनीयः ॥

morphosis into a creeper in the grove of Kartikeya. In this, way is the rule to be applied, according to circumstances, distributively or collectively,* [—each well-deservingorill-deserving person being understood to receive rank, or years, or enjoy-ment, one or more of them, or all of them, or none of them,—and so on through the string of permutations and combinations possible.

e. Now he mentions the fruit of the stock of works divided according to its division† [into merit and demerit].

सतिमूले तद्विपाको जात्यायुर्भोगाः ॥ १३ ॥

The fruit of works. *Aph.* 13—While there is the root, fructification is rank, years, and enjoyment.]

a. The 'afflictions' above-mentioned are the 'root;' whilst these remain unsubdued, of these acts, virtuous or vicious, 'rank, years and enjoyment,' are the 'fructification,' i. e. the fruit. 'Rank' means the being a man [or a god, or a beast,] or the, like. 'Years' mean abiding for a long time in the body. 'Enjoyments' mean sense-objects, the senses, and the aggregate of pleasures and pains, because the word *bhoga* [—here rendered 'enjoyment'—] is formed [from the root *bhuj*] so as to denote the object, the instrument, or the state‡ [of enjoyment].

b. The gist of this is this, that the mental deposits of works, collected, from time without beginning, in the ground of the mind as they by degrees arrive at maturation, so do they existing in lesser or greater measure. [—the sum of the merit

---

* तथाहि कानिचित्पुण्यानि कर्माणि देवताराधनादीनि तीव्रसंवेगेन कृतानीहैव जन्मनि फलं जात्यायुर्भोगलक्षणं प्रयच्छन्ति यथा नन्दीश्वरस्य भगवन्महेश्वराराधन बलादिहैव जन्मनि जात्यादयो विशिष्टाः प्रादुर्भूताः । एवमन्येषां विश्वामित्रादीनां तपःप्रभावाज्जात्यायुषी । केषांश्चिज्जातिरेव । यथा तीव्रसंवेगेन दुष्टकर्मकृतां नहुषादीनां जात्यन्तरादिपरिणाम उर्वश्याश्च कार्तिकेयवने लतारूपतया । एवं व्यस्तसमस्तरूपत्वेन यथायोगं योज्यम् ॥

† इदानीं कर्माशयस्य स्वभेदाभिन्नं फलमाह ॥

‡ मूलमुक्तलक्षणा. क्लेशाः । तेष्वनभिभूतेषु सत्सु तेषां कर्मणां कुशलाकुशलरूपाणां विपाकः फलं जात्यायुर्भोगाभवन्ति । जातिर्मनुष्यत्वादिः । आयुश्च

being lesser than that of the demerit, or conversely—], lead to their effects in the shape of rank [raised or lowered—], years, and enjoyment* [or experience of good or ill].

c. In respect of the 'rank,' &c., which have been declared to be the fruit of acts, he states, according to the works that are the cause of each, which is the cause of that effect.†

ते ल्हादपरितापफलाः पुण्यापुण्यहेतुत्वात् ॥ १४ ॥

What works have what fruits.

Aph. 14.—These have joy or suffering as their fruits, accordingly as the cause is virtue or vice.

a. 'Joy' means pleasure; 'suffering' means pain. Those the fruit of which are joy and suffering, are what are so named [—i. e. are what are denoted in the aphorism by the compound term here analysed]. By 'virtue' (*punya*) is meant any good deed; by 'vice,' its opposite. Of what things these two, viz., virtue and vice, are the causes, the nature of these things [is what is meant by the compound term *punyapunyahetutwat*; and it is] thereby‡ [—or accordingly as the cause is virtue or vice, that the effect is joy or suffering].

b. What is asserted is this, that the rank, years, and enjoyment, originating in good works, are pleasant fruits; and what originate in evil acts are painful fruits.§

c. This twofold character [of the fruit of works] is in respect

---

रकालं कायसम्बन्धः । भोगा विषया इन्द्रियाणि सुखदुःखसंविच्च कर्मकरणभावसाधनव्युत्पत्त्या भोगशब्दस्य ॥

* इदमत्र तात्पर्यं चित्रभूमावनादिकालसञ्चिताः कर्मवासना यथा यथा पाकमुपयान्ति तथा तथा गुणप्रधानभावेन स्थिता जात्यायुर्भोगलक्षणं स्वकार्यमारभन्ते ॥

† उक्तानां कर्मफलत्वे जात्यादीनां स्वकारणकर्मानुसारेण कार्यकर्तृत्वमाह ॥

‡ ल्हादः सुखं । परितापः दुःखं ॥ ल्हादपरितापौ फलं येषां ते तथोक्ताः । पुण्यं कुशलं कर्म । ते पुण्यापुण्ये कारणे येषां तेषां भावस्तस्मात् ॥

§ एतदुक्तम्भवति पुण्यकर्मारब्धाजात्याभोगा ल्हादफलाः । अपुण्यारब्धाः परितापफलाः ॥

of mortals simply; but to the Yogi *all* [mundane experience] is sorrow, as he proceeds to state.*

परिणामतापसंस्कारदुःखैर्गुणवृत्तिविरोधाच्च सर्वं दुःखमेवविवेकिनः ॥१५॥

Pleasure and pain alike vexatious to the Yogi. *Aph.* 15.—And, to the discriminating, *all* is grief simply, since the modifications due to the Qualities are adverse [to the summum bonum] through the vexations of the various forms [of Nature], and of anxiety and impressions self-continuant.

a. That is to say.—[in the opinion] of him who understands discriminatively the 'affections,' &c., *every* instrument of experience [whether of pleasure or of pain] that comes under his view, is, like food with poison in it, a grief only,—something felt to be against the grain.†

b. Since the Yogi who has become a complete adept is distressed even by the slightest pain,—as the eye-ball, and no other member, experiences great pain from the mere touch of a thread of wool, so the discriminating [votary of Quietude] is averse to the adherence of even a very little pain;—*how* is it [that he shrinks from such pains]? To this he replies, 'through the vexations of the various forms, and of anxiety, and of impressions self-continuant.‡

c. Since there is increase of desire in proportion as more objects are enjoyed, and since these [objects] are causes of other pains occasioned by their non-attainment, they are really nothing else than griefs [—according to the principle that the nature of the cause is not other than the nature of the product

---

* एतस्य प्राणिमात्रापेक्षया द्वैविध्यं योगिनस्तु सर्वं दुःख मित्याह ॥

† परिज्ञातक्लेशादिविवेकस्य परिदृश्यमानं सकलमेव भोगसाधनं सविषान्नवत् दुःखमेव प्रतिकूलवेदनीयमित्यर्थः ॥

‡ यस्मादत्यन्ताभिजातो योगी दुःखलेशेनाप्युद्विजते यथाक्षिपात्रमूर्णातन्तुस्पर्शमात्रेणैव महतीं पीडामनुभवति नेतरदङ्गं तथा विवेकी स्वल्पदुःखानुषङ्गेनापि विरज्यते । कथमित्याह परिणामतापसंस्कारदुःखैः

—]; thus is it that the various forms [of Nature presented to us in the shape of objects] are sorrow.*

d. While the means of enjoyment are being enjoyed, since there must ever exist an aversion towards what is hostile to that [enjoyment,—so that thus ever "surgit amari aliquid medio defonte leporum"—], even at the time of experiencing pleasure, the pain of distress is hard to be got rid of,—such is what constitutes the pain [called] anxiety.†

e. As for the fact that 'impressions self-continuant' are griefs,—the sense of enjoyment, and the sense of suffering, that arises on the contact of objects which one desires or does not desire, originates in one's [mental] field a corresponding self-continuant impression. Again we [thence] experience sensations of the same sort, so that, since, through the emergence of innumerable self-continuant impressions, the mundane state is never cut short, everything whatever is a grief.‡

f. 'And since the modifications due to the Qualities, are adverse.' Of the qualities, viz., Purity, Passion, and Darkness the modifications [or psychical influences] which arise in the shape of Pleasure, Pain, and Indifference, are opposed to one another, since they reciprocally are overpowered or do overpower. These are but griefs, since they are, in absolutely every instance, the cause of grief§ [—grief continuing while the mundane state due to the Qualities continues.]

---

* विषयाणामुपभुज्यमानानां यथायथं गर्द्धाभिवृद्धेस्तदप्राप्तिकृतस्य दुःखान्तरसाधनत्वाच्चास्त्येव दुःखरूपतेति परिणामदुःखत्वम् ॥

† उपभुज्यमानेषु तत्प्रतिपन्थिनं प्रति द्वेषस्य सर्वदैवावस्थितत्वात् सुखानुभवकाले ऽपि तापदुःखं दुष्परिहारमिति तापदुःखता ॥

‡ संस्कारदुःखत्वं । स्वाभिमतानभिमतविषयसन्निधाने सुखसंविद्दुःखसंविच्चोपजायमाना तथाविधमेव स्वक्षेत्रे संस्कारमारभते । पुनस्तथाविधसंविदनुभव इत्यपरिमितसंस्कारोत्पत्तिद्वारेण संसारानुच्छेदात्सर्वस्यैव दुःखत्वम् ॥

§ गुणवृत्तिविरोधाच्चेति । गुणानां सत्त्वरजस्तमसां या वृत्तयः सुखदुःखमोहरूपाः परस्परमभिभाव्याभिभावकत्वेन विरुद्धा जायन्ते । तासां सर्वत्रैव दुःखानुबन्धात् दुःखत्वं ॥

g. What is asserted is this, that to the discriminating one, who desires entire and complete cessation of suffering, the whole quaternion [enumerated in the aphorism] are causes of the alleged description* [i. e., causes of grief]. Hence, since all objects exhibit themselves in the shape of vexations, therefore the harvest of all works is in the shape of vexation alone.†

h. This, that, since the aforesaid fund of 'afflictions,' the harvest of [each one's] stock of works, takes its rise in Ignorance, and since Ignorance, as being in the shape of false knowledge, is to be expelled by correct knowledge, and since correct knowledge consists in the ascertainment of what is to be rejected and what to be accepted, with the means [of rejection, &c.,]—in order [—I repeat—] to declare this, he says.‡—

हेयं दुःखमनागतम् ॥ १६ ॥

What is to be shunned. *Aph.* 16.—What is to be shunned is pain not yet come.

a. Since what *has* been is past, and what is *being* experienced is incapable of being shunned [*whilst* being experienced] it is only mundane pain not yet arrived that is to be shunned:—such is what is here asserted.§

b. He states the cause of that which is to be shunned.§

द्रष्टृदृश्ययोः संयोगो हेयहेतुः ॥ १७ ॥

---

* एतदुक्तम्भवति । ऐकान्तिकीमात्यन्तिकीश्च दुःखनिवृत्तिमिच्छतो विवेकिन उक्तरूपकारणं चतुष्टयं । यावत्सर्वे विषया दुःखरूपतया प्रतिभान्ति तस्मात्सर्वकर्म विपाको दुःखरूप एवेति ॥

† तदेवमुक्तस्य क्लेशकर्माशयविपाकराशेरविद्याप्रभवत्वादविद्यायाश्च मिथ्याज्ञानरूपतया सम्यग्ज्ञानस्य ससाधनहेयोपादेयावधारणरूपत्वात् तदभिधानायाह ॥

‡ भूतस्य अतिक्रान्तत्वादनुभूयमानस्यच त्यक्तुमशक्यत्वादनागतमेव संसारदुःखं हातव्यमित्युक्तंभवति ॥

§ हेयहेतुमाह ॥

The origin of evil. *Aph.* 17.—The cause of what is to be shunned is the conjunction of the seer with the visual.

a. The 'seer'—in the shape of Thought. The 'visual' means the principle of understanding [which does not itself see, but is Thought's organ]. The conjunction of these two, occasioned by the absence of discriminative knowledge,—their contact as the experienced [—for all that seems external is developed out of the principle of the understanding—]and the experiencer,—*this* is the cause or reason 'of what is to be shunned,'—of pain—of the world in the shape of a modification of the Qualities;—because when *this* surceases, the mundane state surceases,—such is the meanning.*

a. We have spoken of 'the conjunction of the seer with the visual.' Among these things, of the 'visual' he states the nature, the products, and the motive.†

प्रकाशक्रियास्थितिशीलम्भूतेन्द्रियात्मकं भोगापवर्गार्थं दृश्यम् ॥ १८ ॥

The nature and purpose of the visible. *Aph.* 18.—The visual [—including the visible—]whose habit is illumination, action, and rest, and which consists of the Elements and the Organs, is for the sake of experience and emancipation.

a. 'Illumination' is the property of 'Purity.' 'Action,' in the shape of exertion, is that of 'Passion.' 'Rest,' in the shape of fixation, is that of 'Darkness.' Of which these,—illumination, action, and rest,—are the habit, or the essential nature,—*that* is what is so described [—i. e. described in the aphorism by the compound epithet here analysed]. Thus has its nature been set forth.‡

---

* द्रष्टा चिद्रूपः । दृश्यं बुद्धितत्त्वं । तयोरविवेकख्यातिपूर्वको यो ऽसौ संयोगो भोग्यभोक्तृत्वेन सन्निधानं सहेयस्य दुःखस्य गुणपरिणामरूपस्य संसारस्य हेतुः कारणं तन्निवृत्त्या संसारनिवृत्तिर्भवतीत्यर्थः ॥

† द्रष्टृदृश्ययोः संयोग इत्युक्तं । तत्र दृश्यस्य स्वरूपं कार्यं प्रयोजनञ्चाह ॥

‡ प्रकाशः सत्त्वस्य धर्मः । क्रिया प्रवृत्तिरूपा रजसः । स्थितिर्नियमरूपा तमसः । ताः प्रकाशक्रियास्थितयः शीलं स्वाभाविकं रूपं यस्य तत्तथाविधमिति स्वरूपमस्य निर्दिष्टम ॥

b. 'Consisting of the Elements and the Organs.' The 'Elements,' according to their division into the Gross and the Subtile, are Earth, &c., and the rudiments of Odour; &c. The 'Organs,' according to their division into the organs of knowing, the organs of action, and the internal organ, are of three sorts. Of which this two-fold character of percept and perception is 'what it consists of,'—a modification not other than itself,—*that* is what is so described [—i. e. described as 'consisting of the Elements and the Organs']. Thus have its products [—which are not other than Nature herself—] been stated.*

c. 'Experience' means what has been already defined [at § 13. *a*]. 'Emancipation' is the surcease, occasioned by discriminative knowledge, of the mundane state. Of which these two experience and emancipation, are the motive or purpose, *that* is what is so described [—i. e. described by the compound epithet now analysed—], that is to say 'the visual including the visible.]'†

d. And since this, the 'visible' which consists of modification in the shape of various conditions, requires to be known as what is to be shunned in order to declare its conditions, he says.‡

विशेषाविशेषलिङ्गमात्रालिङ्गानि गुणपर्वाणि ॥ १९ ॥

The aspects of the Qualities.

Aph. 19.—The divisions [of condition] of the Qualities are (1) the diverse, (2) the non-diverse, (3) the merely [once] resolvable, and (4) the irresolvable.

a. The divisions, i. e. the several conditions, of the Qualities, are to be understood to be four,—such is what we are here in-

* भूतेन्द्रियात्मकमिति । भूतानि स्थूलसूक्ष्मभेदेन पृथिव्यादीनि गन्धतन्मात्रादीनि च । इन्द्रियाणि बुद्धीन्द्रियकर्मेन्द्रियान्तःकरणभेदेन त्रिविधानि । उभयमेतद्ग्राह्यग्रहणरूपमात्मा स्वरूपाभिन्न परिणामः यस्य तत्तथाविधमित्यनेन कार्यमस्योक्तम् ॥

† भोगः कथितलक्षणः । अपवर्गो विवेकख्यातिपूर्विका संसारनिवृत्तिः । तौ भोगापवर्गावर्थः प्रयोजनं यस्य तत्तथाविधं दृश्यमित्यर्थः ॥

‡ तस्य च दृश्यस्य नानावस्थारूपपरिणामात्मकस्य हेयत्वेन ज्ञातव्यत्वादवस्थाः कथयितुमाह ॥

formed of. Among these, the 'diverse' are the gross elements and the organs; the 'non-diverse' are the subtile elements and the internal organ; the 'merely [once] resolvable' is intellect [—which is resolvable into the Undiscreet, but not further—]; the 'irresolvable' is the Undiscreet [or nature]:—thus has it been declared.*

b. The four conditions [of development] of the Qualities are set forth as necessarily requiring to be known at the time of Concentration, because we recognise the Undiscreet, which consists of the three Qualities, as being present everywhere that these are,† [—so that if we did not know these, then the Undiscreet, the cause of bondage, might be present undetected].

c. Since the visible requires first to be known as that which is to be shunned, having thus explained it, with its conditions, in order now to explain what is to be accepted [and not to be got rid of—viz.] the 'seer,'—he says.‡

द्रष्टा दृशिमात्रः शुद्धो ऽपि प्रत्ययानुपश्यः ॥ २० ॥

Soul defined. *Aph.* 20.—The 'seer' [soul] is vision simply, though pure, looking directly on ideas.

a. The 'seer,' i. e. Soul, is 'vision simply,' i. e., mere Thought. This 'though pure,' i. e. though abiding as itself, without becoming modified, or the like. 'Looking directly on ideas:'—'ideas' are thought coloured by objects:—it looks 'directly on' these,—immediately,—without the intervention of successive stages, or the like. What is asserted is this, that, whilst it is only the

---

† गुणानां पर्वाण्यवस्थाविशेषाश्चत्वारो ज्ञातव्या इत्युपदिष्टम्भवति । तत्र विशेषा महाभूतेन्द्रियाणि । अविशेषास्तन्मात्रान्तःकरणे । लिङ्गमात्रंबुद्धिः । अलिङ्गमव्यक्तमित्युक्तम् ॥

‡ सर्वत्र त्रिगुणरूपस्याव्यक्तस्यान्वयित्वेन प्रत्यभिज्ञानादवश्यं ज्ञातव्यत्वेन योगकाले चत्वारि पर्वाणि निर्दिष्टानि ॥

§ एवं हेयत्वेन दृश्यस्य प्रथमं ज्ञातव्यत्वात्तदवस्थासहितं व्याख्यायोपादेयं द्रष्टारं व्याकर्तुमाह ॥

intellect that becomes coloured by the object, Soul is spectator merely through proximity.*

b. It alone is the experiencer ;—so he says.*—

तदर्थ एव दृश्यस्यात्मा ॥ २१ ॥

Soul is the experiencer.

Aph. 21.—For the sake of it alone is the entity of the visible.

a. The 'entity,' the self, of the 'visible' which has been already defined [§17. *a.*],—this is 'for the sake of *it*;'—the bringing about that '*it*,' the soul, shall be an experiencer, is its aim, to the exclusion in short of any selfish end. For Nature, energizing, energizes not with a view to any purpose of her own, but with the design "Let me bring about Soul's experience,"†

b. If thus the motive be only the effecting of Soul's experience, then, when this has been effected, it should cease striving for that in the absence of a motive:—and, when it is free from alteration, since it is pure [—exhibiting neither the Qualities of Passion nor of Darkness when all three are in calm equipoise—], all souls should be freed from bondage, and the mundane state should be cut short. Having pondered this doubt, he says.‡—

---

* द्रष्टा पुरुषो दृशिमात्रश्चेतनामात्रः । मात्रग्रहणं धर्मिधर्म निरासार्थं केचिद्धि चेतना मात्मनः धर्म मिच्छन्ति स शुद्धोऽपि । परिणामित्वाद्यभावेन स्वप्रतिष्ठोऽपि । प्रत्ययानुपश्यः । प्रत्यया विषयोपरक्तानि ज्ञानानि । तानि अनु अव्यवधानेन प्रतिसङ्क्रामाद्यभावेन पश्यति । एतदुक्तम्भवति । जातविषयोपरागायामेव बुद्धौ सन्निधानमात्रेणैव पुरुषस्य द्रष्टृत्वमिति ॥

† स एव भोक्तेति आह ॥

‡ दृश्यस्य प्रागुक्तलक्षणस्य आत्मा यत्स्वरूपं स तदर्थस्तस्य पुरुषस्य भोक्तृत्व सम्पादनं नाम स्वार्थपरिहारेण प्रयोजनं । नहि प्रधानं प्रवर्तमानमात्मनः किञ्चित्प्रयोजनमपेक्ष्य प्रवर्त्तते किन्तु पुरुषस्य भोक्तृत्वं सम्पादनायेति ॥

‡ यद्येवं पुरुषस्य भोगसम्पादनमेव प्रयोजनं तदा सम्पादिते तस्मिंस्तन्निष्प्रयोजनं विरतव्यापारं स्यात् । तस्मिंश्च परिणामशून्ये शुद्धत्वात् सर्वे द्रष्टारो बन्धरहितास्युःततश्च संसारोच्छेद इत्याशंक्याह ॥

कृतार्थम्प्रति नष्टमप्यनष्टं तदन्यसर्वसाधारणत्वात् ॥ २२ ॥

The emancipation of one entails not that of others.

Aph. 22.—Though it has ceased to be, in respect of him who has effected what is required, it has not ceased [in regard to all], because it is common to others besides him

a. Although, since it causes experience just till there is discriminative knowledge, it ceases to be, i. e., desists from acting, in respect of some soul which has effected the end [of discerning discriminatively],still, since it is common to all souls, it continues, as regards others, with its operations undestroyed. Therefore, since Nature is common to all experiencers, it never ceases ; nor does the emancipation of one involve the emancipation of all :—such is what is asserted.*

b. Having explained the 'visible' and the 'seer,' in order to explain their conjunction, he says—†

स्वस्वामिशक्त्योः स्वरूपोपलब्धिहेतुःसंयोगः ॥ २३ ॥

The conjunction of soul and nature what.

Aph. 23.—The conjunction is the cause of the apprehension of the actual condition of the natures of the possessed and the possessor.

a. He characterises this through its effect‡ [—telling us not what the conjunction is, but what it is the cause of].

b. 'The nature of the possessed' is the nature of the visible. 'The nature of the possessor' is the nature of the 'seer.' Moreover, the apprehension of the nature of these two, correlated as the known and the knower,—that which is the cause of *this* is the conjunction [here spoken of];—and this is none other

---

* यद्यपि विवेकख्यातिपर्यन्ताद्भोगसम्पादनात्कमपि कृतार्थं पुरुषं प्रति तन्नष्टं विरतव्यापारं तथापि सर्वपुरुषसाधारणत्वादन्यान् प्रत्यनष्टव्यापारमवतिष्ठते । अतः प्रधानस्य सकलभोक्तृसाधारणत्वान्न कदाचनापि विनाश एकस्य मुक्तौ वा न सर्वेषां मुक्तिप्रसङ्ग इत्युक्तम्भवति ॥

† दृश्यद्रष्टारौ व्याख्याय संयोगं व्याख्यातुमाह ॥

‡ कार्यद्वारेणास्य लक्षणं करोति ॥

than the nature of their cognate habit as the experienced and the experiencer. Because, of these two, which are from everlasting and all-pervading, there is no conjunction other than their essential character. That the experienced's character as something experienced and the experiencer's character as an experiencer, has existed from everlasting,—this alone is the conjuction* [or relation between the two].

c. Moreover he states the cause thereof.†

तस्य हेतुरविद्या ॥ २४ ॥

The cause of the conjunction. *Aph.* 24.—The cause thereof is what is to be quitted—viz., Ignorance.

a. That which has been already described [§4] as Ignorance, in the shape of delusion, consisting in the confounding the unreal with the real, is declared to be of that conjunction in the shape of the absence of discriminative knowledge, the cause,—what is to be quitted,—the [grammatical] object of the act of 'quitting.'‡

b. What, again, is the 'quitting' thereof? To this he replies.§

तदभावात्संयोगाभावो हानं तद्दृशेः कैवल्यम् ॥ २५ ॥

The quitting of conjunction what. *Aph.* 25.—The 'quitting' consists in the surcease of the conjunction, on that [Ignorance];—*this* is the isolation of the soul.

a. 'Of that,' i. e., of Ignorance, eradicated by its essential opposite, viz., right knowledge, 'the surcease,'—when this takes

---

* स्वशक्तिः दृश्यस्य स्वभावः । स्वामिशक्तिर्द्रष्टुः स्वरूपं । तयोर्द्वयोरपि संवेद्य संवेदकत्वेन व्यवस्थितयोर्या स्वरूपोपलब्धिस्तस्याः कारणं यस्संयोगः । सचसहजभोग्यभोक्तृभावस्वरूपान्नान्यः । नहि तयोर्नित्ययोर्व्यापकयोश्च स्वस्वरुपादीतिरिक्तः कश्चित्संयोगः। यदेव भोग्यस्य भोग्यत्वं भोक्तुश्चभोक्तृत्वमनादिसिद्धं स एव संयोगः

† तस्यापि कारणमाह ॥

‡ या पूर्वं विपर्यासात्मिका मोहरूपाऽविद्या व्याख्याता सा तस्याऽविवेकख्यातिरूपस्य संयोगस्य कारणं हेयं हानक्रियाकर्मोच्यते ॥

§ किम्पुनस्तद्धानमित्याह ॥

place, the surcease also of its effect, viz., of the conjunction, is what is called the 'quitting' of it.*

b. What is meant is as follows;—abandonment does not apply in the case of this as in that of a circumscribed body [from which you may disjoin yourself by moving away into a portion of space unoccupied by it]; but, when discriminative knowledge has been produced, the conjunction, which was due to the absence of discriminative knowledge, ceases quite of its, own accord;—such is the 'quitting' of it. And, moreover quitting which there is of conjunction [with Nature], being for all eternity, is what is called the isolation *(kaivalya)* of the soul [thereafter existing entirely] *alone* (*kewala*).†

c. Thus have the nature, the cause, and the effect, of the conjunction [of soul with Nature] been declared.‡

d. Now, by means of declaring the means of 'quitting' [what ought to be quitted], he states [by implication] the cause of [the attainment of] what [condition] ought to be accepted§ [as the most desirable possible].

विवेकख्यातिरविप्लवा हानोपायः ॥ २६ ॥

Themeans of quitting the conjunction.

Aph. 26.—The means of quitting [the state of bondage] is discriminative knowledge not discontinuous.

a. The 'knowledge,'—the perfect cognizance, of the distinction, in this shape, viz., that the Qualities are one thing and Soul is another thing, is 'the means,' the cause, 'of quitting,' i. e., of abandoning, the visible [for phenomenal]. *What* sort

---

* तस्या अविद्याया स्वरुपविरुद्धेन सम्यग् ज्ञानेनोन्मूलिताया योऽयमर्मवस्त-स्मिन् सति तत्कार्यस्य संयोगस्याप्यभावस्तद्धानमित्युच्यते ॥

† अयमर्थो नैतस्य मूर्त्तद्रव्यवत् परित्यागो युज्यते किन्तु जातायां विवेकख्यातम वविवेकख्यातिनिमित्तसंयोग स्वयमेव निवर्त्तत इति तस्य हानं । यदेवच संयोगस्य हानं तदेव नित्य केवलस्यापि पुरुषस्य कैवल्यं व्यपदिश्यते ॥

‡ तदेवं संयोगस्य स्वरूपं कारणं कार्यं चाभिहितम् ॥

§ अथ हानोपायकथनद्वारेणोपादेय कारणमाह ॥

of [knowledge]? 'Not discontinuous.' That [knowledge] is 'not discontinuous,' in respect of which there is no skipping—no breaks between and between, in the shape of non-abstraction* [or re-conjunction of soul with the things of sense].

b. The import here is this, that, when Ignorance is dissolved by force of meditating on what is opposed to it, that advent which there is of a reflection, in the soul, of the introspective intellect, where the conceit of being knower or agent has been laid aside, and when it is unoppressed by the filth of Passion and Darkness, is what is called discriminative knowledge, [—or the knowledge of the non-identity of soul and Nature]. And when this prevails permanently, there simply becomes, through the cessation of the rule of the visible, *isolation*.†

c. While telling of what description is the discernment of that soul in which discriminative knowledge has taken place, he declares [by implication] the nature of discriminative knowledge itself.‡

तस्य सप्तधा प्रान्तभूमौ प्रज्ञा ॥ २७ ॥

Discriminative knowledge of what nature.

Aph. 27.—Of that [enlightened soul] the perfect knowledge, up to the ground of the limit, is of seven kinds.

a. 'Of that' [soul] in which discriminative knowledge has sprung up; 'the perfect knowledge'—in the shape of the discrimination which it behooves us to understand; 'up to the

---

* अन्ये गुणा अन्य पुरुष इत्येवंविधस्य विवेकस्य ख्यातिः ॥ प्रख्या सा हानस्य दृश्यपरित्यागस्योपायः कारणं । कीदृशी अविप्लवा । न विद्यते विप्लवो विच्छेदोऽन्तरान्तरा व्युत्थानरूपो यस्या सा ऽविप्लवा ॥

† इदमत्र तात्पर्यम् प्रतिपक्षभावनाबलादविद्याप्रविलये विनिवृत्तज्ञातृत्वकर्तृत्वाभिमानाया रजस्तमोमलानभिभुताया बुद्धेरन्तर्मुखाया या चिच्छायासंक्रान्ति. सा विवेक ख्यातिरित्युच्यते । तस्याश्च संततमविच्छेदेन प्रवृत्तायां दृश्याधिकारनिवृत्तेर्भवत्येव कैवल्यम् ॥

‡ उत्पन्नविवेकख्यातेः पुरुषस्य यादृशी प्रज्ञा भवति तां कथयन् ॥ विवेकख्यातेरेव स्वरूपमाह ॥

ground to the limit,' i. e., as far as is the extent of all the meditation that has a support [—see B.1.§17, *j*,—]; is of seven sorts.*

b. Among these [seven], that which consists in liberation from the products [of mind] is of four sorts,—(1) "That which is to be known is known by me; (2) "There is nothing that ought to be known;" (3) "My afflictions' are destroyed,—there is nothing of mine requiring to be destroyed;" (4) "Knowledge has been attained by me, discriminative knowledge has been attained by me;"—and so, by the abandonment of all other impressions, in that state of things, just such perfect knowledge takes place [as is spoken of in the aphorism]. Such perfect knowledge, being pure knowledge, the object of which is some product [of mind], is what is called 'liberation from the products.'†

c. 'Liberation from the mind' is of three sorts,—(1) "My mind has done its office [in enabling me to discern the distinction of soul and nature];" (2) "And the Qualities have lost their influence [over me],—like stones that have fallen from a mountain-peak which will not again resume their place; for why should these, when tending towards resolution into their cause, spring up again in the absence of the fundamental reason [for their springing up] which is called 'delusion,' and in the absence of a motive?"—(3) "And my meditation is such as has become one with soul;—such being the case, I exist in my real nature." Such is the threefold 'liberation from mind.'‡

---

* तस्योत्पन्नविवेकज्ञानस्य ज्ञातव्यविवेकरूपा प्रज्ञा । प्रान्तभूमौ सकलसालम्बनसमाधिभूमिपर्यन्तं । सप्तप्रकाराभवति ॥

† तत्र कार्यविमुक्तिरूपा चतुःप्रकारा । ज्ञातं मया ज्ञेयं । न ज्ञातव्यं किञ्चिदस्ति । क्षीणा मे क्लेशा । न मे किञ्चित् क्षेतव्यमस्ति । अधिगतं मया ज्ञानं प्राप्तं मया विवेकख्यातिरिति प्रत्ययान्तरपरिहारेण तस्यामवस्थायामीदृश्येवप्रज्ञा जायते । ईदृशी प्रज्ञा कार्यविषयं निर्मलं ज्ञानं कार्यविमुक्तिरित्युच्यते ॥

* चित्तविमुक्तिस्त्रिधा । चरितार्था मे बुद्धिः । गुणाश्च कृताधिकारा गिरिशिखरनिपतिता इव ग्रावाणो पुनः स्थितिं न यास्यन्ति स्वकारणे प्रलयाभिमुखानां मोहाभिधानमूलकारणाभावान्निष्प्रयोजनत्वाच्चामीषां कुतः प्ररोहः । स्वात्मीभूतश्च मे समाधिः तस्मिन् सति स्वरूपप्रतिष्ठोऽहमिति । ईदृशी त्रिप्रकारा चित्तविमुक्तिः ॥

d. So then, when there has sprung up such a sevenfold perfect knowledge, reckoning as far as to the limit [where meditation ceases to rest upon an object], we say that soul is *alone** [*kevala*, or in the desiderated state of *kaivalya*].

e. It has been stated [§26] that discriminative knowledge is the cause of the removal of the Conjunction [between soul and nature]; but what is the cause of *that*? To this he replies.†

योगाङ्गानुष्ठानादशुद्धिक्षये ज्ञानदीप्तिराविवेकख्यातेः ॥ २८ ॥

Ascetic practices clear the way to discriminative knowledge.

Aph. 28.—Till there is discriminative knowledge, there is, from the practice of the things subservient to the *Yoga*, an illumination [more or less brilliant] of knowledge [which is operative] in the removal of impurity.

a. The 'things subservient to the *Yoga*, are what will be mentioned [in §29]. 'From the practice' of these, i. e. from the practice of them preceded by a knowledge of them,—'till there is discriminative knowledge,'—that 'illumination of knowledge' which, more or less, as a modification of the pure [or enlightening] principle, is [operative] 'in the removal of impurity'—in the removal of impurity in the shape of the 'afflictions' whose characteristic is their hiding the light of the pure principle of the mind,—until discriminative knowledge [takes place], *that* is the cause of this knowledge [of the distinction between soul and nature];—such is the meaning.‡

b. 'From the practice of the things subservient to the *Yoga*,—in the removal of impurity,'—has been said:—what, then, are those 'things subservient to the Yoga'? So he enunciates them.§

---

* तदेवमीदृश्यां सप्तविधप्रान्तभूमिप्रज्ञायामुपजातायां पुरुषः केवल इत्युच्यते ॥

† विवेकख्यातिस्संयोगाभावे हेतुरित्युक्तं । तस्यास्तूत्पत्तौ किन्निमित्तमित्यत आह ॥

‡ योगाङ्गानि वक्ष्यमाणानि । तेषामनुष्ठानाद् ज्ञानपूर्वकादभ्यासादाविवेकख्यातेरशुद्धिक्षये चित्तसत्त्वस्य प्रकाशावरणलक्षणक्लेशरूपाशुद्धिक्षये या ज्ञानदीप्तिस्तारतम्येन सात्त्विकः परिणामो विवेकख्यातिपर्यन्तस्स तस्याः ख्यातेर्हेतुरित्यर्थः ॥

§ योगाङ्गानुष्ठानादशुद्धिक्षय इत्युक्तं । कानि पुनस्तानि योगाङ्गानीति तेषामुद्देशमाह ॥

यमनियमासनप्राणायामप्रत्याहारधारणाध्यानसमाधयोऽष्टावङ्गानि॥ २९ ॥

The eight subservients of Concentration.

Aph. 29.—The eight things subservient [to Concentration] are (1) forbearance, (2) religious observance, (3) postures, (4) suppression of the breath, (5) restraint, (6) attention, (7) contemplation, and (8) meditation.

b. Some of these, as 'attention,' &c., are immediately subservient, since they are directly conducive to meditation. Some as 'forbearance', 'religious observance,' &c., conduce to meditation by means of their eradicating [all] hesitation about things opposed to it, such as killing, &c. Of 'postures', and the rest [in the list,] the conduciveness is successive, it being, e. g., when one has succeeded in regard to 'posture', that there is steadiness in 'suppression of breath';—and so it is to be inferred also in respect of the others [in succession.]*

b. He describes these in their order.†

अहिंसासत्यास्तेयब्रह्मचर्यापरिग्रहा यमः ॥ ३० ॥

Forbearance what.

Aph. 30.—'Forbearance' (*yama*) consists of not killing, veracity, not stealing, continence, and not coveting.

a. Among these [—to speak first of the first—], 'killing' is acting for the purpose of removing life; and this is a cause of all evils. The absence of this is what is meant by 'not killing.' Since 'killing' must be abstained from at *all* times, its opposite, 'not killing' is set down first‡ [in the list.]

b. 'Veracity' means conformity, in speech and mind, to fact. Its opposite is falsehood. 'Theft' is the taking away another's

---

* इह कानिचित् समाधेस्साक्षादुपकारकत्वेनान्तराण्यङ्गानि यथा धारणादीनि । कानिचित् प्रतिपक्षभूतहिंसादिवितर्कोन्मूलनद्वारेण समाधेरुपकुर्वन्ति यथा यमनियमादयः । तत्रासनादीनामुत्तरोत्तरमुपकारकत्वं यथा सत्यासनजये प्राणायामस्थैर्यं । एवमुत्तरत्रापि न्याय्यम् ॥ † क्रमेणैषां स्वरूपमाह ॥

‡ तत्र प्राणवियोगप्रयोजनव्यापारो हिंसा । साच सर्वानर्थहेतुः ॥ तदभावोऽहिंसा । हिंसायास्सर्वकालमेव परिहार्यत्वात्प्रथमं तदभावाया अहिंसाया निर्देशः ॥

property. Its absence is 'not stealing.' 'Continence is the subjection of one's members. 'Not coveting' means not desiring for one's self means of enjoyment.*

c. These five, 'not killing,' &c., which are meant by the word 'forbearance,' are laid down as things conducive to Concentration.†

d. He states a peculiarity of these.‡

एते जातिदेशकालसमयानवच्छिन्नाः सार्वभौममहाव्रतम् ॥ ३१ ॥

Honesty independent of circumstances.

Aph. 31.—These, without respect to rank, place, time, or compact, are the universal great duty.

a. 'Rank' means Bráhman-hood, &c. 'Place' means a place of pilgrimage, &c., 'Time' means the fourteenth of the month, or other [date which may affect the meritoriousness or otherwise of this or that otherwise perhaps indifferent act]. 'Compact' means that a Bráhman, for example, is the motive [of our doing or leaving undone.] The aforesaid 'forbearances,' viz. 'not killing,' &c., without respect to these four [considerations], abiding in all places—i. e. [as the moral law written on the heart, in all] understandings,—are what are called 'the great duty.'§.

b. To explain :—'I will not kill a Bràhman,'—'I will not kill any one at a place of pilgrimage,'—'I will not kill any one on the fourteenth of the month,'—'I will not kill, except for the benefit of a god, a Bràhman, or the like,'—[well, the 'forbear—

---

* सत्यं वाङ्मनसयोर्यथार्थत्वं । तदभावोऽसत्यं । स्तेयंपरस्वापहरणं । तदभावोऽस्तेयं । ब्रह्मचर्यं उपस्थसंयमः । अपरिग्रहो भोगसाधनानामस्वीकरणं ॥

† त एते ऽहिंसादयः पञ्च यमशब्दवाच्या योगाङ्गत्वेनानिर्दिष्टा ॥

‡ एषां विशेषमाह ॥

§ जातिर्ब्राह्मणत्वादिः । देशस्तीर्थादिः । कालश्चतुर्दश्यादिः । समयो ब्राह्मणप्रयोजनादिः । एतैश्चतुर्भिरनवच्छिन्नाः पूर्वोक्ता अहिंसादयो यमाः सर्वासु क्षित्यादिषु चित्तभूमिषु भवा महाव्रतमित्युच्यते ॥

ances, must be] without this fourfold qualification,—unqualified, —thus 'I will not kill any one, anywhere, at any time, or for any purpose whatever.' And the same holds in respect of 'truth' and the rest, *mutatis mutandis*. It is these thus unqualified, and acted upon in their full generality, that are called 'the great duty.'*

c. He states what are 'religious observances' (*niyama*).†

शौचसन्तोषतपःस्वाध्यायेश्वरप्रणिधानानि नियमाः ॥ ३२ ॥

Religious observances. *Aph.* 32.—Religious observances (*niyama*) are (1) purification, (2) contentment (3) austerity, (4) inaudible mutterings, and (5) persevering devotion to the Lord.

a. 'Purification' (*shaucha*) is of two sorts, external, and internal. The external is the cleansing of the body by earth, water, &c. The internal is the washing away the impurity of the mind by means of benevolence, &c.‡

b. 'Contentment' (*santosha*) means contentedness. The rest have been already described. These, viz. 'purification,' and the rest, are what are meant by the term 'religious observances.'§

c. 'How are these subservient to Concentration? To this he replies.||

वितर्कबाधने प्रतिपक्षभावनम् ॥ ३३ ॥

---

* तद्यथा । ब्राह्मणं न हनिष्यामि तीर्थे कञ्चन न हनिष्यामि चतुर्दश्यां न हनिष्यामि देवब्राह्मणाद्यर्थंव्यतिरेकेण न हनिष्यामीत्येवं चतुर्विधावच्छेदव्यतिरेकेण कञ्चित् क्वचित् कदाचित् कस्मिंश्चिदप्यर्थे न हनिष्यामीत्यनवच्छिन्नाः । एवं सत्यादिषु यथायोगं योज्यं । इत्थमनियतीभूताः सामान्येनैव प्रवृत्ताः महाव्रतमित्युच्यते ॥ † नियमानाह ॥

‡ शौचं द्विविधं बाह्यमाभ्यन्तरञ्च । बाह्यं मृज्जलादिभिः कायप्रक्षालनम् । अभ्यन्तरं मैत्र्यादिभिश्चित्तमलप्रक्षालनम् ॥

§ सन्तोषस्तुष्टिः । शेषाः प्रागेव भूतव्याख्यानाः । एते शौचादयो नियमशब्दवाच्याः ॥ || कथमेषां योगाङ्गत्वमित्यत आह ॥

How these things are of use.

Aph. 33.—In excluding things questionable, the calling up something opposite [is serviceable].

a. 'Killing,' &c., as opponents of Concentration, are 'things questionable,' because they are doubted about [—it being questionable what real good they can do]. If these are excluded when things opposed to them are called up, then concentration is facilitated. Hence 'forbearance' and 'religious observances' really are subservient to Concentration.*

b. Now he states, in order, the nature, the divisions, the kind, the cause, and the fruit, of the 'things questionable' (*vitarka*).†

वितर्का हिंसादयः कृतकारितानुमोदिता लोभक्रोधमोह पूर्वका मृदुमध्याधिमात्रा दुःखाज्ञानानन्तफला इति प्रतिपक्षभावनम् ॥ ३४ ॥

Account of objectionable things.

Aph. 34.—The 'things questionable,' killing, &c.; whether done, caused to be done, or approved of; whether resulting from covetousness, anger, or delusion; whether slight, of intermediate character, or beyond measure; have no end of fruits [in the shape of] pain and ignorance;—hence the calling up of something opposite [is every way advisable].

a. These the 'killing,' &c., aforesaid are first divided tripartitely through the difference of 'done,' 'caused to be done, and 'approved of.' Among these, those are 'done,' which are carried into effect by one's self. Those are 'caused to be done,' which are brought about by the employment of the incentive expression 'Do it, do it.' Those are 'approved,' which, when being done by another, are consented to by the expression 'Well done, well done.' And this threefold character is mentioned in order to debar hallucination in regard to these respectively; otherwise some dull-witted one might reflect thus,

---

* वितर्क्यन्त इति वितर्का योगपरिपन्थिनो हिंसादयः । तेषां प्रतिपक्षभावने सति यदि बाधा भवति तदा योगस्सुकरो भवतीति भवत्येव यमनियमानां योगाङ्गत्वम् ॥ † इदानीं वितर्काणां स्वरूपं भेदं प्रकारं कारणं फलञ्च क्रमेणाह ॥

"The killing was not done by me myself, therefore the blame is not mine."*

b. In order to declare the causes of these ['questionable things'], he says, 'resulting from covetousness, anger, or delusion.'†

c. Although 'covetousness' is the one first specified yet, since the source of *all* the 'afflictions' is delusion, whose mark is the conceit that what is *not* soul is soul, *this* we must be sure is the root, because, when *it* takes place, 'covetousness' 'anger' and the rest arise in consequence of there having gone before the division of *self* and *other one* [—but for the existence of which delusive division there would have been no room for either covetousness or anger]. We mean, then, that every class of evils results from delusion.‡

d. 'Covetousness' is a thirst. 'Anger' is an inflamed condition of the mind, which uproots all discrimination between what ought to be done and what ought not to be done.§

e. 'Killing,' &c., moreover, which are severally threefold through the distinction between 'done,' &c., [§34. *a.*], are divided tripartitely through their having as their cause 'delusion,' &c., [§34. *b*]. He mentions, of these again, a threefold character, through their difference of state, as 'slight, of intermediate character, and beyond measure.' The 'slight,' or slow,

---

* एते पूर्वोक्ता हिंसादयः प्रथमं त्रिधा भिद्यन्ते कृतकारितानुमोदितभेदेन। तत्र स्वयं निष्पादिताः कृताः । कुरुकुर्विति प्रयोजकव्यापारेण समुत्पादिताः कारिताः अन्येन क्रियमाणाः साधु साध्वित्यङ्गीकृता अनुमोदिताः । एतच्च त्रैविध्यं परस्परव्यामोहनिवारणायोच्यते । अन्यथा मन्दमतिरेवं मन्येत न मया स्वयं हिंसा कृतेति नास्ति मे दोष इति ।

† एतेषां कारणप्रतिपादनायाह लोभक्रोधमोहपूर्वका इति ॥

‡ यद्यपि लोभः क्रोधः प्रथमं निर्दिष्टस्तथापि सर्वक्लेशानां मोहस्यानात्मन्यात्माभिमानलक्षणस्य निदानत्वात तस्मिन् सति स्वपरविभागपूर्वकत्वेन लोभक्रोधादीनामुद्भवान्मूलत्वमवसेयं । मोहपूर्विका । सर्वा दोषजातिरित्यर्थः ॥

§ लोभस्तृष्णा । क्रोधः कृत्याकृत्यविवेकोन्मूलकः प्रज्वलनात्मकश्चित्तधर्मः ॥

are those that are neither fierce nor middling. Those 'of intermediate character,' are what are neither slow nor fierce. Those that are 'beyond measure' are what are vehement, neither middling nor slight. Thus the nine divisions, since there is thus a further threefold character, become twenty-seven.*

f. The 'slight,' &c., moreover severally may be of three sorts through the distinction of slight, intermediate, and excessive. These are to be combined accordingly as they can combine. For example, the 'slightly slight,' the 'slightly intermediate,' the 'slightly excessive,' and so on.†

g. He mentions their fruit, saying, 'having no end of fruits [in the shape of] pain and ignorance.' 'Pain' is a state of mind, dependent on the Quality of passion, exhibiting itself as something repugnant. 'Ignorance' is false knowledge, in the shape of doubt or error. Those ['questionable things'] of which the endless, or unlimited, fruits are these two, viz. pain and ignorance, are what are so spoken of‡ [—i. e. spoken of by the compound epithet here analysed].

h. Thus it is enjoined, that the Yogi, by meditating on 'something opposite' is to get rid of these ['questionable things'] which he has understood by means of the division of natures, causes, &c.,§ [that has been now set forth].

---

* प्रत्येकं कृतादिभेदेन त्रिप्रकारा अपि हिंसादयो मोहादिकारणत्वेन त्रिधा भिद्यन्ते । तेषामेव पुनरवस्थाभेदेन त्रैविध्यमाह मृदुमध्याधिमात्राः । मृदवो मन्दा न तीव्रा नापि मध्यमाः । मध्या न मन्दा नापि तीव्राः । अधिमात्राः तीव्रा न मध्या नापि मन्दा इति नव भेदा इत्थं त्रैविध्ये सति सप्तविंशतिः ॥

† मृद्वादीनामपि प्रत्येकं मृदुमध्याधिमात्रभेदात् त्रैविध्यं सम्भवति । तद्यथायोगं योज्यं तद्यथा । मृदुमृदुर्मृदुमध्यो मृदुतीव्र इत्यादि ॥

‡ एषां फलमाह दुःखाज्ञानानन्तफला इति । दुःखं प्रतिकूलतयावभासमानो राजसश्चित्तधर्मः । अज्ञानं मिथ्याज्ञानं संशयविपर्ययरूपं । ते दुःखाज्ञाने अनन्तमपरिच्छिन्नं फलं येषां ते तथोक्ताः ॥

§ इत्थं तेषां स्वरूपकारणादिभेदेन ज्ञातानां प्रतिपक्षभावनया योगिना परिहारः कर्त्तव्य इत्युपदिष्टम्भवति ॥

i. With a view to declare, in order, how perfections arise, consequent on these ['forbearances,' &c.], when by practice, they have reached their highest degree, he says.*—

तत्सन्निधौ वैरत्यागः ॥ ३५ ॥

Influence of the Yogi that is harmless.

Aph. 35.—When harmlessness is complete, near him, there is abandonment of enmity.

a. When the harmlessness of him that practices harmlessness is complete, even natural enemies, as the snake and the mungoose, abandon [when near him] their enmity, and abide in amity;—that is to say, those that delight in destroying, leave off their distructiveness.†

b. What happens in respect of him that practices veracity? To this he replies.

सत्यप्रतिष्ठायां क्रियाफलाश्रयत्वम् ॥ ३६ ॥

Influence of veracity.

Aph. 36.—When veracity is complete, he is the receptacle of the fruit of works.

a. For works, such as sacrifices, being performed, give fruits such as Paradise. But of that Yogi who practises veracity, the veracity rises to such a degree that the Yogi receives the fruit even without the works being performed. At his bidding, the fruit of works accrues to any one soever, even though not performing the work:—such is the meaning.‡

b. He states the fruit accruing to him that practises abstinence from theft.§

---

* एषामभ्यासात् प्रकर्षमागच्छतामनुनिष्पादिन्यः सिद्धयो यथा भवन्ति तथा क्रमेण प्रतिपादयितुमाह ॥

† तस्याहिंसां भावयतो ऽहिंसाप्रतिष्ठायां सहजविरोधिनामप्यहिनकुलादीनां वैरत्यागो निर्मत्सरतयावस्थानं भवति । हिंसारताः हिंस्रत्वं परित्यजन्तीत्यर्थः ॥

‡ सत्याभ्यासवतः किं भवतीत्याह ॥

§ क्रियमाणा हि क्रियाः यागादिकाः फलं स्वर्गादिकं प्रयच्छन्ति । तस्य तु सत्याभ्यासवतो योगिनस्तथा सत्यं प्रकृष्यते यथा अकृतायामपि क्रियायां योगी फलमाप्नोति । तद्वचनाद्यस्य कस्यचित् क्रियामकुर्वतोऽपि क्रियाफलं भवतीत्यर्थः ॥

§ अस्तेयाभ्यासवतः फलमाह ॥

अस्तेयप्रतिष्ठायां सर्वरत्नोपस्थानम् ॥ ३७ ॥

The reward of not thieving.

Aph. 37.—When abstinence from theft is complete, all jewels come near him.

a. When he practises abstinence from theft, then, on its reaching its highest degree, the jewels that exist in every quarter come to him even though he covet them not.*

b. He states the fruit of the practice of continence.†

ब्रह्मचर्यप्रतिष्ठायां वीर्यलाभः ॥ ३८ ॥

The reward of continence.

Aph. 38.—When continence is complete, there is gain of strength.

a. He, indeed, that practises continence, when it is complete, there is revealed in him excessive strength, or power. For continence is the preserving of one's manly vigour; and from this [continence] being of a high degree, vigour in body, organs, and mind, attains a high degree.‡

b. He states the fruit of the practice of non-covetousness.§

अपरिग्रहस्थैर्ये जन्मकथन्तासम्बोधः ॥ ३९ ॥

The reward of non-covetousness.

Aph. 39.—When non-covetousness is established, there is knowledge of all about [former] states of existence.

a. 'All about it' means the condition how [—*kathantá* being the abstract of the indeclinable *katham*]. 'All about states of existence,' such is the meaning of *janmakathantà.* The 'knowledge' thereof, the perfect understanding. That is to say, he knows perfectly every thing in regard to the

---

* अस्तेयं यदाभ्यस्यति तदा तस्य प्रकर्षाभिरभिलाषस्यापि सर्वतो दिक्स्थानि रत्नान्युपतिष्ठन्ते ॥ † ब्रह्मचर्याभ्यासस्य फलमाह ॥

‡ यः किल ब्रह्मचर्यमभ्यस्यति तस्य तत्प्रकर्षादतिशयं वीर्यं सामर्थ्यमाविर्भवति । वीर्यनिरोधो हि ब्रह्मचर्यं तस्य प्रकर्षाच्छरीरेन्द्रियमनःसु वीर्यं प्रकर्षमागच्छति॥

§ अपरिग्रहाभ्यासस्य फलमाह ॥

K

question 'Who was I in a former state of existence? What sort of person? The doer of what actions?'*

b. It is not merely the coveting of the means of enjoyment that is [here meant by] covetousness. Covetousness is [meant] even as far as the soul's coveting a body. Since a body is an instrument of enjoyment whilst *it* exists, from its association with desires, our energy being directed to the external, no real knowledge reveals itself. When, again, without regard to coveting a body, &c., one betakes one's self to indifference, then, since one abandons desire, &c., the acquaintance with past and future states of existence becomes indeed a cáuse of right knowledge to the indifferent† [person, who thus discerns how little there is deserving of a wise man's regard in any mundane condition whatever].

c. The fruits of the 'forbearances' have been stated. Now he mentions [those of] the 'religious observances.'‡

शौचात्स्वाङ्गजुगुप्सा परैरसंसर्गः ॥ ४० ॥

Mental result of purifications.

Aph. 40.—From 'purification,' results loathing for one's own members, and non-intercourse with others.

a. He who practises 'purification,' to him there springs up a loathing, an aversion, even for his own members, through his thoroughly discerning the cause and nature [of a body];—"This body is impure; any fondness for it is not to be entertained;"—and so for the same reason, there is 'non-intercourse,'

---

* कथमित्यस्य भावः कथन्ता । जन्मनः कथन्ता जन्मकथन्ता । तस्याः सम्बोधः सम्यक् ज्ञानं । जन्मान्तरे कोऽहमासं कीदृशः किङ्कार्यकारीति जिज्ञासायां सर्वमेव सम्यक् जानातीत्यर्थः ॥

† न केवलं भोगसाधनपरिग्रह एव परिग्रहः । यावदात्मनः शरीरपरिग्रहोऽपि परिग्रहः । भोगसाधनत्वाच्छरीरस्य तस्मिन् सति रागानुबन्धाद्बहिर्मुखायामेव प्रवृत्तौ न तात्त्विकज्ञानप्रादुर्भावः । यदा पुनः शरीरादिपरिग्रहनैरपेक्ष्येण माध्यस्थ्यमवलम्ब्यते तदा मध्यस्थस्य रागादित्यागात्सम्यग्ज्ञानहेतुर्भवत्येव पूर्वापरजन्मसम्बोधः॥

‡ उक्ता यमानां सिद्धयः । अथ नियमानाह ।

the absense of intercourse, the avoidance of intercourse, 'with others,' 'with other possessors also of bodies;—such is the meaning. For whoso loathes his own body, through his discernment of this or that fault, how must he judge of intercourse with the similar bodies of others?*

b. He states another fruit of this same 'purification.'†

सत्त्वशुद्धिसौमनस्यैकाग्र्येन्द्रियजयात्मदर्शनयोग्यत्वानि च ॥४१॥

Other results of purifications. *Aph.* 41.—And purity in the Quality of Goodness, complacency, intentness, subjugation of the senses, and fitness for the beholding of soul, [are fruits of 'purification'].

a. 'Are' is required to complete the sentence.‡

b. The 'Quality of goodness' is what consists of light, joy &c., [—see Sánkhya Aphorisms B. I. §62]; its 'purity' is its not being oppressed by Passion and Darkness. 'Complacency' is mental joy, from there not being the oppression of distress. 'Intentness' is steadiness of the mind on an object to which the senses are confined. 'Subjugation of the senses' is the abiding in themselves of the senses averted from objects. The 'fitness' of the mind means its power of beholding soul, —[this 'beholding' being] in the shape of the knowledge of the distinctness§ [of soul from nature].

---

* यः शौचं भावयति तस्य स्वाङ्गेष्वपि कारणस्वरूपपर्यालोचनद्वारेण जुगुप्सा घृणा समुपजायते अशुचिरयं कायो नात्राग्रहः कर्त्तव्य इत्यमुनैव हेतुना परैरन्यैश्च कायवद्भिरसंसर्गः संसर्गाभावः संसर्गपरिवर्ज्जनमित्यर्थः । यः किल स्वमेव कायं जुगुप्सते तत्तदवद्यदर्शनात्कथं परकीयैस्तथाभूतैः कायैस्संसर्गमनुभवति ॥

† शौचस्यैव फलान्तरमाह ॥

‡ भवन्तीति वाक्यशेषः ॥

§ सत्त्वं प्रकाशसुखाद्यात्मकं । तस्य शुद्धिः रजस्तमोभ्यामनभिभवः । सौमनस्यं खेदाननुभवेन मानसी प्रीतिः । एकाग्रता नियतेन्द्रियविषये चेतसः स्थैर्यं । इन्द्रियजयो विषयपराङ्मुखानामिन्द्रियाणां स्वात्मन्यवस्थानं । आत्मदर्शने विवेकख्यातिरूपे चित्तस्य योग्यत्वं समर्थत्वं ॥

c. These, 'purity in the Quality of Goodness, and the rest, manifest themselves in succession, in the case of him that practises purifications. That is to say, from 'purification' comes 'purity in the Quality of Goodness;' from 'purity in the Quality of Goodness,' 'complacency'; from 'complacency,' 'intentness'; from 'intentness,' 'subjugation of the senses;' and from 'subjugation of the senses,' 'fitness for the beholding of soul.'*

d. He states the fruit of the practice of contentment.†

सन्तोषादनुत्तमस्सुखलाभः ॥ ४२ ॥

The fruit of contentment.

Aph. 42.—From contentment there is acquired superlative felicity.

a. From contentment reaching its highest degree, there is revealed to the Yogi such an inward joy that the external enjoyment of objects is not equal to a hundredth part of it.‡

b. He states the fruit of 'austerity' *(tapas)*.§

कायेन्द्रियसिद्धिरशुद्धिक्षयात्तपसः ॥ ४३ ॥

The fruit of austerity.

Aph. 43.—The perfection of the bodily senses, by the removal of impurity, [is the fruit] of austerity.

a. 'Austerity,' when thoroughly practised, brings 'perfection,' i. e. a heightening, of the bodily senses, through the removal of the impurity, consisting in the 'afflictions,' &c., of the mind.||

b. What is meant is this;—by the *chándráyana* ['species

---

* शौचाभ्यासवत एते सत्त्वशुद्ध्यादयः क्रमेणप्रादुर्भवन्ति। शौचात् सत्वशुद्धिः। सत्त्वशुद्धेः सौमनस्यं। सौमनस्यादैकाग्र्यं। ऐकाग्र्यादिन्द्रियजयः। इन्द्रियजयादात्मदर्शनयोग्यतेति॥ † सन्तोषाभ्यासस्य फलमाह॥

‡ सन्तोषप्रकर्षेण योगिनस्तथाविधमान्तरं सुखमाविर्भवति यस्य बाह्यं विषयसुखं शतांशेनापि न समम्॥ § तपसः फलमाह॥

|| तपः समभ्यस्यमानं चेतसः क्लेशादिलक्षणाशुचिक्षयद्वारेण कायेन्द्रियाणां सिद्धिमुत्कर्षमादधाति॥

of fast], and the like, there is the removal of the 'afflictions' [§ 3] of the mind. By the removal of these there is developed, in the senses, the power of, for example, discerning the subtile, the hidden, and the infinite; and, in the body, [the power of assuming] at will either an atomic or an enormous bulk, &c.*

c. He states the fruit of 'inaudible muttering' *swádhyayá.*†

स्वाध्यायादिष्टदेवतासम्प्रयोगः ॥ ४४ ॥

The fruit of inaudible muttering.

Aph. 44.—Through inaudible muttering there is a meeting with one's favourite deity.

a. When 'inaudible muttering,' in the shape of charms and spells directed [to some deity or other], is at its height, there takes place, in the case of the Yogi, a meeting with the 'favourite' deity, i. e. with the one to whom this [inaudible muttering] was directed. That is to say, the deity becomes visible‡ [—and most probably says "Ask a boon"].

b. He sates the fruit of 'persevering devotion to the Lord' (*Ishwara-pranidhana*).§

समाधिसिद्धिरीश्वरप्रणिधानात् ॥ ४५ ॥

The fruit of persevering devotion to the Lord.

Aph. 45.—Perfection in meditation comes from persevering devotion to the Lord.

a. As for this species of faith in the Lord, there is developed therefrom Meditation, which has been already described,—because that Divine Lord, being pleased, having removed the obstructive 'afflictions,' elicits meditation.||

---

* अयमर्थः । चान्द्रायणादिना चित्तक्लेशक्षयः ॥ तत्क्षयादीन्द्रियाणां सूक्ष्मव्यवहितविप्रकृष्टदर्शनादिसामर्थ्यमाविर्भवति कायस्य यथेच्छमणुमहत्त्वादीनि ॥

† स्वाध्यायस्य फलमाह ॥

‡ अभिप्रेतमन्त्रजपादिलक्षणे स्वाध्याये प्रकृष्यमाणे योगिन इष्टया अभिप्रेतया देवतया सम्प्रयोगो भवति । सा देवता प्रत्यक्षीभवतीत्यर्थः ॥

§ ईश्वरप्रणिधानस्य फलमाह ॥

|| ईश्वरे यो ऽयं भक्तिविशेषः तस्मात्समाधेरुक्तलक्षणस्याविर्भावो भवति यस्मात्स भगवानीश्वरः प्रसन्नः सन्नन्तरायरूपान् क्लेशान्परिहृत्य समाधिमुद्बोधयति ॥

b. Having spoken of the 'forbearances' and the 'religious observances' [§29], he speaks of the 'postures' (*ásana*).*

स्थिरसुखमासनम् ॥ ४६ ॥

Postures what.

Aph. 46.—A 'posture' is what is steady and pleasant.

a. A 'posture' means what one sets one's self in,—such as the *padma*, the *danda*, the *swastika*, &c., [with the precise character of which we are not at present concerned]. When this is 'steady,'—not wavering,—and 'pleasant,'—not uncomfortable,—then this serves as a subservient to Concentration.†

b. He mentions a plan for producing steadiness and pleasantness in this same.‡

प्रयत्नशैथिल्यानन्त्यसमापत्तिभ्याम् ॥ ४७ ॥

'Postures' how managed.

Aph. 47.—Through slightness of effort and through attaining to the infinite [do 'postures,' become steady and pleasant].

a. The construction [with the preceding aphorisms] is this, that that,—viz., 'posture,' becomes steady and pleasant through slightness of effort and through attaining to the infinite.§

b. When, he forms the wish—"Let me establish [myself in such and such] a posture,"—that 'posture' is effected with slight effort, with little trouble; and when the mind attains the boundlessness that belongs to space,—i.e. when in thought one has identified one's self with it,—then, from there being neither body nor self-consciousness, the 'posture' is no cause of pain;—when *this* command over the 'postures' has been

---

* यमनियमानुक्त्वासनमाह ॥

† आस्यते अनेनेत्यासनं । पद्मासनदण्डासनस्वस्तिकासनादि । तद्यदा स्थिरं निष्कम्पं सुखं अनुद्वेजनीयं भवति तदा तद्योगाङ्गतां भजते ॥

‡ तस्यैव स्थिरसुखत्वापत्त्यर्थमुपायमाह ॥

§ तदासनं प्रयत्नशैथिल्येनानन्तसमापत्त्याच स्थिरं सुखं भवतीति सम्बन्धः ॥

attained, the tremblings, &c. [B. I. §31], which are obstacles to meditation, no longer prevail.*

c. He mentions a fruit of this when accomplished.†

ततो द्वन्द्वानभिघातः ॥ ४८ ॥

Fruit of the 'postures.'

Aph. 48.—Thence there is no assault by the pairs.

a. When this command of the 'postures' has been attained, the Yogi is not assailed by 'the pairs,' cold and heat, hunger and thirst, &c.;—such is the meaning.‡

b. Next after the mastering of the 'postures,' he speaks of the 'regulation of the breath' (*pranayama*).§

तस्मिन् सति श्वासप्रश्वासयोर्गतिविच्छेदः प्राणायामः ॥ ४९ ॥

Regulation of the breath.

Aph. 49.—When this has taken place, there is regulation of the breath, a cutting short of the motion of inspiration and expiration.

a. When steadiness in a 'posture' has taken place, that species of auxiliary of Concentration, viz., 'regulation of the breath,' to which this [steadiness of posture] is conducive, is to be practised. Of what sort is this? In the shape of 'a cutting short of the motion of inspiration and expiration.'||

b. 'Inspiration and expiration,' are what have been described [B. I. §31, *e*]. What is called 'regulation of the breath,' is the 'cutting short,' or restraining, 'of the motion,' or flow, in the

---

* यदा यदासनं बध्नामीति इच्छां करोति प्रयत्नशैथिल्ये ऽप्यक्लेशेनैव तदा तदासनं निष्पद्यते । यदा आकाशगते आनन्त्ये चेतसः समापत्तिः क्रियते अवधानेन तादात्म्यमापद्यते तदा देहाहङ्काराभावान्नासनं दुःखजनकं भवति । अस्मिंश्चासनजये सति समाध्यन्तरायभूता न प्रभवन्त्यङ्गमेजयत्वादयः ॥

† तस्यैवानुनिष्पादितस्य फलमाह ॥

‡ तस्मिन्नासनजये सति द्वन्द्वैः शीतोष्णक्षुत्तृष्णादिभिर्योगी नाभिहन्यत इत्यर्थः॥

§ आसनजयादनन्तरं प्राणायाममाह ॥

|| आसनस्थैर्ये सति तन्निमित्तकः प्राणायामलक्षणो योगाङ्गविशेषो ऽनुष्ठेयो भवति । कीदृशः । श्वासप्रश्वासयोर्गतिविच्छेदलक्षणः ॥

places external or internal [—see §51—], of these two by means of the threefold process of [regulated] expiration, retention, and inspiration,* [—see B. I. §34, *a*].

c. In order that this same may be easily understood he states the nature of it, with its divisions.†

स तु बाह्याभ्यन्तरस्तम्भवृत्तिर्देशकालसंख्याभिः परिदृष्टो
दीर्घसूक्ष्मः ॥ ५० ॥

This explained.

Aph. 50.—But this, which is (1) outer, (2) inner, and (3) steady, peculiarised by place, time, and number, is long or short.

a. 'That which is outer' is the expiration, or expelling; 'that which is inner' is the inspiration, or filling; 'that which abides steady,' within, is called *kumbhaka*. It is called ***kumbhaka*** because, when it takes place, the vital spirits rest motionless like water in a jar (*kumbha*).‡

b. This threefold regulation of the breath, further peculiarised by place, time, and number, is termed 'long or short.' 'Peculiarised by place,' e. g., [see the direction] "As regards beginning and end, twelve from the nose;"—that is to say, as far as twelve inches, beginning from the nose. 'Peculiarised by time,' as, "For the duration of thirty six *matras*," &c. 'Peculiarised by number,'—e. g. the first *udvata* is made by so many inspirations and expirations, so many times; and the employment of number is had recourse to in order that this may be known [by substituting the definite number for the indefinite 'so many']. By *udvaṭa* is meant the impinging of the air sent [upwards, in

---

* श्वासप्रश्वासौ कृतलक्षणौ । तयोस्त्रिधा रेचनकुम्भनपूरणद्वारेण बाह्याभ्यन्तरेषु स्थानेषु गतेः प्रवाहस्य विच्छेदो धारणं प्राणायाम उच्यते ॥

† तस्यैव सुखावगमाय विभज्य स्वरूपं कथयति ॥

‡ बाह्यवृत्तिः श्वासो रेचकः । अन्तर्वृत्तिः प्रश्वासः पूरकः । अन्तस्तम्भवृत्तिः कुम्भकः । तस्मिन् जलमिव कुम्भे निश्चलतया प्राणा अवस्थाप्यन्ते इति कुम्भकः ॥

speaking,] from the pit of the stomach, on the head,* [from which it is supposed to be reflected down again, so passing out of the mouth].

b. Having mentioned three regulations of the breath, in order to declare a fourth one, he says.†

बाह्याभ्यन्तरविषयाक्षेपी चतुर्थः ॥ ५१ ॥

A special variety. *Aph.* 51.—The fourth recognises both the outer and the inner spheres.

a. The 'outer sphere' of the breath is that [space] from beginning to end [—reckoning from the nose—] of twelve [inches;—see §50,*b*]. The 'inner sphere' is the heart, the navel, the plexus, &c. The fourth regulation of the breath is that which, in the shape of motionlessness, is a cutting off of the motion [of the breath], recognising, i. e. having an eye upon, both those two spheres.‡

b. The distinction between this and the third one, viz. the *kumbhaka* [§50, *a*,] is this. That one [—the *kumbhaka*—], without paying any regard to the two spheres, the outer and the inner, suddenly, like a lotus dropped upon a heated stone, at once arrives at the condition of rigidity;—but *this* one is a restrainment that has respect to the two spheres.*

---

* त्रिविधोऽयं प्राणायामो देशेन कालेन संख्यया चोपलक्षितो दीर्घसूक्ष्मसंज्ञको भवति । देशेनोपलक्षितो यथा नासाद्वादशान्तादौ नासामारभ्य द्वादशाङ्गुलपर्यन्तमित्यर्थः । कालेनोपलक्षितो यथा षट्त्रिंशन्मात्रादिप्रमाणः । संख्ययोपलक्षितो यथा इयतो वारान् कृत एतावद्भिः श्वासप्रश्वासैः प्रथम उद्घातो भवति एतज्ज्ञानाय संख्याग्रहणमुपात्तं । उद्घातो नाभिमूलात्प्रेरितस्य वायोः शिरस्यभिहननम् ॥

† त्रीन् प्राणायामानभिधाय चतुर्थमभिधातुमाह ॥

‡ प्राणस्य बाह्यो विषयो द्वादशान्तादिः । अन्तरो विषयो हृदयनाभिचक्रादिः तौ द्वौ विषयावाक्षिप्य पर्यालोच्य यो निष्टम्भरूपो गतिविच्छेदः स चतुर्थः प्राणायामः ॥

§ तृतीयस्मात्कुम्भकादयमस्य विशेषः । स बाह्याभ्यन्तरौ विषयावपर्यालोच्यैव सहसा तप्तोपलनिपतितजलन्यायेन युगपत् स्तम्भवृत्त्या निष्पद्यते । अस्य तु विषयद्वयाक्षेपको निरोधः ॥

c. This also, like the former [§50, *b*], is to be regarded as being peculiarised by time, space, and number.*

d. Of this [regulation of the breath] which is of four descriptions, he mentions the fruit.†

ततः क्षीयते प्रकाशावरणम् ॥ ५२ ॥

The fruit of the regulation of the breath.

Aph. 52.—Thereby is removed the obscuration of the light.

a. 'Thereby,' i. e. by that regulation of the breath' there is 'removed,' or destroyed, that 'obscuration' which, in the shape of the 'afflictions' [§3], there is 'of the light,' that belongs to the Pure Quality of the mind;—such is the meaning.‡

b. He mentions another result.§

धारणासु च योग्यता मनसः ॥ ५३ ॥

A further result.

Aph. 53.—And the mind becomes fit for acts of attention.

a. 'Acts of attention' are what will be spoken of [in the sequel]. The mind, freed from its defects by the several kinds of regulation of the breath, wherever it is directed to, there it remains fixed, and does not suffer distraction.||

b. He defines 'restraint' (*pratyáhára*).$

स्वस्वविषयसम्प्रयोगाभावे चित्तस्य स्वरूपानुकार इवेन्द्रियाणां प्रत्याहारः ॥ ५४ ॥

'Restraint' what.

Aph. 54.—'Restraint' is as it were the accommodation of the senses to the nature of the mind in the absence of concernment with each one's own object.

---

* अयमपि पूर्ववद्देशकालसंख्याभिरुपलक्षितो द्रष्टव्यः ॥

† चतुर्विधस्यास्य फलमाह ॥

‡ ततः तस्मात्प्राणायामात् प्रकाशस्य चित्तसत्त्वगतस्य यदावरणं क्लेशरूपं तत् क्षीयते विनश्यतीत्यर्थः ॥

§ फलान्तरमाह ॥

|| धारणा वक्ष्यमाणाः । तासु प्राणायामैः क्षीणदोषं मनो यत्र यत्र धार्यते तत्र तत्र स्थिरं भवति न विक्षेपं भजते ॥

$ प्रत्याहारस्य लक्षणमाह ॥

a. It is called 'restraint,' because, when it exists, the senses are restrained, are withheld, from their respective objects. And how is this effected? He replies;—'of the senses,' Sight, &c., there is 'each one's own object,' as Colour, &c:—'concernment' therewith is any energizing with respect thereto:—the 'absence of this is the abiding in their mere nature after having abandoned all regard to such things. When this takes place, the senses simply accommodate themselves to the nature of the mind; for, all the senses are observed to follow obsequiously the mind, as the bees their leader. Hence, when the mind is restrained [from the exercise of its functions], these [senses], are restrained; and their accommodation to the nature thereof [under such circumstances] is what is called 'restraint.'*

b. He states the fruit.†

ततः परमा वश्यतेन्द्रियाणाम् ॥ ५५ ॥

The fruit of restraint.

Aph. 55.—Therefrom is there complete subjection of the senses.

a. For, when 'restraint' is practised, the senses become so subjected, so subdued, that, even when attracted towards external objects, they will not go;—such is the meaning.‡

Recapitulation.

b. Thus, then, [—to recapitulate briefly—] of Concentration, which was defined in the First Beok, having declared that appendage, viz., the 'Practical [part of] Concentration' [§.1], the fruit of which is the alleviat-

* इन्द्रियाणि स्वस्वविषयेभ्यः प्रत्याह्रियन्ते प्रतिकूलतया आह्रियन्ते ऽस्मिन्निति प्रत्याहारः। स च कथं निष्पद्यत इत्याह। चक्षुरादीनामिन्द्रियाणां स्वः स्वो विषयो रूपादिः। तेन सम्प्रयोगस्तदाभिमुख्येन प्रवर्त्तनं। तदभावस्तदाभिमुख्यं परित्यज्य स्वरूपमात्रे ऽवस्थानं। तस्मिन् सति चित्तस्वरूपमात्रानुकारीणीन्द्रियाणि भवन्ति यतश्चित्तमनुवर्तमानानि मधुकरराजमिव मधुकरमक्षिकाः सर्वाणीन्द्रियाणिप्रतीयन्ते। अतश्चित्तनिरोधे तानि प्रत्याहृतानि भवन्ति। तेषां तत्स्वरूपानुकारः प्रत्याहार उक्तः॥ † फलमाह॥

‡ अभ्यस्यमाने हि प्रत्याहारे तथा वश्यान्यायत्तानीन्द्रियाणि सम्पद्यन्ते यथा बाह्यविषयाभिमुखतां नीयमानान्यपि न यान्तीत्यर्थः॥

ing of the 'afflictions' [§2]; having mentioned the names of the 'afflictions' [§3], their cause and source [§4], their nature and fruit [§5—11]; having stated also the division, cause, nature and fruit, of works [§12]; the nature and cause of fructification are set forth [§13—14.] Then, since the 'afflictions,' &c., are to be got rid of, and since it is impossible to get rid of them without knowing what they are, and since knowledge is dependent on instruction, and since the instruction assumes four aspects, as it respects (1) what is to be got rid of, (2) what is not [desired] to be got rid of, (3) what is constituted by the cause, and (4) what is the cause constitutive, and since, without [an explanation of what is meant by the expression] 'getting rid of,' the nature of 'what is to be got rid of' cannot be explained, [therefore] having set forth the fourfold arrangement, with [an explanation of what is meant by] 'getting rid of,' and with [an account of] the cause of each thing severally [§15—27]; having explained, along with the fruits, the nature of those appliances, 'forbearance' &c., which stand in the relation of causes, immediate or mediate, in respect of the constitutive cause [of emancipation], viz., 'discriminative knowledge' [§28—46]; having exhibited the 'postures,' &c., as far as 'attention,' arranged according to their mutual relation as conduced to and conducers [§47—52]; their fruits, along with the respective characters thereof, have been set forth [§53—55].*

c. Thus this 'Concentration,' having, through 'forbearance,'

---

* तदेवं प्रथमपादोक्तलक्षणस्य योगस्याङ्गभूतं क्लेशतनूकरणफलं क्रियायोगमभिधाय क्लेशानामुद्देशं कारणं क्षेत्रं स्वरूपं फलं चोक्त्वा कर्म्मणामपि भेदं कारणं स्वरूपं फलं चाभिधाय विपाकस्य स्वरूपं कारणं चाभिहितम् ततस्त्याज्यत्वात्क्लेशादीनां ज्ञानव्यतिरेकेण त्यागस्याशक्यत्वात् ज्ञानस्य च शास्त्रायतत्वात् शास्त्रस्य च हेयाहेयकारणोपादेयोपादानकारणत्वेन चतुर्व्यूहत्वाद्धेयस्य हानव्यतिरेकेण स्वरूपानिष्पत्तेर्हानसहितं चतुर्व्यूहं स्वस्वकारणसहितमभिधाय उपादानकारणभूताया विवेकख्यातेः कारणभूतानामन्तरङ्गबहिरङ्गभावेन स्थितानां योगाङ्गानां यमादीनां स्वरूपं फलसहितं व्याकृत्य धारणापर्यन्तानां आसनादीनां परस्परमुपकार्योपकारकभावेनावस्थितानामुद्देशमभिधाय परस्परलक्षणपूर्वकं फलमभिहितम् ॥

'religious observances,' &c., attained to the condition of a seed, and having sprouted by means of the 'postures' and 'regulation of the breath,' and having blossomed by means of 'self-restraint,' will fructify by means of 'attention,' 'contemplation,' and 'meditation' [§29]. Thus has the Book on the Means been explained.*

d. Thus has been completed the Second Book—that on the Means—of the commentary called the *Rája Martanda*, composed by the illustrious great king and governor, king Bhoja Rájâ, on the Aphorisms of Patanjali's System of the Yoga.†

---

* तदयं योगो यमनियमादिभिः प्राप्तबीजभाव आसनप्राणायामैरङ्कुरितः प्रत्याहारेण कुसुमितो धारणाध्यानसमाधिभिः फलिष्यतीति व्याख्यातः साधनपादः ॥

† इति श्री राजाधिराजभोजदेवविरचितायां राजमार्तण्डाभिधायां पातञ्जलयोगशास्त्रसूत्रवृत्तौ द्वितीयः साधनपादः समाप्तः ॥

END OF BOOK II.

THE

SANKHYA

OR

YOGA APHORISMS

OF

PATANJALI.

BOOK III.

a. May that Lord of Spirits (Shiva)—by the recollection of whose Lotus-Feet the superhuman faculties, Anima &c., are (at the disposal) of devotees, be (helpful) for (the attainment) of prosperity !*

b. Thus then, to discuss the three Yogangas, Dharana &c, which have been generally stated before (see Aph. 29th. Book I. P. 25) and to explain, by stating the appellation of Sanyama, the external and internal and other Siddhis (the superhuman faculties), Patanjali begins to define the three Yogangas of which he declares [first] the nature of Dharana (attention).†

देशबन्धश्चित्तस्य धारणा ॥ १ ॥

Dharana defined. *Aph.* 1.—Fixing the internal organ [Chitta] on a place is Dharana (attention).

a. "On a place" i. e. at the circle of the navel, &c. The fixing of the internal organ, by abstracting it from all other ob-

---

* यत्पादपद्मस्मरणादणिमादिविभूतयः । भवन्ति भाविनामस्तु भूतनाथः स भूतये ॥

† तदेवं पूर्वोद्दिष्टं धारणाद्यङ्गत्रयं निर्णेतुं संयमसंज्ञाभिधानपूर्वं बाह्याभ्यन्तरादिसिद्धिप्रतिपादनाय लक्षयितुमुपक्रमते । तत्र धारणायाः स्वरूपमाह ।

jects, is called Dharana (attention) of the internal organ, (Chitta).*

b. Having defined Dharana, he (Patanjali) proceeds to state Dhyana (contemplation).†

तत्र प्रत्ययैकतानता ध्यानम् ॥ २ ॥

Dhyana defined. *Aph.* 2.—A course of uniform (fixed on only one object) modification of knowledge at that place (where the internal organ is fixed in Dharana) is Dhyana (contemplation).

a. A course of uniform modification of knowledge at that place where the internal organ is fixed in attention by avoiding the otherwise (not uniform) modification of knowledge, is called Dhyana (contemplation).‡

b. [It is to be observed here that in this philosophy the usual tenet is, that knowledge in the shape of Dhyana does not take place unless it has recourse to a certain place. Therefore, the definition speaks of a course of uniform modification of knowledge at that place, where the internal organ is fixed in attention, Dharana.]

a. He explains (now) Samádhi, the last of the Yogángas (things subservient to the Yoga.)§

तदेवार्थमात्रनिर्भासं स्वरूपशून्यमिव समाधिः ॥ ३ ॥

Samádhi defined. *Aph.* 3.—The same (contemplation) when it arises only about a material substance or object of sense, (and therefore) is (then) like a non-existence of itself (that is like ignorance) is Samádhi (meditation).

---

* देशे नाभिचक्रादौ चित्तस्य बन्धो विषयान्तरपरिहारेण यत् स्थिरीकरणं सा चित्तस्य धारणेत्युच्यते ।

† धारणामभिधाय ध्यानमभिधातुमाह ।

‡ तत्र तस्मिन् देशे यत्र चित्तं धृतं तत्र प्रत्ययस्य ज्ञानस्य या एकतानता विसदृशपरिणामपरिहारद्वारेण यदेव धारणायामालम्बनीकृतं तदालम्बनतयैव निरन्तरमुत्पत्तिः सा ध्यानमुच्यते । § चरमं योगाङ्गं समाधिमाह ।

b. [The true meaning of this aphorism is this, that knowledge in the shape of contemplation always takes place about the following three, i. e. the material substance whether it be animate or inanimate, such as a cow, a jar &c., the term cow, jar &c., and the knowledge itself; but when it takes place only about the material substance and not about the latter two, then such a knowledge in the shape of contemplation is called Samádhi.]

c. The term Samádhi means literally that state (of knowledge) in which the mind, having avoided the obstacles (see Aph. 30th, Book I), is well fixed on, or confined to one object only.*

a. In order to give a technical term for the use of the three Yogángas just defined, he says.†

त्रयमेकत्र संयमः ॥ ४ ॥

Sanyama defined. *Aph.* 4.—These three (when they operate only) on one object, constitute Sanyama.

b. The three which are characterized as Contemplation, Attention and Meditation, when they operate on only one object, are called in this philosophy by the appellation of Sanyama.‡

a. He explains the fruit (result) of Sanyama.§

तज्जयात् प्रज्ञालोकः ॥ ५ ॥

The fruit produced by Sanyama. *Aph.* 5.—By subduing Sanyama, a discerning principle is developed.

b. "By subduing Sanyama" i. e. by rendering it natural (easily attainable) through endeavours, a principle, distinguishing things from others, is developed; that is to say, the intellect well apprehends a thing to be known.||

---

* सम्यक् आधीयत एकाग्रीक्रियते विक्षेपान् परिहृत्य यत्र मनः स समाधिः ।

† उक्तलक्षणस्य योगाङ्गत्रयस्य व्यवहाराय तान्त्रिकीं संज्ञां कर्तुमाह ॥

‡ एकस्मिन् विषये ध्यानधारणासमाधिलक्षणं त्रितयं प्रवर्तमानं संयमसंज्ञया शास्त्रे व्यवह्रियते ॥ § तस्य फलमाह ॥

|| तस्य संयमस्य जयादभ्यासेन सात्म्योत्पादनात् प्रज्ञाया ज्ञातव्यविवेकरूपाया आलोकः प्रसरो भवति । प्रज्ञा ज्ञेयं सम्यगवभासयतीत्यर्थः ॥

v. He explains the use of Sanyama.*

तस्य भूमिषु विनियोगः ॥ ६ ॥

The use of Sanyama. *Aph.* 6.—Sanyama is to be used in the modifications (of the internal organ *Chitta*)

b. "In the modifications (of the internal organ)" in the shapes characterised by the rough (Sthula) and fine (Sukshma) objects, Sanyama is to be used, that is, to make the modifications fit, by Sanyama, for the future fruit just defined. When it is known that the lower modifications of the internal organ are subdued, Sanyama is then to be used in the superior modifications to subdue them, because, the Soul would never gain the fruit (aimed at) without subduing the lower modifications, though attempting to subdue the superior ones by Sanyama.†—[The meaning of the whole is this, that a man should proceed towards concentration by gradually acquiring control over the modifications of the internal organ, in the shapes of the rough and fine objects. When the superhuman faculties Anima &c., attainable by the conquest of the respective modifications of the internal organ, are at his disposal, he is to know that those modifications are subdued, and then he should proceed further to subdue the other ones, otherwise, he is not to expect to gain access to Concentration (Yoga)].

a. In (the Second Book called) Sàdhanapàda, he, having enunciated the eight Yogangas—things subservient to concentration (See Aph. 29), has defined (only) five (of them, i. e. forbearance—Yama &c.); but why has he not (there) defined the last three, attention &c.? With reference to this he declares as follwows :—‡

* तस्योपयोगमाह ॥

† तस्य संयमस्य भूमिषु स्थूलसूक्ष्मालम्बनभेदेन स्थितासु चित्तवृत्तिषु विनियोगः कर्तव्यः । अधरामधरां चित्तभूमिं जितां ज्ञात्वोत्तरस्यां भूमौ संयमः कार्यः नह्यसावात्माऽजिताधरभूमिरुत्तरस्यां भूमौ संयमं कुर्वाणः फलभाग् भवति ॥

‡ साधनपादे योगाङ्गान्यष्टावुद्दिश्य पञ्चानां लक्षणं विधाय त्रयाणां कथं न कृतमित्याशङ्क्याह ।

त्रयमन्तरङ्गं पूर्वेभ्यः ॥ ७ ॥

The three Yogangas interior to the meditation called Samprajnatasamadhi.

Aph. 7.—The three Yogangas (i. e. attention, contemplation, and meditation) are more interior (i. e. immediately subservient to that kind of meditation in which there is distinct recognition i. e. Samprajnatasamadhi,—See Aph. 17. Book.1) than the first (five Yogangas, forbearance &c.)

b. The first (five) Yogangas, forbearance (Yama) &c, are not immediately subservient to that kind of meditation in which there is distinct recognition (i. e. Samprajnatasamadhi) but as the three (Yogangas, attention &c.) are immediately subservient to accomplish its nature, these three therefore are more interior —Antaranga—to it than the first five.*

a. He declares (now) that these three (Yogangas) also are exterior (Bahiranga) to the other kind of meditation in which distinct recognition is lost (i. e. Asamprajnatasamadhi—See Aph. 18. Book. 1.)†

तदपि बहिरङ्गं निर्बीजस्य ॥ ८ ॥

The very three are exterior to the meditation called Asamprajnatasamadhi.

Aph. 8.—Those three also are exterior to the meditation without a seed (Nirbija).

b. "Nirbija" i. e, that which has no support to depend on, that is to say, that kind of meditation in which recognition of an object is lost. To this kind of meditation, these three yogangas are not immediately subservient, and therefore these also are exterior (Bahiranga) to this kind of meditation.‡

a. Now, being desirous to explain the Siddhis (Superhuman faculties which arise from the Yogangas); to bring under discus-

---

* पूर्वेभ्यो यमादिभ्यो योगाङ्गेभ्यः पारम्पर्य्येण समाधेरुपकारकेभ्यो धारणादियोगाङ्गत्रयं संप्रज्ञातस्य समाधेरन्तरङ्गं समाधिस्वरूपनिष्पादनात् ।

† तस्यापि समाध्यन्तरापेक्षया बहिरङ्गत्वमाह ।

‡ निर्बीजस्य निरालम्बनस्य शून्यभावनापरपर्यायस्य समाधेरेतदपि योगाङ्गत्रयं बहिरङ्गं पारम्पर्य्येणोपकारकत्वात् ।

sion the particular circumstances of Sanyama (which has been defined before—See Aph. 4. Book III.) he declares the three modifications (of the internal organ) successively.*

व्युत्थाननिरोधसंस्कारयोरभिभवप्रादुर्भावौ
निरोधलक्षण चित्तान्वयो निरोधपरिणामः ॥ ९ ॥

The modification in the shape of Nirodha defined.

Aph. 9.—Out of the two trains of self-reproductive thought, resulting from the Vyutthana and the Nirodha, when the former is subdued and the latter is manifested, and, at that moment of manifestation the internal organ (Chitta) is concerned in both of the trains, then, such modification of the iternal organ is the modification in the shpe of Nirodha.

b. "Vyutthana" consists of the three modifications of the internal organ in the shape of Kshipta (cast), Mudha (darkened) and Vikshipta (better than kshipta): [That is the first is that modification of the internal organ in which it, by passion, is entirely cast in, i. e. engaged in the thought of an object; the second is that in which it, by darkness, takes the shape of sleep and the third is that in which it is better than kshipta, i.e. in which, though it is inclined towards concentration, still it, every now and then, becomes engaged with other objects—see the sentence, given below, of the Commentary on the Yogabhashya, by Vidnyanabhikshu.]† "Nirodha," is that modification in which the internal organ has only a pure element (Sattva) as an object of thought. From these two, result the two trains of self-reproductive thought, out of which, in succession, when the former is overcome, i. e. become incapable of producing any effect on account of its being hidden, and the latter is manifested, i. e., come in

* इदानीं योगाङ्गसिद्धिरास्थ्यातुकामः संयमस्य विषयपरिशुद्धिं कर्तुं क्रमेण परिणामत्रयमाह ।

† क्षिप्तमित्यादि क्षिप्तं रजसा विषयेष्वेव वृत्तिमत् मूढं तमसा निद्रादिवृत्तिमत् क्षिप्ताद्विशिष्टं विक्षिप्तं सत्त्वाधिक्येन समादधदपि चित्तं रजोमात्रयाऽन्तरान्तरा विषयान्तरवृत्तिमत् । विज्ञानभिक्षुः ॥

veiw in the present way and at that moment of Nirodha (just expounded), the connection of the internal organ with both of the trains is called the modification (of the internal organ) in the shape of Nirodha.—The meaning is this, that when the quality in the shape of the train resulting from the Vyutthtna has disappeared, and that in the shape of the train resulting from the Nirodha becomes manifest, and the internal organ appears to be connected with both of the trains, then such modification of the internal organ is (technically) termed Nirodhaparinama. Though the internal organ is not fixed (because it consists of) the three principles of existence, i. e., Sattva (truth or existence), Rajas (passion or foulness) and Tamas, (darkness or ignorance) which always vary (according to the technicality of the Yoga and Sankhya Philosophies) still this modification of the internal organ is called the fixed modification (of it).*

a. He states the (special) fruit of it.†

तस्यप्रशान्तवाहिता संस्कारात् ॥१०॥

The fruit resulting from the Nirodha-parinàma.

Aph. 10.—A uniform flow (of modifications of the internal organ arises) from the (aforesaid) train of self-reproductive thought.

b. "A uniform flow &c." that is to say, the internal organ takes a uniform shape on account of its being deprived of the

---

* व्युत्थानं क्षिप्तमूढविक्षिप्ताख्यं भूमित्रयं निरोधः प्रकृष्टसत्त्वस्याङ्गितया चेतसः परिणामस्ताभ्यां व्युत्थाननिरोधाभ्यां यौ जनितौ संस्कारौ तयोर्यथाक्रममभिभवप्रादुर्भावौ यदा भवतः । अभिभवो न्यग्भूततया कार्यकरणासामर्थ्येनावस्थानम् । प्रादुर्भावो वर्तमानेऽध्वन्यभिव्यक्तरूपतयाऽवस्थानं तदा निरोधलक्षणे चित्तस्योभयवृत्तित्वादन्वयो यः स निरोधपरिणाम इत्युच्यते । अयमर्थः । यदा व्युत्थानसंस्काररूपो धर्मस्तिरोभूतो भवति निरोधसंस्काररूपश्चाविर्भवति धर्मिरूपतया च चित्तमुभयत्रान्वयित्वेनावस्थितं प्रतीयते तदा स निरोधपरिणामशब्देन व्यपदिश्यते । चलत्वाद्गुणवृत्तस्य यद्यपि चेतसो निश्चलत्वं नास्ति तथाप्येवंभूतः परिणामः स्थैर्यमुच्यते ।

† अस्यैव फलमाह ।

obstacles (Vikshepas or Antaráyas, sickness, langour &c.—see Aph. 30. Book I).*

a. Having described the modification in the shape of Nirodha (hindrance) he declares (now) the modification in the shape of Samádhi (meditation).†

सर्वार्थतैकाग्रतयोः क्षयोदयौ चित्तस्य समाधिपरिणामः ॥ ११ ॥

The modification in the shape of Samádhi (meditation) defined.

Aph. 11.—Out of the two (properties) of the internal organ—chitta— which consist of Sarvárthatá (that is its comprehension of several objects) and Ekágratá (i. e. its intentness on a single point); (when) the first is utterly destroyed and the second is manifested—(at that time the connection of the internal organ with both of the properties or the state in which it exists as Dharmí, i. e. endowed with the two properties) is the modification of the internal organ in the shape of Samadhi (meditation).

b. "Sarvárthatá" i. e. that property, in the shape of an obstacle, of the internal organ—chitta—which consists of its comprehension of several objects on account of its being changeable. "Ekágratá" (literally means intentness on a single point, but here it) means a uniform modification of the internal organ having its support on only one object. This also is a property of the internal organ. Out of these two, (when) the destruction (of the first) and the manifestation (of the 2nd) i. e. the destruction or an utter conquest of the first property characterised as Sarvárthatá and the manifestation or development of the 2nd one distinguished as Ekágratá, take place successively, (at that time), the connection of internal organ, which has (then) an abundance of the principle Sattva—truth—with both of the properties or its existence as Anvayi (or Dharmi i. e. endowed with the two properties just mentioned) is technically called the modification in the shape of Samadhi—meditation.

---

* तस्य चेतस उक्तान्निरोधसंस्कारात् प्रशान्तवाहिता भवति । परिहृतविक्षेपतया सदृशप्रवाहपरिणामीशालिचित्तं भवतीत्यर्थः ।

† निरोधपरिणाममभिधाय समाधिपरिणाममाह ॥

This modification differs from the former one only in this respect, that there, the subjugation and manifestation of the Sanskaras—trains of self-reproductive thought, that is, the subjugation of the former train of self-reproductive thought, resulting from Vyutthana before defined and the manifestation or the state of not being subdued, of the latter one, resulting from Nirodha—hindrance—are to take place. But here, (i. e. in the modification in the shape of Samadhi—meditation) the destruction and manifestation of the properties—Dharmas (and not of the Sanskaras), that is, the destruction or entering past way, on account of utter negligence, of the property of an obstacle in the shape of Sarvarthata and the production or manifestation, in the present way, of the property characterised as Ekagrata, (are to take place).*

a. (He) declares (now) the third modification of the internal organ (in the shape of) intentness on a single point (Ekagrata).†

शान्तोदितौ तुल्यप्रत्ययौ चित्तस्यैकाग्रतापरिणामः ॥ १२ ॥

The third modification in the shape of intentness on a single point defined.

Aph. 12.—(When) the two particular states or modifications (pratyayas), the one tranquil (Santa) and the other reason (Udita), of the internal organ become equal, then its connection with both of the states is (its) modification in the shape of an intentness on a single point (Ekàgrata).

b. The one particular state of the obstructed internal organ

---

* सर्वार्थता चलत्वान्नानाविधार्थग्रहणं चित्तस्य विक्षेपो धर्मः । एकस्मिन्नेवालम्बने सदृशपरिणामितैकाग्रत्वं तदपि चित्तस्य धर्मः । तयोर्यथाक्रमं क्षयोदयौ सर्वार्थतालक्षणस्य धर्मस्य क्षयोऽत्यन्तमभिभव एकाग्रतालक्षणस्य धर्मस्य प्रादुर्भावो ऽभिव्यक्तिश्चित्तस्योद्रिक्तसत्त्वस्यान्वयितया ऽवस्थानं समाधिपरिणाम इत्युच्यते । पूर्वस्मात् परिणामादस्यायं विशेषः । तत्र संस्कारलक्षणयोर्धर्मयोरभिभवप्रादुर्भावौ पूर्वस्य व्युत्थानसंस्कारस्वरूपस्य धर्मस्य न्यग्भावः । उत्तरस्य निरोधसंस्कारस्वरूपस्योद्भवो ऽनभिभूतत्वेनावस्थानमिह तु क्षयोदयाविति । सर्वार्थतारूपविक्षेपस्यात्यन्ततिरस्कारादनुत्पत्तिरतीते ऽध्वनि प्रवेशः क्षयः । एकाग्रतालक्षणस्य धर्मस्योद्भवो वर्तमाने ऽध्वनि प्रकटत्वम् ।

† तृतीयमेकाग्रतापरिणाममाह ।

is tranquil (Santa) i. e. entered the past way; and the other risen i. e. agitated in the present way, (when) both of these states also become equal or similar; as the internal organ, being abstracted from all other objects, has only one one object, as its support, to contemplate with, (then) the abiding (Avasthana) of the internal organ is in the shape of intentness on a single point (Ekagrata).*

a. To explain the (same) nature (of the modifications) about other things, as has been stated as to those of the internal organ, (he) says (as follows).†

एतेन भूतेन्द्रियेषु धर्मलक्षणावस्थापरिणामा व्याख्याताः ॥ १३ ॥

The modifications of the Elements and organs explained.

Aph. 13.—By this (exposition of the modifications of the internal organs) the (three) modifications in the shape of property (Dharma), indication (Lakshana) and position (Avastha) in (or of) the Elements and organs, have been (sufficiently) explained.

b. "By this (exposition)" of the threefold modification of the internal organ (see Aphs. 9, 11, 12) the three modifications under the distinction of property, indication and position, have been explained or are to be understood, in (or of) the gross (Sthula) and subtle (Sukshma) Elements and both the organs i. e. those of perception and action as they are characterised. [Now, the commentator explains these three successively.]

1st. (When) a Dharmi (i. e. that which is endowed with a property) is taken into consideration, leaving its former property, it embraces another one, (then) this its embracing of another property is the modification (of it) in the shape of property. As for example. [Take a lump of clay which is called Dharmi, as it is endowed with a property in the shape of lumpiness.]

---

* समाहितस्यैव चित्तस्यैक प्रत्ययौ वृत्तिविशेषः शान्तोऽतीतमध्वानं प्रविष्टः। अपरस्तूदितो वर्तमानेऽध्वनिस्फुरितो द्वावपि समाहितचित्तत्वेन तुल्यावेकरूपालम्बनत्वेन सदृशौ प्रत्ययावुभयत्रापि समाहितस्यैव चित्तस्यान्वयित्वेनावस्थानं स एकाग्रता परिणाम इत्युच्यते। † चित्तपरिणामोक्तं रूपमन्यत्रातिदिशन्नाह।

(When) the Dharmi clay (as it is called) by quitting the property in the shape of lumpiness, assumes another one in the shape of jar-hood (then) this modification (which the clay has now undergone) is called the modification of property.

2nd. The modification in the shape of indication is as follows, (when) the same jar, by leaving the way called Anagata (not come in view) embraces the way called Vartamana (present) and again by quitting it when it takes the way called Atita (past,) (then), this sort of modification is called the modification in the shape of indication. The following example will sufficiently illustrate this. A stone has a statue already hidden in it and the sculptor only removes the outer parts of it to make it apparent. In the same manner, the jar exists already in the lump of clay and it only becomes visible when the potter removes the superfluous parts from it; therefore, according to the technicality of this Philosophy, the jar is said to exist in the Anagata way, before it becomes visible. On its being visible, it is said to be in the present way and when it is destroyed it is said to be in the way called Atita—past.]

3rd. The modification in the shape of position is as follows. In any two similar—i. e. belonging to the present way—moments, the same jar exists (and hence it is said) to be Anvayi (to the moments i. e. connected with both of them, but not without being changed, because, comparatively speaking, the jar was new in the first moment and became old in the next one), for the three visible principles of existence (Guna) cannot exist even in a single moment without being changed. (This) kind of modification which the jar, existing in the present way, undergoes every moment, is called the modification in the shape of position).*

---

* एतेन त्रिविधोक्तेन चित्तपरिणामेन भूतेषु स्थूलसूक्ष्मेषु इन्द्रियेषु बुद्धिकर्म-लक्षणभेदेनावस्थितेषु धर्मलक्षणावस्थाभेदेन त्रिविधः परिणामो व्याख्यातोऽवगन्तव्यः । अवस्थितस्य धर्मिणः पूर्वधर्मनिवृत्तौ धर्मान्तरापत्तिर्धर्मपरिणामः । यथा मृल्लक्षणस्य धर्मिणः पिण्डरूपधर्मपरित्यागेन घटरूपधर्मान्तरस्वीकारो धर्मपरिणाम

a. Well then, what is a Dharmi? with reference to this query, he declares the definition of Dharmi.*

शान्तोदिताव्यपदेश्य धर्मानुपाती धर्मी ॥ १४ ॥

Dharmi what? *Aph.* 14.—A Dharmi is that which follows upon (or has) the properties in the shape of Santa (tranquil), Udita (risen) and Avyapadeshya (incapable of denomination).

b. "Santas" are those (properties) which have done their respective functions, i. e. entered the past (Atita) way; "risen" are those (properties) which having abandoned the way not come in view (Anagata) perform their own functions, and "incapable of denomination" are those (properties) which exist in the shape of Shakti (literally power, but here the Anagata way as the word is used here according to the technicality of the Mimansa Philosophy and consequently) these cannot be particularly denominated. As for example, (these are those properties which stand in this form) "all consists of all" &c. [It will be clear from the following tenet of this Philosophy that "all things are eventually dissolved into nature—Prakriti; and consequently a jar can easily be denominated a cloth and conversely. So, in short, it can be said that all consists of all and hence they cannot be particularly named, as jar, cloth &c.]

By the word Dharma (property) is meant here a power itself limited, as being capable of doing a fixed action. (Thus) a Dharmi is that which follows upon (at different times) or has, being Anvayi (i. e. connected with them), all the three properties (just defined). As for example, gold in the form of a Ruchaka (chain) has a property in the shape of a chain and by quitting that property assumes another one in the shape of Svastika (a particular kind of ornament). Then though the

---

इत्युच्यते । लक्षणपरिणामो यथा तस्यैव घटस्यानागताध्वपरित्यागेन वर्तमानाध्वस्वीकारस्तत्परित्यागेन चातीताध्वपरिग्रहः । अवस्थापरिणामो यथा तस्यैव घटस्य प्रथमद्वितीययोः सदृशयोः धर्मलक्षणयोरन्वायित्वेन । यतश्चलं गुणवृत्तं नापरिणममानं क्षणमप्यस्ते, ।

* ननु कोऽयं धर्मीत्याशङ्क्य धर्मिणो लक्षणमाह ।

N

properties (in question) differ from each other in some way, still the gold follows when it is commonly taken in the shape of Dharma (property) it appears then to follow as a distinct one, [because every body can easily perceive that a garland differs from the Svastika, though both of them are nothing but gold.]*

a. To remove the doubt how the same Dharmi is to undergo the various modifications, (he) declares (as follows).†

क्रमान्यत्वं परिणामान्यत्वे हेतुः ॥ १५ ॥

Aph. 15.—The altered state of the order (of the threefold modification just defined) is indicative of the variety of the modifications (which the same Dharmi is to undergo).

An indication of the various modifications of the same Dharmi.

b. The apparent state, changeable in every moment, of the order (of the modifications) of the properties defined before, is indicative of the variety of the modifications. The meaning is this, that the apparent order (of the modifications of the properties) that a lump of clay (is produced) from the power of the earth thence the several part of the jar and then the jar, indicates the state of variety of the modifications. By the same argument, the order of modifications of the indication and position, is also to be understood indicative of the variety of the modifications of the same Dharmi (i. e. as a jar) (in this manner) all things appear to undergo a certain change according to fixed order, and hence it is proved that the variety of the modifications (of the same Dharmi) is indicated by that of the order

---

* शान्ता ये कृतस्वस्वव्यापारा अतीतेऽध्वन्यनुप्रविष्टाः । उदिता येऽनागतमध्वानं परित्यज्य स्वस्वव्यापारंकुर्वन्ति अव्यपदेश्या ये शक्तिरूपेण स्थिता व्यपदेष्टुं न शक्यन्ते यथा सर्वं सर्वात्मकमित्येवमादयः । नियतकार्यकारणरूपयोग्यतयाऽवच्छिन्ना शक्तिरेवेह धर्मशब्देनाभिधीयते तंत्रिविधमपि धर्मं योऽनुपतत्यनुवर्तते ऽन्वयित्वेन स्वीकरोति स शान्तोदिताव्यपदेश्यधर्मानुपाती धर्मीत्युच्यते । यथा सुवर्णं रुचकरूपधर्मपरित्यागेन स्वस्तिकरूपधर्मान्तरपरिग्रहे सुवर्णरूपतयाऽनुवर्तमानं तेषु धर्मेषु कथञ्चित् भिन्नेषु धर्मिरूपतया सामान्यात्मना धर्मरूपतया विशेषात्मना स्थितमनुपातित्वेनावभासते ।

† एकस्य धर्मिणः कथमनेके परिणामा इत्याशङ्कामपनेतुमाह ।

(just explained). Some of the properties of the internal organ, and all of its objects &c, are apprehended by perception (Pratyaksha) as happiness &c., and position and others (respectively) and some are understood only by inference (Anumana) as property, train of self-reproductive thought, the way not come in view &c. It is always to be observed that Dharmi differs and does not differ from itself*(accordingly as it is connected with the modifications of the position and the way not come in view—as the compound word Anagatadhva means).

a Now, in order to explain the Siddhis—Superhuman faculties—by showing (first)the particular circumstances of the before-mentioned Sanyama—restraint i. e. the circumstances where Sanyama is to be used to attain to the Siddhis, he declares (as follows).†

परिणामत्रयसंयमादतीतानागतज्ञानम् ॥ १६ ॥

The superhuman faculty which consists in a knowledge of past and future events.

Aph. 16.—A knowledge of past and future events (comes to an ascetic) from (his rendering) Sanyama—restraint—about the three modifications (just explained).

b. "From rendering Sanyama about the three modificatoins (just explained)" in the shape of property, indication and position (i. e. from acquiring control over them from rendering Sanyama regarding them) an ascetic knows well the past and future events. The true meaning is this that this (particular)

---

* धर्माणामुक्तलक्षणानां: यः क्रमस्तस्य यत्प्रतिक्षणमन्यत्वं परिदृश्यमानमस्योक्तलक्षणस्यान्यत्वे नानाविधत्वे हेतुर्लिङ्गं ज्ञापकं भवति । अयमर्थः योऽयं नियतक्रमोमृच्चूर्णान्मृत्पिण्डस्ततः कपालानि तेभ्यश्च घट इत्येवंरूपः परिदृश्यमानः परिणामस्यान्यत्वमावेदयति । तस्मिन्नेव धर्मिणि यो लक्षणपरिणामस्यावस्थापरिणामस्य च क्रमः सोऽप्यनेनैव न्यायेन परिणामान्यत्वे गमकोऽवगन्तव्यः । सर्व एव भावा नियतेनैव क्रमेण प्रतिक्षणं परिणममाना दृश्यन्ते । अतः सिद्धं क्रमान्यत्वात्परिणामान्यत्वम् । सर्वेषां चित्तविषयादीनां परिणममानानां केचिद्धर्माः प्रत्यक्षेणैवोपलभ्यन्ते यथासुखादयः संस्थानादयश्च । केचिच्चैकान्तेनानुमानगम्याः । यथा धर्मसंस्कारशक्तिप्रभृतयः । धर्मिणश्चभिन्नाभिन्नरूपतया सर्वत्रानुगमः ।

† इदानीमुक्तस्य संयमस्य विषयप्रदर्शनद्वारेण सिद्धीः प्रतिपादयितुमाह ।

property is in this Dharmi, this is the way which it belongs to, and this is the position it possesses. Moreover on its coming from the Anagatadva—the way not come in view—, it has performed its respective function in the present way and entered now the past way. When all this the ascetic (clearly perceives) by getting rid of the obstacles from Sanyama—restraint—, then he knows whatever is past and whatever is to come or arise (in future) because the capacity of the internal organ to comprehend all objects, on account of its consisting of the manifestation of the pure truth (Sattva) is taken away by (i. e. is hidden under) the obstacle ignorance (Avidya) &c. and when these obstacles are removed by (adopting) special measures, then the capacity of beholding all objects, is manifested in the internal organ (which then becomes) like a cleared mirror by the force or intentness on a single point (Ekagrata).*

a. (He) declares (now) another siddhi.†

शद्धार्थप्रत्ययानामितरेतराध्यासात्संकरस्तत्प्रवि-

भागसंयमात्सर्वभूतरुतज्ञानम् ॥ १७ ॥

The superhuman faculty which consists in a knowledge of the speech of all living beings.

Aph. 17.—A confusedness of Shabda (an uttered sound or a word) Artha i. e. (class, quality, action &c.) and Pratyaya (knowledge) arises from comprehending these three indiscriminately. (But when an ascetic views these separately by performing Sanyama—restraint—with regard to them, a knowledge (is produced in him) of the speech of all

---

* धर्मलक्षणावस्थाभेदेन यत्परिणामत्रयमुक्तं तत्र संयमात् तस्मिन्विषये पूर्वोक्तस्य संयमस्य करणादतीतानागतज्ञानं योगिनः सम्यगाविर्भवति । इदमत्र तात्पर्यम् । अस्मिन् धर्मिण्ययं धर्म इदं लक्षणमियमवस्था चानागतादध्वनः समेत्य वर्तमाने ऽध्वनि स्वं व्यापारं विधायातीतमध्वानं प्रविशतीत्येवं परित्यक्तविक्षेपतया यदा संयमं करोति तदा यत्किञ्चिदतिक्रान्तमनुत्पन्नं वा तत्सर्वं योगी जानाति । यतश्चित्तस्य शुद्धसत्त्वप्रकाशरूपत्वात्सर्वार्थग्रहणसामर्थ्यमविद्यादिभिर्विक्षेपैरजस्रं परिह्रियते । यदा तु तैस्तैरुपायैर्विक्षेपाः परिह्रियन्ते तदा निवृत्तमलस्येवादर्शस्य सर्वार्थग्रहणसामर्थ्यमेकाग्रताबलादाविर्भवति । † सिद्ध्यन्तरमाह ।

living beings (i. e. he has a power of understanding their speech.)

b. "Shabda" is that (uttered sound) which is cognizable by the organ of hearing; it consists of letters whose order is fixed and it is productive of knowledge of a fixed object. [This definition of Shabda is given here according to the technicality of the Nyáya Philosophy, and according to that of the grammarians it is as follows.] Sabda is (that sound in the utterance of which) no order of its constituent letters is to be conceivable and (hence) which is Sphotatma (i. e. from which, class, quality, action &c. become plain at once) and which can (only) be understood by a mind cultivated by science. According to both of these technicalities, it (Shabda) consists of term and sentence, because these two can indicate their own fixed objects.

"Artha" (means literally sense, but here it means) class, quality, action &c, "Pratyaya" (means) knowledge, i. e., a modification of the internal organ, in the form of an object. A confusedness (arises) by forming the same notion of them or supposing the Shabda, Artha and Pratyaya (just expounded) to be identical though they are different from each other, in their use. An illustration of this is as follows. (Suppose) when a person is asked to bring a cow, he then comprehends indiscriminately these three, i. e., the material substance indicated by the term cow, possessed of the dewlap &c., and possessing the characteristic implied by the term cow its indicatory term cow and the knowledge by which the material substance is conceived: but he does not perceive them so discriminately that the term cow, is indicatory of this (material substance); that this is to be declared by the term cow, and that this is the knowledge by which the two former are conceived. Thus, when he is asked what is this substance, what is this term and what is this knowledge, he then, gives the same answer "cow" to all these questions. If he does not conceive the identity of these three, how does he give the same answer to all these questions? In this state, he who, having made this distinction that indicativeness is the essential nature of Shabda (term), that the state of having to be declared is the essential nature of Artha (before defined,) and that luminousness is the essential nature of Dnyan (knowledge), performs Sanyama—restraint—; acquires the knowledge of or understands the speech or language of all living beings, i. e., of animals, wild and domestic, birds, reptiles &c., that is whatever cry or whatever word (is uttered) he knows it all, viz., that the sound was uttered with such and such a motive.*

a. (He) mentions another Siddhi.†

संस्कारसाक्षात्करणात् पूर्वजातिज्ञानम् ॥ १८ ॥

The superhuman faculty which consists in a knowledge of the class &c. experienced in the former birth.

Aph. 18.—A knowledge of the class (&c., experienced) in a former birth (arises) from presenting to our mind (Sakshatkarana)—the trains of self-reproductive thought—Sanskaras (of the internal organ).

b. Sanskaras—the trains of self-reproductive thought which consist of the present consciousness of past perceptions of the internal organ are twofold. Some of these produce only a memory (of the events formerly experienced) and others are the causes of the modifications in the shape of class, age, and experience of pleasure and distress as they are called virtue and

---

* शब्दः श्रोत्रेन्द्रियग्राह्यो नियतक्रमवर्णात्मा नियतैकार्थप्रतिपत्त्यवच्छिन्नः यदि वा क्रमरहितः स्फोटात्मा ध्वनिःशास्त्रसंस्कृतबुद्धिग्राह्यः। उभयथापि पदरूपो वाक्यरूपश्च तयोरेकार्थप्रतिपत्तौ सामर्थ्यात्। अर्थो जातिगुणक्रियादिः प्रत्ययो ज्ञानं विषयाकारा बुद्धिवृत्तिः। एषां शब्दार्थज्ञानानां व्यवहारे इतरेतराध्यासाद्भिन्नानामपिबुद्ध्येकरूपतासंपादनात्संकीर्णत्वम्। तथाहि गामानयेत्युक्ते कश्चिद्गोलक्षणमर्थं गोत्वजात्यवच्छिन्नं सास्नादिमत्पिण्डरूपं शब्दं च तद्वाचकं ज्ञानं च तद्ग्राहकमभेदेनैवाध्यवस्यति न त्वस्य गोशब्दो वाचकोऽयं गोशब्दस्य वाच्यस्तयोरिदं ग्राहकं ज्ञानमिति भेदेन व्यवहरति। यथाहि कोऽयमर्थः कोऽयं शब्दः किमिदं ज्ञानमिति पृष्टः सर्वत्रैकरूपमेवोत्तरं ददाति गौरिति स यद्येकरूपतां न प्रतिपद्यते कथमेकमेवोत्तरं प्रयच्छति। एतस्मिन् स्थिते योऽयं प्रविभाग इदं शब्दस्य तत्त्वं यद्वाचकत्वं नाम। इदमर्थस्य यद्वाच्यत्वम्। इदं ज्ञानस्य यत्प्रकाशकत्वमिति। प्रविभागं विधाय तस्मिन् प्रविभागे यः संयमं करोति तस्य सर्वेषां भूतानां मृगपशुपक्षिसरीसृपादीनां यद्रुतं यः शब्दस्तत्र ज्ञानमुत्पद्यतेऽनेनाभिप्रायेणैतेनायं शब्दः समुच्चारित इति सर्वं जानाति।

† सिद्ध्यन्तरमाह।

vice. When (an ascetic) performs Sanyama—restraint—with regard to the Sanskaras (just illustrated); that is, when he remembers only through an abstract meditation and without any exciting cause, all that is past, reflecting that he has experienced such and such thing—this is the result of the former set of the Sanskaras—and that he has performed such and such action, then he clearly sees the class &c., experienced in the former birth when the trains of self-reproductive thought are thus gradually awakened.*

a. (He) explains (now) another Siddhi.†

प्रत्ययस्य परचित्तज्ञानम् ॥ १९ ॥

The superhuman faculty which consists in the penetration of the mind of other persons.

Aph. 19.—The mind of other persons becomes known to (an ascetic when he performs Sanyama—restraint) with regard to the Pratyaya—knowledge—(contained in it, i. e., in the mind of other persons).

b. When (an ascetic) performs Sanyama with regard to the Pratyaya—knowledge—obtained by any characteristic such as complexion of the face then he knows the mind or another person that is, (he) knows even the qualities which have entered into the mind of others, whether their mind is impassioned (Saraga) or dispassionate (Virága).‡

a. (He now) declares a peculiarity of this same knowledge of the mind of other persons.§

---

* द्विविधाश्चित्तस्य वासनारूपाः संस्काराः केचित् स्मृति मात्रोत्पादनफलाः केचिज्जात्यायुर्भोगलक्षणविपाकहेतवो यथा धर्माधर्माख्याः तेषु संस्कारेषु यदा संयमं करोति एवं मया सोऽर्थोऽनुभूत एवं मया सा क्रिया निष्पादितेति पूर्ववृत्तं सर्वमनुसंदधानो भावनयैवप्रबोधकमन्तरेणोद्बुद्धसंस्कारः सर्वमतीतं स्मरति क्रमेण। साक्षात्कृतेषु बुद्धेषु संस्कारेषु पूर्वजन्मानुभूतानपि जात्यादीन् प्रत्यक्षेण पश्यति।

† सिद्ध्यन्तरमाह।

‡ प्रत्ययस्य केनचित् मुखरागादिना लिङ्गेन गृहीतस्य यदा संयमं करोति तदा परकीयस्य चित्तस्य ज्ञानमुत्पद्यते। सरागमस्य चित्तं विरागं वेति। परचित्तगतानपि धर्मान जानातीत्यर्थः।

§ अस्यैव परचित्तज्ञानस्यस्य विशेषमाह।

न तत्सालम्बनं तस्याविषयीभूतत्वात् ॥ २० ॥

The mind of other persons is comprehended without its object.

Aph. 20.—It (i. e. the mind of other persons) is not comprehended with its Alambana—support, i. e., object (to an ascetic) because it was not the object (of Sanyama which he, the ascetic, made use of in comprehending the mind.)

b. The mind of other persons cannot be understood together with its Alambana—support—i. e. object, because it is not recognized by any characteristic. For by the characteristic the mind only of others is understood, but it is not known what its object is and whether it be blue or yellow. It cannot be known what that object is because Sanyama cannot be performed with regard to it since it is not recognized. Hence the mind of others is not comprehended together with its Alambana, object—as it is not recognized. But the properties of the internal organ—chitta, i. e. mind—are comprehended. When an ascetic performs Pranidhana, i. e. Sanyama with a view of discovering what mind has for its object, then a knowledge of that object also arises in him by that Sanyama (restraint).*

a. (He now) states another Siddhi.†

कायरूपसंयमात्तद्ग्राह्यशक्तिस्तम्भे चक्षुःप्रकाशासंयोगेऽन्तर्धानम् ॥ २१ ॥

The superhuman faculty which consists in the disappearing of an ascetic.

Aph. 21.—By performing Sanyama—restraint—about form (the property) of body (defined in Aph. 11. See the Nyaya Philosophy p. 16), its power of being apprehended (by the organ of sight) being checked, and luminousness, the property of the

---

* तस्य परस्य यच्चित्तं तत्सालम्बनं स्वकीयालम्बनेन सहितं न शक्यते ज्ञातुमालम्बनस्य केनचिल्लिङ्गेनाविषयी कृतत्वात् । लिङ्गाच्चित्तमात्रं परस्यावगतं न तु नीलविषयमस्य चित्तं पीतविषयमिति वा । यच्च न गृहीतं तत्र संयमस्य कर्तुमशक्यत्वात् न भवति परचित्तस्य यो विषयस्तत्र ज्ञानं तस्मात् परकीयं चित्तं नालम्बनसहितं गृह्यते तस्यालम्बनस्यागृहीतत्वात् । चित्तधर्माः पुनर्गृह्यन्त एव यदा किमनेनालम्बितमिति प्रणिधानं करोति तदा तत्संयमात् तद्विषयमपि ज्ञानमुत्पद्यत एव । † सिद्ध्यन्तरमाह ।

organ of sight having no connection (with its object, i. e. the form, the result) is the disappearance of the ascetic.

b. The form (Kupa) of the body (kaya) is a property to be apprehended by the organ of sight. By performing Sanyama with reflection "Form consists in this body" (and no-where else) the power belonging to that form of being apprbended by the organ of sight is arrested through being subjected to that notion. On the cessation of the connection of the organ of sight with luminousness, luminousness being a property of *Sattva*, [that is to say] when there is no function of apprehending that [form], the disappearance of the ascetic takes place, i. e. he is not seen by any body.*

एतेन शब्दाद्यन्तर्धानमुक्तम् ॥ २२ ॥

Aph. 22.—By this, a concealment (Antardhana) of speech (Shabda) &c. is also stated.

a. "By this," i. e. by explaining the means of disappearance of form, (See the preceding Aph.) a concealment of speech (Shabda) &c. cognizable by the organ of hearing and other organs is (also) to be understood as stated.†

[That is to say that the speech of an ascetic cannot be heard by any body if he performs Sanyama—restraint—about it, and this is the case with all other qualities of the organs of perception.] [It is to be observed here that Bhojarája, the commentator of this work, maintains that this Aphorism belongs to the text and consequently gives a comment upon it; but this is not the case, because, Vijnana Bhikshu, the expositor of the Bhashya, says that the author of the Bhashya removes the deficiency of Patanjali by stating the following sentence

---

* कायः शरीरं तस्य रूपं चक्षुर्ग्राह्यो गुणस्तस्मिन् काये रूपमिति संयमात् तस्य रूपस्य चक्षुर्ग्राह्यत्वरूपा या शक्तिस्तस्याः स्तम्भे भावनावशात्प्रतिबन्धे चक्षुः प्रकाशासंयोगे चक्षुषः प्रकाशः सत्त्वधर्मस्तस्यासंयोगे तद्ग्रहणस्य व्यापाराभावे योगिनोऽन्तर्धानं भवति । न केनचिदसौ दृश्यत इत्यर्थः ।

† एतेन रूपाद्यन्तर्धानोपायप्रदर्शनेन शब्दादीनां श्रोत्रादिग्राह्याणामन्तर्धानमुक्तं वेदितव्यम् ।

एतेन शब्दाद्यन्तर्धानमुक्तम् । in his Bhashya. Therefore it is not one of the Aphorisms of the text but a sentence of the Bhashya.]

a. (He now) states another Siddhi.*

सोपक्रमं निरुपक्रमं च कर्म तत्संयमादपरान्तज्ञान-
मरिष्टेभ्यो वा ॥ २३ ॥

The superhuman faculty which consists in a fore knowledge of death.

Aph. 23.—An action (karma) is two-fold; one accompanied by anticipation of consequences (Sopakrama) and other destitute of it (Nirupakrama) :—from performing Sanyama—restraint—with regard to this two-fold action, a knowledge (arises in an ascetic) of the separation from (his) body—Aparanta—(i. e. death). Or (the time of death is known) from portents (Arishta).

b. The action, performed before (i. e. in the former birth) the consequence of which is years (Ayus) is two-fold, Sopakrama and Nirupakrama. Of these, Sopakrama is that which has an inclination to produce a fruit or anticipate consequences. As, for example, a wet cloth spread in a warm place dries quickly [This action is called Sopakrama]. Nirupakrama is the converse of it, as the same cloth folded and (put) in a cold place dries after a long time. A knowledge of the separation of body —Aparanta—i. e. death, arises in him who performs Sanyama in (the above-mentioned) two-fold action, so that he discovers what action anticipates consequences quickly and what after a long time, from steadfastness of contemplation (Dhyana). (That is to say) he knows undoubtedly that he shall be deprived of his body (in other words that he shall die) at such and such time and such and such place.

"Or from portents," which are three-fold according to the distinction of Adhyatmika, Adhibhautika, and Adhidaivika. Of these, the Adhyatmikas are such as (when a man) shutting his ears does not hear the sound of the vital air (diffused, throughout his body &c. Adhibhautikas are such as a sudden

---

* सिद्ध्यन्तरमाह ।

appearance of a deformed person &c. and Adhidaivikas are such as seeing unexpectedly such things as paradise (Svarga) &c. which are incapable of being seen. From these (i. e. from seeing these), a man knows the time of separation from his body (Aparanta) i. e., death. Though the persons who are not ascetic know for the most part (the time of their death) from (seeing) the portents; still they know it generally (and not particularly and consequently their knowledge of it) is doubtful. But ascetics know it (i. e., their death) invariably like a thing before their eyes (pratyaksha) on account of (their knowing) the fixed time and place (i. e. they know certainly when and at what place they will die.)*

a. He now proceeds to declare the Siddhis resulting from the purifying processes (see Aph. 33. Book I. P. 39).†

मैत्र्यादिषु बलानि ॥ २४ ॥

Superhuman faculties about benevolence, &c.

Aph. 24.—(Superhuman) faculties (are manifested in an ascetic by performing restraint) in benevolence, &c.

b. By performing restraint in benevolence, tenderness, complacency, and disregard (towards objects) the faculties of

---

* आयुर्विपाकं यत्पूर्वकृतं कर्म तद् द्विप्रकारं सोपक्रमं निरुपक्रमं च तत्र सोपक्रमं यत् फलजननायोपक्रमेण कार्यकरणाभिमुख्येन सह वर्तते । यथोष्णप्रदेशे प्रसारितमार्द्रं वस्त्रं शीघ्रमेव शुष्यति । उक्तरूपाद्विपरीतं निरुपक्रमं यथा तदेवार्द्रं वासः संवर्तितमनुष्णदेशे चिरेण शोषमेति । अस्मिन् द्विविधे कर्मणि यः संयमं करोति किं कर्म शीघ्रविपाकं किं चिरविपाकमिति । एवं ध्यानदार्ढ्यादपरान्तज्ञानमस्योत्पद्यते । अपरान्तः शरीरवियोगस्तस्मिन् ज्ञानममुष्मिन् देशेऽमुष्मिन् काले मम शरीरवियोगो भविष्यतीति निःसंशयं जानाति । अरिष्टेभ्यो वाऽरिष्टानि त्रिविधान्याध्यात्मिकाधिभौतिकाधिदैविकभेदेन । तत्राध्यात्मिकानि पिहितकर्णः कोष्ठस्यवायोर्घोषं न शृणोतीत्येवमादीनि । आधिभौतिकान्यकस्माद्विकृतपुरुषदर्शनादीनि । आधिदैविकान्यकाण्डएव द्रष्टुमशक्यस्वर्गादिपदार्थदर्शनादीनि । तेभ्यः शरीरवियोगकालं जानाति । यद्यप्ययोगिनामप्यरिष्टेभ्यः प्रायेण ज्ञानमुत्पद्यते तथापि तेषां सामान्याकारेण तत्संशयरूपं योगिनां पुनर्नियतकालदेशतया प्रत्यक्षवदव्यभिचारी ।

† परिकर्मनिरयन्दभूताः सिद्धीः प्रतिपादयितुमाह ।

Sanyam about them are manifested (in an ascetic). He has such an excellent command over benevolence, tenderness, complacency, and disregard, that he can contract friendship &c. with all (persons).*

a. (He) declares (now) another Siddhi.†

बलेषु हस्तिबलानि ॥ २५ ॥

Aph. 25.—The faculties of an elephant &c. (are manifested in an ascetic by performing restraint) in these faculties.

b. The ascetic who performs restraint in the faculties of an elephent &c. gets these manifested in him. That is to say; every faculty whether of an elephant, wind, or of a lion, in which he performs restraint by paying close attention, is manifested in him on account of his having command over every one of them.‡

a. He (now) states another Siddhi.§

प्रवृत्त्यालोकन्यासात्सूक्ष्मव्यवहितविप्रकृष्टज्ञानम् ॥ २६ ॥

Expedient for the knowledge of minute, concealed and distant objects.

Aph. 26.—A knowledge of the minute, concealed and distant (objects of sense arises in an ascetic) by his throwing the light of immediate cognition—Pravritti (on them).

b. Pravritti, the immediate cognition which is sensuous and luminous, as it is stated before (see Aphs. 35, 36, Book 1. P. 31 & 32):—by placing the spreading light of the pure element—Sattva which exists in immediate cognition, i. e., by brooding on the objects of sense modified in the spreading light of the pure element of immediate cognition, the organs of sense and

---

* मैत्रीकरुणामुदितोपेक्षासु यो विहितः संयमस्तस्य बलानि मैत्र्यादीनां संबन्धीनि प्रादुर्भवन्ति मैत्रीकरुणामुदितोपेक्षास्तथाऽस्य प्रकर्षं गच्छन्ति यथा सर्वस्य मित्रत्वादिकं संप्रतिपद्यते । † सिद्ध्यन्तरमाह ।

‡ हस्त्यादिसंबन्धेषु बलेषु कृतसंयमस्य तद्बलानि हस्त्यादिबलान्याविर्भवन्ति । तदयमर्थो यस्मिन् हस्तिबले वायुवेगे वा सिंहवीर्ये वा तन्मयीभावेन संयमं करोति तत्सर्वसामर्थ्ययुक्तत्वात्सर्वमस्य प्रादुर्भवतीत्यर्थः । § सिद्ध्यन्तरमाह ।

the mind (of an ascetic) acquire a particular power (and then), a knowledge arises (in him) of minute objects, atoms &c., concealed objects, wealth hidden in a certain place &c., and distant objects, the life-prolonging medicine or elixir—Rasáyana, &c.*

a. He (now) states another Siddhi.†

भुवनज्ञानं सूर्येसंयमात् ॥ २७ ॥

Aph. 27.—A knowledge of (seven) worlds (arises in an ascetic) by his performing restraint in regard to the (luminous body) the sun.

b. He, who performs restraint with regard to the luminous sun, knows exactly about the cities consisting of the seven worlds which are Bhur-loka, the earth; Bhuvarloka, the space between the earth and the sun. Swarga-loka—, the heaven of Indra and others. In the preceding aphorism, the light of pure element (is to be understood) as stated as a support (for fixation of the mind) and in this the elemental light. This is the difference only.‡

a. He states another Siddhi through the very support of the elemental light.§

चन्द्रे ताराव्यूहज्ञानम् ॥ २८ ॥

An expedient.

Aph. 28 A knowledge of forms of the asterisms (arises in an ascetic) when he performs restraint with regard to the Moon.

---

* प्रवृत्तिर्विषयवती ज्योतिष्मती च प्रागुक्ता तस्या योऽसावालोकः सात्त्विकप्रकाशप्रसरस्तस्य निखिलेषु विषयेषु न्यासात्तद्वासितानां विषयाणां भावनात्सान्तःकरणेषु प्रकृष्टशक्तिमापन्नेषु सूक्ष्मस्य परमाण्वादेर्व्यवहितस्य भूम्यन्तर्गतस्य निधानादेर्विप्रकृष्टस्य मेरुपरपार्श्ववर्तिनोरसायनादेर्ज्ञानमुत्पद्यते । † सिद्ध्यन्तरमाह ।

‡ सूर्ये प्रकाशमये यः संयमं करोति तस्य सप्तसु भूर्भुवःस्वःप्रभृतिषु लोकेषु यानि भुवनानि तत्सन्निवेशभाञ्जिपुराणि तेषु यथावदस्य ज्ञानमुत्पद्यते । पूर्वस्मिन् सूत्रे सात्त्विकः प्रकाश आलम्बनतयोक्त इह तु भौतिक इति विशेषः ।

§ भौतिकप्रकाशद्वारेणैव सिद्ध्यन्तरमाह ।

b. "Forms of the asterisms," i. e., the particular figures of the fixed stars :—a knowledge arises (in an ascetic) about these (when) he performs restraint with regard to the Moon. As the lustre of the asterisms is destroyed by the light of the sun and consequently a knowledge cannot be obtained about them, this expedient is therefore separately stated.*

a. He states another Siddhi.†

ध्रुवे तद्गतिज्ञानम् ॥ २९ ॥

Aph. 29. A knowledge of the motion of the stars (arises in an ascetic by his performing restraint) with regard to the polar star (Dhruva).

b. An ascetic when he performs his restraint with regard to the fixed polar star, the principal of all constellations, knows the fixed time and fixed amount of the motion of every star. (The true) meaning of the Aphorism is this that the ascetic knows all this that such and such a (heavenly body) is a star and such and such a heavenly body is a planet. This star will reach such and such a sign of the Zodiac by such and such a fixed time. This (sort of) knowledge of time is the result of the restraint (performed with regard to the polar star).‡

a. Having stated the external Siddhis, he (now) proceeds to explain the internal ones.§

नाभिचक्रे कायव्यूहज्ञानम् ॥ ३० ॥

Aph. 30. A knowledge of the particular structure of the body (arises in an ascetic who performs his restraint) with regard to the circle of the navel.

---

* ताराणां यो व्यूहो विशिष्टः सन्निवेशस्तस्मिन् चन्द्रे कृतसंयमस्य ज्ञानमुत्पद्यते । सूर्यप्रकाशेन हततेजस्कत्वात् ताराणां सूर्यसंयमात्तज्ज्ञानं न शक्नोति भवितुमिति पृथगयमुपायो ऽभिहितः । † सिद्ध्यन्तरमाह ।

‡ ध्रुवे निश्चले ज्योतिषां प्रधाने कृतसंयमस्य तासां ताराणां या गतिः प्रत्येकं नियतकालंनियतदेशं च तस्य ज्ञानमुत्पद्यते । इयं ताराऽयं ग्रह इयता कालेनइमां राशिमिदं नक्षत्रं यास्यतीति सर्वं जानातीति सूत्रार्थः इदं कालज्ञानमस्य फलमित्युक्तं भवति । § बाह्याः सिद्धीः प्रतिपाद्यान्तराः प्रतिपादयितुमुपक्रमते ।

b. The particular structure of the body; that is, the constitution of the essential humour (Rasa), the excretion (Mala), the principle (Dhátu) and veins &c. of the body:—a knowledge about this structure arises in an ascetic by his performing restraint with regard to the circle of the navel situated in the body called Nábhi which is endowed with sixteen angles. The true meaning of this is that the circle of the navel being situated in the middle of the body is a root or origin of veins &c. which are extended throughout (the body), and consequently by performing restraint with regard to the circle of the navel, the whole constitution of the body becomes exactly known to the ascetic.*

a. He (now) states another Siddhi.†

कण्ठकूपे क्षुत्पिपासानिवृत्तिः ॥ ३१ ॥

Aph. 31. A cessation of hunger, thirst, &c. (takes place in an ascetic by performing his restraint with regard to the well of (his) throat.

b. There is a place like a pit below the tongue in the throat (which is called the well) of the throat; a contact of the vital airs with this well causes the manifestation of hunger, thirst, &c. And these inclinations cease in an ascetic who performs a restraint with regard to that (well), *i. e.*, a superhuman faculty of this nature (is invariably at the command of an ascetic) on account of his brooding upon this stream (*i. e.* the well of the throat which is situated) below the uvula.‡

a. He (now) states another Siddhi.§

---

* शरीरमध्यवर्ति नाभिसंज्ञकं यत्षोडशारं चक्रं तस्मिन् कृतसंयमस्य योगिनः कायगतो योऽसौ व्यूहो विशिष्टरसमलधातुनाड्यादीनामवस्थानं तत्रज्ञानमुत्पद्यते । इदमुक्तं भवति । नाभिचक्रं शरीरस्य मध्यवर्ति सर्वतःप्रसृतानां नाड्यादीनां मूलभूतमतस्तत्र कृतावधानस्य समग्रः सन्निवेशो यथावत् आभाति । † सिद्ध्यन्तरमाह ।

‡ कण्ठे गले कूपः कण्ठकूपो जिह्वातोऽधस्तात् कूप इव कूपो गर्ताकारः प्रदेशः प्राणादेर्यत्संस्पर्शनात्क्षुत्पिपासादयः प्रादुर्भवन्ति तस्मिन् कृतसंयमस्य योगिनः क्षुत्पिपासादयो निवर्तन्ते घण्टिकाधस्तात्स्रोतस्यवधार्यमाने तस्मिन्भाविते भवत्येवंविधा सिद्धिः । § सिद्ध्यन्तरमाह ।

कूर्मनाड्यां स्थैर्यम् ॥ ३१ ॥

Aph. 32. A firmness (of mind takes place when an ascetic performs his restraint) with regard to the vein (called) kúrma (tortoise).

b. A firmness of mind is produced when the ascetic performs his restraint with regard to the vein called kúrma which is situated below the well of the throat:—that is fickleness of mind does not take place when the ascetic (by the efficacy of his meditation) enters the spot (i. e., the vein) or firmness is produced in the body (of the ascetic) that it, is cannot be moved by anything.*

a. He now states another Siddhi.†

मूर्द्धज्योतिषि सिद्धदर्शनम् ॥ ३२ ॥

Aph. 33. (The ascetic) sees Siddhas, the divine personages or spirits (when he performs his restraint) with regard to the light—Jyotis—of the head.

b. An aperture called Brahmarandhra in the skull (of every body) is a light (Jyotis) on account of its being a reservoir of light:—as the spreading light of a gem situated in the inside of a house collects in the keyhole of the door, so in the same manner the luminousness of sattva of mind, being spread, collects in the aperture called Brahmarandhra of the skull. (Therefore) when the ascetic performs his restraint with regard to this aperture or light (as just expounded), he catches sight of the divine spirits who dwell in the (wide) space between the earth and sky and who cannot be seen by any other beings (but the ascetic); that is, he sees and converses with them.‡

---

* कण्ठकूपस्याधस्तात्या कुर्माख्या नाडी तस्यां कृतसंयमस्य चेतसः स्थैर्यमुत्पद्यते । तत्स्थानमनप्रविष्टस्य चञ्चलता न भवतीत्यर्थः यदि वा काये स्थैर्यमुत्पद्यते न केनचित्स्पन्दयितुं शक्यत इत्यर्थः । † सिद्धयन्तरमाह ।

‡ शिरः कपाले ब्रह्मरन्ध्राख्यं छिद्रं प्रकाशाधारत्वात् ज्योतिः । यथा गृहाभ्यन्तरस्थस्य मणेः प्रसरन्ती प्रभा कुञ्चिकाविवरप्रदेशेसं घट्टे तथा हृदयस्थः सात्विकः प्रकाशः प्रसृतस्तत्र संपीडितत्व भजते । तत्र कृतसंयमस्य ये द्यावापृथिव्योरन्तरालवर्तिनः सिद्धा दिव्याः पुरुषास्तेषामितरप्राणिभिरदृश्यानां दर्शनं भवति तान् स पश्यति तैश्च संभाषत इत्यर्थः ।

a He (now) states another expedient for omniscience.*

प्रातिभाद्वा सर्वं सर्वनिमित्तानपेक्षम् ॥ ३४ ॥

Aph. 34. Or (the ascetic) disregarding all other instrumental causes (knows) every thing from (only) Prátibha (a knowledge called Tàraka).

b. A right knowledge instantly produced from (the operations of) mind only is called Pratibha, and a restraint being performed with regard to this, Taraka (i. e. preserver) a knowledge antecedent to a discriminating faculty of mind Vivekakhyati, arises. As the twilight appears before sun-rise, so Taraka, a knowledge concerning all things, manifests (itself in the ascetic) before the Vivekakhyati. That is, when this is the case, (the ascetic), having then no need of any other restraint, knows every thing.†

a. He (now) states another Siddhi.‡

हृदये चित्तसंवित् ॥ ३५ ॥

Aph. 35. A knowledge about mind—Chitta— (arises in an ascetic, when he performs his restraint) with regard to the internal organ—Hridaya.

b. "Hridaya" a particular part of the body:—in this part there is the site of the internal organ within a small inverted lotus, and when the ascetic performs his restraint with regard to that site, a knowledge of his own mind as well as that of others arises in him, that is, he knows all fancies of his own mind as well as the passions &c. of the minds of others.§

---

* सर्वज्ञत्व उपायान्तरमाह ।

† मनोमात्रजन्यमविसंवादकं द्रागुत्पद्यमानं ज्ञानं प्रतिभा तस्यां संयमे क्रियमाणे प्रातिभं विवेकख्यातेः पूर्वभावि तारकं ज्ञानमुदेति । यथोदेष्यति सवितरि पूर्वं प्रभा प्रादुर्भवति तद्वद्विवेकख्यातेः पूर्वं तारकं सर्वविषयकं ज्ञानमाविर्भवति । तस्मिन् साति संयमान्तरानपेक्षः । सर्वं जानातीत्यर्थः

‡ सिद्ध्यन्तरमाह ।

§ हृदयं शरीरस्य प्रदेशविशेषस्तस्मिन्नधोमुखस्वल्पपुण्डरीकाभ्यन्तरेऽन्तःकरणस्य स्थानं तत्र कृतसंयमस्य स्वपराचित्तज्ञानमुत्पद्यते स्वचित्तगताः सर्वा वासनाः पराचित्तगतांश्च रागादीन् जानातीत्यर्थः

a. He (now) states another Siddhi.*

पुरुषसत्त्वयोरत्यन्तासंकीर्णयोः प्रत्ययाविशेषो भोगः परार्थान्य-
स्वार्थसंयमात् पुरुषज्ञानम् ॥ ३६ ॥

The expedient for the knowledge of the person—Purusha.

Aph. 36. From conceiving indifferently the knowledge of the person (soul) and sattva (purity or the principle of understanding, Buddhitattva—) which are entirely different from each other, (a knowledge of joy and affliction arise and) that is enjoyment (Bhoga). This enjoyment is another's object (Parártha), and an object different from this is the proper object (Svártha—of the principle of understanding) and from performing restraint with regard to this proper object, a knowledge of the person (arises in an ascetic).

b. "Sattva," (purity) is a particular modification of nature which consists of illumination and joy (and it is what is called the principle of understanding, Buddhitattva.) The person (soul) is an experiencer—in the form of the ruler. These are entirely unmixed. The meaning is that, these are quite different (from each other) on account of their being severally experience and experiencer, conscious and unconscious. From sattva's acting the part of the agent (karta), in consequence of conceiving identically the knowledge of the (two, i. e., sattva and soul,) a knowledge (sanvit) or a modification consisting of joy and pain (arises) and it is (what is called) Bhoga enjoyment. By sattva's not regarding this enjoyment as its own object it is the object of another—Parartha—i. e. it is for the sake of soul and an object different from this is sattva's own object (svartha). This object is clinging only to the nature of soul, the consciousness. That is, it is an object or reflection of consciousness (chichchhayasankranti) in sattva when it is free from egoism. When an ascetic performs his restraint with regard to that (svartha of soul) a knowledge concerning the soul arises (in him), i. e., the ascetic knows that the soul is conscious of

* सिद्ध्यन्तरमाह ।

only this sort of knowledge, the clinging to the consciousness which consists in the sattva; and it (the soul) being intelligent becomes not the object of knowledge inasmuch as there would arise a difficulty from its becoming knowable (jneya) as there is a total contrariety of the intelligent and knowable.*

a. He (now) states the fruit of the same restraint.†

ततः प्रातिभश्रावणवेदनादर्शास्वादवार्ता जायन्ते ॥ ३७ ॥

The fruit of the preceding superhuman faculty.

Aph. 37 From that, Prátibha, (Táraka a knowledge concerning all things, see Aph. 34. Book 3, and the knowledge caused by the organs) hearing, touch, sight, taste, and smell arises in (the ascetic).

b. "From that" (i. e.) from practising the restraint with regard to soul—Purusha— (the following knowledge arises in the ascetic (when) he is even Vyutthita, i. e., not devoted to meditation. In this case, from the manifestation of the aforesaid knowledge, Pratibha, he sees subtile objects, &c. He recognises the sound produced in heaven from the eminent practice, gained by the force of restraint, in the knowledge produced from the organ of hearing. A knowledge arises (in him) with regard to touch of the objects in heaven from Vedana, an appellation, technically used in Tantra (science) for a faculty of mind by which a knowledge produced from the organ of touch or tangibility is meant. A knowledge about the divine form arises (in an ascetic) from the excellent Adarsha —a faculty of mind by which the forms (situated) all around

* सत्वं प्रकाशसुखात्मकप्राधानिकः परिणामविशेषः पुरुषो भोक्ताऽधिष्ठातृरूपस्तयोर्भोग्यभोक्तृत्वरूपत्वात चेतनाचेतनत्त्वाच्चात्यन्तासंकीर्णत्वं भिन्नत्वमित्यर्थः । तयोः प्रत्ययस्याविशेषोऽभेदेनाप्रतिभासनं तस्मात्सत्वस्यैव कर्तृताप्रत्ययेनया सुखदुःखसंवित्स भोगः । सत्वस्य स्वार्थनैरपेक्षेण परार्थः पुरुषार्थः तस्मादन्यो यः स्वार्थः पुरुषस्वरूपमात्रालम्बनःपरित्यक्ताहङ्कारे सत्वे या चिच्छायासंक्रान्तिस्तत्र कृतसंयमस्य पुरुषविषयं ज्ञानमुत्पद्यते तदेवं रूपं स्वालम्बनं ज्ञानं सत्वनिष्ठं पुरुषो विजानाति न पुनः पुरुषो ज्ञाता ज्ञानस्य विषयभावमापद्यते ज्ञेयत्त्वापत्तेः । ज्ञातृत्वज्ञेयत्वयोश्चात्यन्तविरोधात ।

† अस्यैव संयमस्य फलमाह ।

are seen and consequently (it means) the knowledge caused by the organ of sight. Asvada, a faculty of mind—by which (a thing) is tasted; and thus it means the knowledge caused by the organ of taste. It being excellent, a knowledge about the divine taste arises (in the ascetic). Varta, or Gandhasanvitti, is a knowledge caused by the organ of smell, because the organ of smell is called by the term Vritti in technical language of science (Tantra) as there is an object of smell in it; and this faculty being excellent, a divine odour is experienced (by the ascetic).‡

a. He (now) states the respective provinces of these particular fruits.*

ते समाधावुपसर्गा व्युत्थानेसिद्धयः ॥ ३८ ॥

Aph. 38. These fruits are obstacles in the way of meditation and superhuman faculties (in the state of) non-meditation (Vyutthana).

b. The aforesaid particular fruits become obstacles to the ascetic closely devoted to meditation (because his) meditation becomes relaxed by reason of joy, wonder &c. but in the state of non-meditation Vyutthána—(that is) in the state of action, these fruits become the superhuman faculties on account of their yielding the particular fruits.‡

---

* ततः पुरुषसंयमादभ्यस्यमानात् व्युत्थितस्यापि ज्ञानानि जायन्ते। तत्र प्रातिभं पुर्वोक्तं ज्ञानं तस्याविर्भावात्सूक्ष्मादिकमर्थं पश्याति। श्रावणं श्रोत्रेन्द्रियजं ज्ञानं तस्माच्च प्रकृष्टाद्दिव्यं दिवि भवं शब्दं जानाति। वेदना स्पर्शेन्द्रियजं ज्ञानं विद्यतेऽनयेति कृत्वा तान्त्रिकया संज्ञया व्यवन्हियते तस्माद्दिव्यस्पर्शविषयंज्ञानमुपजायते। आदर्शश्चक्षुरिन्द्रियजं ज्ञानं। आसमन्तात दृश्यते रूपमनेनेति कृत्वा तस्य प्रकर्षाद्दिव्यरूपज्ञानमुत्पद्यते। आस्वादो रसनेन्द्रियजं ज्ञानमास्वाद्यतेऽनेनेति कृत्वा तास्मिन् प्रकृष्टे दिव्येरसे संविदुपजायते। वार्ता गन्धसंवित्तिर्वृत्तिशब्देन तान्त्रिक्या परिभाषया घ्राणेन्द्रियमुच्यते। वर्तते गन्धविषय इति कृत्वा। वृत्तेर्घ्राणेन्द्रियाज्जाता वार्ता गन्धसंवित्तस्यां प्रकृष्यमाणायां दिव्य गन्धोऽनुभूयते।

† एषां फलविशेषाणां विषयविभागमाह।

‡ ते प्राक् प्रतिपादिताः फलविशेषाः समाधेः प्रकर्षं गच्छत उपसर्गा उपद्रवा

a. He (now) states another Siddhi.*

बन्धकारणशैथिल्यात् प्रचारसंवेदनाच्च चित्तस्य परशरीरावेशः ॥ ३९ ॥

The position when the ascetic knows the mind of another person.

Aph. 39. The mind of (the ascetic) enters the body of others by reason of the laxity of the cause of Bandha—bondage, and by the knowledge of the process—Prachàra—(of mind).

b. A knowledge of the pervading soul and internal organ, entered into (a particular) body only by virtue of some fixed action, which arises in the form of their becoming experiencer and experience is called a bondage to the body (Sharirabandha). When this knowledge, the cause of bondage, i. e. the action called virtue and vice becomes relaxed or diminished, then the ascetic enters &c. The vein-(called) chittavaha, by which the internal organ blows, is a knowledge (sanvedana) of its course of the site of heart towards (external) objects by means of organs, and this vein is (quite) different from the veins through which the humour (Rasa) vital air &c., blow. Therefore, when the internal organ knows the course (just expounded) of its own body and that of others, it enters a living or dead body of another person by means of that course. The organs (too) follow the internal organ entering the body of another (person), as black bees follow the queen bee. After that, the ascetic who has (thus) entered the body of another person, deals with that body as if it were his own body, because, the internal organ and the soul are (at all times) pervading, (but a particular) action becomes the cause of the contraction of their enjoyment, and if it is destroyed by meditation, they

---

विघ्नकारिणः । तत्र हर्षविस्मयादिकारणेन समाधिः शिथिलीभवति व्युत्थाने तु व्यवहारदशायां विशिष्टफलदायकत्वात् सिद्धयो भवन्ति ।

* सिद्ध्यन्तरमाह ।

then receive enjoyment everywhere in consequence of their being independent.*

a. He (now) states another Siddhi. †

उदानजयाज्जलपङ्ककण्टकादिष्वसङ्ग उत्क्रान्तिश्च ॥ ४० ॥

Aph. 40. A disunion (Asanga) with and a rising (Utkranti) from water, mud, thorns &c. (take place) by conquering the Udana, one of the vital airs.

b. The state of the organs, arisen at once like a flame of burning chaff, is called by the word Jivana and it is denominated Prana &c. from the different actions. Of these, one is called Prana from its conducting the air through the mouth and nose from the heart; another Apana, from the region of the navel to the great toe: another, Samana, from conducting air every where having surrounded the region of the navel with it; another, Udana, from its conducting air the upwards from the back of the neck (Krikatika) to the heart and another Vyana, from its conducting the air which pervades the whole body. (The ascetic) disjoins himself from water, (i. e.) with a large river &c. or a great (quantity) of mud or sharp thorns by the quality of going upwards (obtained) by hindrance of all the airs (effected) by his conquering the air Udana by means of restraint. The meaning (of disjunction with water is that the ascetic) being very light like a quantity of cotton, even if immerged in (deep)

---

* व्यापकत्वादात्मचित्तयोर्नियतकर्मवशादेव शरीरान्तर्गतयोरेव भोक्तृभोग्यभावेन यत्संवेदनमुपजायते स एव शरीरबन्ध इत्युच्यते । तद्यदा समाधिवशाद्बन्धकारणं धर्माधर्माख्यं कर्म शिथिलं भवति तानवमापद्यते चित्तस्य योऽसौ प्रचारो हृदयप्रदेशादिन्द्रियद्वारेण विषयाभिमुख्येन प्रसरस्तस्य संवेदनं ज्ञानमियं चित्तवहा नाडी । अनया चित्तं वहति । इयं च रसप्राणादिवहाभ्यो नाडीभ्यो विलक्षणा इति स्वपरशरीरयोर्यदा संचारं जानाति तदा परकीयं शरीरं मृतं जीवच्छरीरं वा चित्तसंचारद्वारेण प्रविशति चित्तं च परशरीरं प्रविशदिन्द्रियाण्यनुवर्तन्ते मधुकरराजमिव मधुमक्षिकास्ततः परशरीरप्रविष्टो योगी स्वशरीरेणेवतेन व्यवहरति । यतो व्यापकयोश्चित्तपुरुषयोर्भोगसंकोचे कारणं कर्माभूत् तच्चेत्समाधिना क्षीणं तदा स्वातन्त्र्यात्सर्वत्रैव भोगनिष्पत्तिः ।

† सिद्ध्यन्तरमाह ।

water, rises to the surface.* [He comes out even if placed under a large quantity of mud and cannot be pricked with sharp thorns, by reason of his subduing the air Udana through the efficacy of his restraint.]

a. He (now) states another Siddhi.†

समानजयात्प्रज्वलनम् ॥ ४१ ॥

Aph. 41. A blazing (takes place) from conquering the air Samana.

b. The ascetic appears as if wonderfully blazing by light of the fire of the stomach (Jatharagni) being uncovered from conquering, i. e., from subduing with restraint, the air called Samana which exists (in the body) surrounding the fire of the stomach.‡

a. He (now) states another Siddhi. §

श्रोत्राकाशयोः संबन्धसंयमाद्दिव्यं श्रोत्रम् ॥ ४२ ॥

Aph. 42. A divine organ of hearing (is developed in the ascetic) by his performing restraint with regard to the connection between (Shrotra) the organ of hearing and (Akasa) the ether.

b. "Shrotra" the organ caused by selfishness which apprehends sound and Akasa, ether, the object of which is the subtle rudiment of Sound (Shabda-tanmatra). "The connection between these," the characteristic of this connection is be-

---

* समस्तानामिन्द्रियाणां तुषज्वालावद्या युगपदुत्थिता वृत्तिः साजीवनशब्दवाच्या तस्याः क्रियाभेदात्प्राणादिभिर्व्यपदेशस्तत्र हृदयान्मुखनासिकाद्वारेण वायोः प्रणयनात्प्राण इत्युच्यते । नाभिप्रदेशात्पादाङ्गुष्ठपर्यन्तमपनयनादपानः । नाभिप्रदेशं परिवेष्ट्यासमन्तान्नयनात्समानः । कृकाटिकादेशादाशिरोवृत्तेरुन्नयनादुदानः व्याप्य नयनात्सर्वशरीरव्यापी व्यानः उदानस्य संयमद्वारेण जयादितरेषां वायूनां निरोधादूर्ध्वगामित्वेन जले महानद्यादौमहति वा कर्दमे तीक्ष्णेषु कण्टकेषु वा न मज्जति अतिलघुत्वात्तूलपिण्डवज्जलादौ मज्जितोऽप्युद्गच्छतीत्यर्थः । † सिद्ध्यन्तरमाह ।

‡ अग्निमावेष्ट्य व्यवस्थितस्य समानाख्यस्य वायोर्जयात् संयमेन वशीकाराभिरावरणस्याग्नेरद्भुतं तेजसा प्रज्वलन्निव योगी प्रतिभाति । § सिद्ध्यन्तरमाह ।

coming site and situated object, i.e., having place. Such is the meaning of the compound word Deshadeshibhavalakshana. [Or Avachchedyavachchedakalakshana, that is, the characteristic of which is being inclosed and encloser. The true meaning of this is that when sound takes place in the ether enclosed by the space of the ear, then only the organ of hearing catches the sound, otherwise not. Such is the connection between ether and the organ of hearing.] And, when the ascetic performs his restraint with regard to that connection, a divine organ of hearing is developed in him,—an organ of hearing which is capable of catching simultaneously subtle, concealed and distant sound.—Such is the meaning.*

a. He (now) states another Siddhi.†

कायाकाशयोः संबन्धसंयमाल्लघुतूलसमापत्तेश्चाकाशगमनम् ॥ ४३ ॥

Aph. 43. (A power) of walking through the air (is developed in the ascetic) by his obtaining a state of lightness like a light piece of cotton, &c, from performing his restraint with regard to the connection which a (man's) body has with air.

b. The ascetic having performed restraint with regard to the connection of a body consisting of five elements with air by its yielding a space to the body, forms an identity with loose cotton &c., and thus having obtained a state of extreme lightness, he walks at will, on the earth at first, and subsequently being able to walk along the spider's threads, sports with the sun's rays and then walks through the air in any way he likes.‡

He now [states] another Siddhi.§

---

* श्रोत्रं शब्दग्राहकमाहङ्कारिकमिन्द्रियमाकाशं व्योम शब्दतन्मात्राकार्यं तयोः संबन्धो देशदेशिभावलक्षणस्तस्मिन् कृतसंयमस्य योगिनो दिव्यं श्रोत्रं प्रवर्तते। युगपत्सूक्ष्मव्यवहितविप्रकृष्टग्रहणसमर्थं भवतीत्यर्थः। † सिद्ध्यन्तरमाह।

‡ कायः पञ्चभौतिकं शरीरं तस्याकाशेनावकाशदातृत्वात् संबन्धस्तत्र संयमं विधाय लघुनि तूलादौ समापत्तिः तन्मयीभावलक्षणां तां च विधाय प्राप्तात्यन्तलघुभावो योगी प्रथमं भुवि यथारुचि संचरन् क्रमेणोर्णनाभतन्तुजालेन संचरमाण आदित्यरश्मिभिश्च विहरन् यथेष्टमाकाशेन गच्छति। § सिद्ध्यन्तरमाह।

बहिरकल्पिता वृत्तिर्महाविदेहा ततः प्रकाशावरणक्षयः ॥ ४४ ॥

Aph. 44. The external modification [of the internal organ] akalpita, thoughtless, is [called] the great incorporeal [modification, mahavideha]: therefrom [results] the destruction of the obscuration of the illumination [of intellect].

The modification which arises outside the body without having dependence thereon, is, by means of the removal of the steadfastness of the selfishness with regard to the body, called "the great incorporeal" [modification "mahavideha"]. "Therefrom"—from the asceticism performed with regard to it: the distruction of the obscuration of the illumination" that is—the annihilation of the obscuration—the afflictions, works &c. [i. e. fructification]—of the light of intellect [or thinking principle] characterised by purity [the quality, sattva], takes place; the meaning is this,—the external modification of the mind, which takes place while selfishness in regard to the body [sharirahankara] exists, is called, kalpita, or thoughtful, and when the modification of the mind arises independently, having laid aside the selfishness with regard to the body, then it is called "akalpita" or thoughtless [modification]: from the restraint performed with regard to this, [akalpita vrittih] all the impurities of the mind ascetic are removed.*

In order to exhibit various methods for the perfection of the meditations [both] with a germ [sabeeja] and without a germ, [nirbeeja], which are conducive to the discernment of the truth he states as follows.†

* शरीराद्बहिर्या मनसः शरीरनैरपेक्ष्येण वृत्तिः सा महाविदेहा नाम विगतशरीराहङ्कारदार्ढ्यद्वारेणोच्यते ततस्तस्यां कृतात् संयमात्प्रकाशावरणक्षयः सात्त्विकस्य चित्तस्य यः प्रकाशस्तस्य यदावरणं क्लेशकर्म्मादि तस्य क्षयः प्रविलयो भवति अयमर्थः शरीराहङ्कारे सति या मनसो बहिर्वृत्तिः सा कल्पितेत्युच्यते यदा पुनः शरीराहङ्कारभावम्परित्यज्य स्वातन्त्र्येण मनसो वृत्तिः साऽकल्पिता तस्यां संयमाद्योगिनः सर्वे चित्तमलाः क्षीयन्ते ॥

† इदानीं तत्त्वदर्शनोपयोगिसबीजनिर्बीजसमाधिसिद्धये विविधोपायप्रदर्शनायाह ।

स्थूलस्वरूपसूक्ष्मान्वयार्थवत्त्वसंयमाद्भूतजयः ॥ ४९ ॥

Aph. 45. The conquering of the elements [takes place from, the asceticism [performed with regard to the five forms of the elements] gross [sthula]—nature, [swarupa], subtile [sukshma], concomitant [anwaya] and possession of objects [arthavattwa].

The ascetic attains victory [over] the elements, that is the elements become subject to him, from the restraint performed in regard to the five properties, grossness &c., [i. e. grossness, nature, subtility, concomitance, possession of objects] of the elements,—earth &c. [It should be borne in mind that each and all of the five elements possess these five properties—forms]: "gross" [or the 1st form] is the phenomenal having appreciable form, of the elements [including in it gross qualities, gross sound &c.]: the "nature" [or second form] of these, [that is of the elements] is characterised respectively by tenuity, viscidity, heat, impulsion and giving space; the "subtile" [or third form] is, the subtile elements, odour &c. [gandhaditanmatra, that is odour, flavour, colour, tangibility and sound], which are determined to be the respective causes of the elements; "concomitants" [or the fourth form] are qualities, which are observed as everywhere co-existing, in the form or shape of light, action and rest, [or revealing, exertion and fixation]; "possession of objects" [or the fifth form] means the power, existing in these qualities, [or in the five elements, earth &c.] called the power of procuring fruition, and emancipation, [bhogapavarga sampadanakhya shaktihi], [and as this power exists in the qualities, and as the qualities, exist in the subtile and other elements &c., every thing is endowed with fruition and emancipation].*

* पञ्चानाम्पृथिव्यादीनां ये पञ्चावस्था विशेषरूपा धर्म्माः स्थूलत्वादयस्तत्र कृतसंयमस्य भूतजयो भवति भूतानि वश्यान्यस्य भवन्तीत्यर्थः। तथाहि भूतानाम्परिदृश्यमानं विशिष्टाकारवत् स्थूलम्। स्वरूपञ्चैषां यथाक्रमङ्कार्श्योष्णताप्रणावकाशदानलक्षणम्। सूक्ष्मन्तु यथाक्रमम्भूतानाङ्कारणभेदेन व्यवस्थितानि गन्धादितन्मात्राणि। अन्वयिनो गुणाः प्रकाशप्रवृत्तिस्थितिरूपतया सर्वत्रैवान्वयित्वेन समुपलभ्यन्ते। अर्थवत्त्वं तेष्वेव गुणेषु भोगापवर्गसम्पादनाख्या शक्तिः॥

Thus [this being the case] the ascetic performing the asceticism in regard to each of the five forms of the five elements differing by the [five] shapes characterised by the [particular] states above described, conquers the elements. For example, the natures of the elements become obedient like cows following their calves, to his [the ascetic's] resolves, who has finished the performing of the restraint [with regard to each of the five forms]—i. e. (who has) first performed [restraint] with regard to gross form [sthula], afterwards with regard to subtile form [sukshma] and so forth in due order, [that is in regard to the remaining successive forms].*

He [now] mentions the result of the conquering of the elements :—†

ततोऽणिमादिप्रादुर्भावः कायसम्पत् तद्धर्मा-
नभिघातश्च ॥ ४६ ॥

Aph. 46. Therefrom spring up [three perfections i. e.] minuteness &c, excellence of body, and non-destruction of the merits of it.

" Minuteness" [anima] attainment of an atomic form—or the power of becoming as minute as an atom , [by this power the ascetic can enter into a diamond &c] ; [by the word ' Et cætera are meant the other seven perfections viz.] ' Magnitude' [mahima] greatness—or the power of magnifying oneself [by this power the ascetic can occupy as much space as he likes]. ' Gravity' [garima] attainment of heaviness—or the power of becoming heavy ; ' Lightness' [laghima] the power of becoming as light as a ball of cotton ; 'Reach' [prapti) the power of touching the moon &c., with the tip of the finger &c. ; ' Irresistible will' [prakamya] means nonfrustration of desires in the corpo-

---

* तदेवं भूतेषु पञ्चसूक्तलक्षणावस्थाभिन्नेषु प्रत्येकस्यं संयमं कुर्वन् योगी भूतजयी भवति तद्यथा प्रथमं स्थूले रूपे संयमं विधाय तदनुसूक्ष्मरूपे इत्येवंक्रमेण तस्य कृतसंयमस्य सङ्कल्पानुविधायिन्यो वत्सानुसारिण्य इव गावो भूतप्रकृतयो भवन्ति ॥

† भूतजयस्य फलमाह ।

real internal organ; 'Dominion' [ishitva] the power of prevailing everywhere; 'Subjection' [vasitva] means that all the elements obey (or are unable to disobey) his (the ascetic's) command. These, viz. 'Minuteness' and the other seven perfections, which are conducive to meditation, result from the conquest of the elements, and [they] are called the eight great perfections [mahasiddhis]; the "Excellence of body" which will be described hereafter [in the next aphorism] is attained by the ascetic [who has conquered the elements]; "Merits of it" mean the qualities of the body [of the ascetic], colour &c., their destruction—annihilation—cannot be effected by anything, for example, fire cannot burn nor can air dry up his [the ascetic's] colour: such and other cases may be considered.*

[Next] He mentions what the 'Excellence of body' is:—†

रूपलावण्यबलवज्रसंहननत्वानि कायसम्पत् ॥ ४७ ॥

Aph. 47. The excellence of body consists of colour, loveliness, strength, and adamantine density.

"The excellence of body" ['kaya-sampat'—which is one of the three perfections that arise from the conquest of the elements] consists of "Colour" ['rupa,'—which means the virtue of becoming white &c. from black &c. and so on]; "Loveliness" [lavanya—excellent beauty—or the virtue of becoming exceedingly beautiful] "Strength" ['bala'—or the power of becoming very strong] and "adamantine density" ['vajrasanhananatva'] i. e. hardness of the body like that of a

---

* अणिमा परमाणुरूपतापत्तिर्महिमा महत्वङ्गरिमा गुरुत्वप्राप्तिः लघिमा लघुत्वम् तूलपिण्डवल्लघुत्वप्राप्तिः प्राप्तिरङ्गुल्यग्रेण चन्द्रादिस्पर्शनशक्तिः प्राकाम्यमिच्छाऽनभिघातः शरीरान्तःकरणे ईशित्वं सर्वत्रप्रभविष्णुता वशित्वं सर्वाण्येव भूतानि तदुक्तमनुगच्छन्ति तएते अणिमाद्याः समाध्युपयोगिनो भूतजयात् प्रादुर्भवन्ति एते अणिमादयो ऽष्टौ महासिद्धय उच्यन्ते कायसम्पत् वक्ष्यमाणा ताम्प्राप्नोति तद्धर्मानभिघातश्च तस्य कायस्य ये धर्म्मारूपादयस्तेषामनभिघातो नाशो नास्य कुतश्चिदपि भवति नास्य रूपमग्निर्दहाति न च वायुः शोषयतीत्यादियोज्यम् ॥

† कायसम्पदमाह ।

diamond [or the power of making the body as hard as a diamond].*

[Having described the conquest of the elements] He now mentions the conquest of the organs of sense :—†

ग्रहणस्वरूपास्मितान्वयार्थवत्त्वसंयमादिन्द्रियजयः ॥ ४८ ॥

Aph. 48. The conquering of the organs of sense result from the restraint performed with regard to perception, nature, egoism, concomitance, and possession of objects.

The ascetic attains victory over the organs of sense, having as aforesaid [Aph. 45] performed restraint with regard to the five states of the organs of sense, viz. "Perception" ['grahana'] the function of the organs of sense directed towards their objects; "Nature" [svarupa] the state of revealing in general—or the eleven organs, viz., [the five organs of action and the five of sense and the mind]; "Egoism" [asmita] notion of selfishness; "Concomitance" and "Possession of objects" are as beforestated. [Aph. 45.]‡

He (now) states the result of the conquering of the organs of sense:—§

ततो मनोजवित्वं विकरणभावः प्रधानजयश्च ॥ ४९ ॥

Aph. 49. Therefrom spring up velocity of mind the state of modification, and the conquest of nature.

"Velocity of mind" ('manojavitva') means attainment of rapid motion by the body like that of mind; [that is, the ascetic can move his body from one place to another as quick as the mind]. "The state of modification" (vikaranabhava) is, the attainment of functions in the organs of sense independent of body; [that is, the modifications of the organs of sense take

---

* वज्रसंहननत्वं वज्रवत्कठिनाङ्गत्वमन्यत्प्रसिद्धम् ॥ † इन्द्रियजयमाह ।

‡ ग्रहणमिन्द्रियाणां विषयाभिमुखी वृत्तिः स्वरूपं सामान्येन प्रकाशत्वमस्मिता अहङ्कारानुगमोऽन्वयार्थवत्त्वे पूर्ववत् । एतेषामिन्द्रियाणामवस्थापञ्चके पूर्ववत् संयमं कृत्वा इन्द्रियजयो भवति ॥ § तस्य फलमाह ।

place independently of the body at any time, whenever the ascetic desires, with regard to any place or object]. "The conquest of nature" [pradhana-jaya, the chief or universal victory,] controlling all things,—[that is altering anything from one state into another at will]. These perfections are attained by the ascetic who has conquered the organs of sense. And these are, here—in this system, called the honey-like [perfections, madhupratika] because like an individual particle of honey each of them is tasteful.*

He [now] mentions the conquering of the organ.†

सत्त्वपुरुषान्यताख्यातिमात्रस्य सर्वभावाधिष्ठातृत्वं सर्वज्ञातृत्वञ्च ॥ ५० ॥

Aph. 50. Omniscience and Supremacy over all existence arise merely [in the ascetic] who has the discriminative knowledge of the element of purity and soul.

[In the ascetic] who has practised asceticism with regard to the clear modification of the pure element [—i, e. with regard to internal organ, antahkarana] arises the knowledge of the difference between the quality of purity [sattwa] and soul [purusha], in the shape of inertness of the notion in regard to the qualities existing as agents, [or in other words, by which knowledge the conceit that, 'the qualities are agents is rendered inert]. From the influence of this [knowledge] arises in the ascetic, situated in the selfsame position, meditation—or recognition—viz, "Supremacy over all existence" and "Omniscience."‡

---

* शरीरस्य मनोवदुत्तमो गतिलाभो मनोजवित्वङ्कायानिरपेक्षाणामिन्द्रियाणां वृत्तिलाभो विकरणभावः सर्ववशित्वम्प्रधानजयः । एताः सिद्धयो जितेन्द्रियस्य प्रादुर्भवन्ति ताश्चास्मिन् शास्त्रे मधुप्रतीका इत्युच्यन्ते यथा मधुन एकदेशोऽपि स्वदते एवंप्रत्यकमेताः सिद्धयः स्वदन्त इति मधुप्रतीकाः ॥

† अन्तःकरणजयमाह ।

‡ तस्मिन् शुद्धे सात्विके परिणामे कृतसंयमस्य या सत्वपुरुषयोरुत्पद्यते सा विवेकख्यातिर्गुणानाङ्कर्तृत्वाभिमान शिथिलीभावरूपा तन्माहात्म्यात् तत्रैव स्थितस्य योगिनः सर्वभावाधिष्ठातृत्वं सर्वज्ञातृत्वञ्च समाधेर्भवति ॥

"Supremacy over all existence" means, overcoming like a master all entities, which are modifications of the qualities [guna] "Omniscience" means, the distinctive knowledge of them [i. e. of entities] as they are in themselves, which exist in the modes as subsided [Santa] emerged [udita] and not yet named—[avyapadeshya]—viz, the things past, present and future. In the state of perfect consciousness of having overcome [them] the perfection which in this system is [technically] called víshoká, or free from sorrow, takes place.*

He [now] states another ground—or position in order :—†

तद्वैराग्यादपि दोषबीजक्षये कैवल्यम् ॥ ५१ ॥

Aph. 51. From an indifference even to this [perfection] through the destruction of the germ of perniciousness, results isolation.

When an indifference even to this perfection [which is called] víshoká—or free from sorrow, results in the ascetic; then through that [indifference] on the absolute destruction—eradication of ignorance which is the germ of the evils—or perniciousness—i.e. desire &c. [—desire and aversion &c.]—isolation—absolute cessation of pain—that is, permanence of soul in its own state—takes place in consequence of the conclusion of the supremacy of the qualities [guna].‡

[Next] He states an expedient for firmness in this meditation.§

स्थान्युपनिमन्त्रणे सङ्गस्मयाकरणम्पुनरनिष्टप्रसङ्गात् ॥ ५२ ॥

---

* सर्वेषाङ्गुणपरिणामानाम्भावानां स्वामिवदाक्रमणं सर्वाधिष्ठातृत्वं तेषामेव शान्तोदिताव्यपदेश्यधर्मित्वेन स्थितानां यथावद्विवेकज्ञानं सर्वज्ञातृत्वम् । एषां चास्मिन् शास्त्रे परस्यां वशीकारसञ्ज्ञायां विशोकानामासिद्धिरित्युच्यते ॥

† क्रमेण भूमिकान्तरमाह ।

‡ तस्यामपि विशोकायां सिद्धौ यदा वैराग्यमुत्पद्यते योगिनस्तदा तस्माद्दोषाणां रागादीनां यद्बीजमविद्यादयस्तस्याः क्षये निर्मूलने कैवल्यमात्यन्तिकी दुःखनिवृत्तिः पुरुषस्य गुणानामधिकारपरिसमाप्तेः स्वरूपप्रतिष्ठत्वम् ॥

§ अस्मिन् समाधौ स्थित्युपायमाह ।

Aph. 52. [The ascetic ought] not to form association and exhibit wonderment at the invitation of the tutelary deities, for evil would again ensue.

There are four [classes of] ascetics viz., (1) he who has performed the practice and in whom the light [that consists of the pure element] has just entered; (2) he who possesses knowledge that holds to the truth; (3) he who has conquered the elements and senses; (4) he who has transcended the objects of meditation. This—the fourth one, in whom has sprung up the seven-fold perfect knowledge, up to the ground of the limit and is realising [or has the immediate cognition of] the last stage, which is technically called, madhumati or honeyed, is invited by tutelary deities [Indra &c.]: that is, they allure him with celestial nymphs and elixirs or ambrosia and the like. He, upon this invitation should neither form association nor exhibit amazement. By association he falls again into the enjoyment of objects; and by wonderment thinking that he has accomplished his objects does not persevere in meditation. Therefore he should avoid association and wonderment.*

He states another expedient in regard to this resultant discriminative knowledge.†

क्षणतत्क्रमयोः सम्बन्धसंयमाद्विवेकजञ्ज्ञानम् । ५३ ॥

Aph. 53. Knowledge springing from discrimination results from asceticism performed with regard to the relation between moments and to their order.

---

* चत्वारो योगिनो भवन्ति तत्राभ्यासवान् प्रवृत्तमात्रज्योतिः प्रथमः । ऋतम्भरप्रज्ञो द्वितीयः । भूतेन्द्रियजयी तृतीयः । अतिक्रान्तभावनीयश्चतुर्थः ॥ तस्य चतुर्थस्य समाधेर्भूतसप्तविधप्रान्तभूमिप्रज्ञस्यान्त्यां मधुमतीसञ्ज्ञाम्भूमिकां साक्षात्कुर्वतः स्थानिनो देवा उपनिमन्त्रयितारो भवन्ति दिव्यस्त्रीरसायनादिकेनोत्कण्ठयन्तीति तस्मिन्नुपनिमन्त्रणे नानेन सङ्गः कर्तव्यो नापि स्मयः । सङ्गति करणे पुनर्विषयभोगे पतति स्मयकरणे कृतकृत्यमात्मानं मन्यमानो न समाधावुत्सहतेऽतः सङ्गस्मययोर्वर्जनन्तेन कर्तव्यम् ॥

† अस्यामेव फलभूतायां विवेकख्यातावुपायान्तरमाह ।

"By moments" is meant the ultimate division of time, which cannot be sub-divided into other periods. "Order" means modification of such moments of time as prior and posterior. From asceticism [performed] with regard thereto [i. e. with regard to both—the moments and their order] the above discriminative knowledge results.*

The meaning is this, when perception even of an exceedingly subtile order of moments has taken place in the ascetic, who has performed asceticism in regard to the order that this moment is posterior to that, and that moment is prior to this; then he perceives other subtile things also, i. e., the great principle, &c.†

With the purpose of citing [another] discrimination of this restraint he states.‡

जातिलक्षणदेशैरन्यतानवच्छेदात् तुल्ययोस्ततः प्रतिपत्तिः ॥ ५४ ॥

Aph. 54. Therefrom results discernment of two similar things, as there is non-discrimination by class, characteristic and place

The causes of distinction of things are "class" [Jati] "characteristic" [lakshana] and "position" [desha]. In some cases the cause of distinction is "class;" for instance, This is an ox, and This is a buffalo. The cause of discrimination of two things of the same class, is "characteristic;" for example, This [cow] is of variegated colour, and that is red. And the cause of discrimination of two things not differentiated by class and possessing similar characteristics is the place seen, as in the case of two emblic myrobalans of equal size, situated in two different places.§

---

* क्षणः स चाल्पः कालावयवो यस्य कलाः प्रविभक्तुं न शक्यन्ते तथाविधानां कालक्षणानां यः पौर्वापर्य्येण परिणामस्तत्रसंयमात् प्रागुक्तविवेकजं ज्ञानमुत्पद्यते॥

† अयमर्थः अयङ्कालक्षणोऽमुष्मात् कालक्षणादुत्तरोयमस्मात्पूर्व इत्येवं विधेक्रमे कृतसंयमस्यात्यन्तं सूक्ष्मेऽपि क्षणक्रमे यदा भवति साक्षात्कारस्तदाऽन्यदपि सूक्ष्मं महदादि साक्षात्करोति ॥ ‡ अस्यैव संयमस्य विवेकोपक्षेपायाह ।

§ पदार्थानाम्भेदहेतवो जातिलक्षणदेशा भवन्ति कचिद्भेदहेतुर्जातिर्यथा गौरियं महिषोऽयमिति जात्या तुल्ययोर्लक्षणम्भेदहेतुर्यथा इयङ्कर्बुरा इयमरुणेति जात्या लक्षणेन चाभिन्नयोर्भेदहेतुर्देशो दृष्टो यथा तुल्यपरिमाणयोरामलयोर्भिन्नदेशास्थितयोः

But distinction cannot be made in each case as of two atoms existing in the same place. When [in the ascetic] who has practised restraint for a discrimination in regard to such objects, knowledge of distinction arises, then from the practice of that, subtile principles are distinctively known. What is meant is this: where it is impossible to know difference by any other means, there, discernment of distinction certainly takes place by asceticism.*

In order to explain the signification [sanjna'] object [vishaya] and nature or characteristic [swabháva] of the above-described knowledge, springing from discrimination, he states.†

तारकं सर्वविषयं सर्वथाविषयमक्रमञ्चेति विवेकजं ज्ञानम् ॥ ५५ ॥

Aph. 55. The knowledge springing from discrimination is [called] saving [knowledge], has all things and the entire nature of all things for its objects, and is non-successive.

The knowledge arisen in its final stage, from the efficacy of the asceticism described above [Aph. 53.] is by [its] significant name called saving [knowledge] for it delivers ascetics from the unfathomable sea of transmigratory existence. He states its object. It has all things for its object that is, all principles [tattwa] i. e. the great principle &c., are its objects. Its "Nature" [swabháva] is that it has all nature [or all states] of things for its object; that is, all principles existing in any mode, i. e., in all different forms, gross, natural and subtile &c., in all states, in all modifications, are its objects. He states another characteristic of it, that it is non-successive, that is, there is no order [priority and posteriority] in perceving without exception all entities modified in various states or forms: therefore it is

---

* यत्र पुनर्भेदो नावधारयितुं शक्यते यथैकदेशस्थितयोः पार्थिवयोः परमाण्वोः। तथाविधे विषये भेदाय कृतसंयमस्य यदा भेदेन ज्ञानमुपजायते तदा तदभ्यासात् सूक्ष्माण्यपि तत्वानि भेदेन प्रतिपद्यन्ते । एतदुक्तम्भवति यत्र न केनाप्युपायेन भेदोऽवधारयितुं शक्यस्तत्र संयमाद्भवत्येव भेदप्रतिपत्तिरिति ॥

† उक्तस्य विवेकजन्यज्ञानस्य संज्ञां विषयं स्वभावञ्च व्याख्यातुमाह ।

called orderless [akrama]. It contemplates simultaneously all nature as if it were an emblic myrobalan-fruit in the hand.*

What results from this saving [knowledge's táraka]? To this he replies:—†

सत्वपुरुषयोः शुद्धिसाम्ये कैवल्यम् ॥ ५६ ॥

Aph. 56. On equalization of clearness of the pure quality [i. e. understanding] and soul, Isolation takes place.

On the quality of clearness of the pure quality [viz., the understanding—the modifications of the pure quality] and soul, the characteristics of which have been described before, Isolation takes place. By "clearness" of the pure quality [i. e. thinking principle, buddhisattwa] is meant its resolution into its cause, by removal of the conceit [or notion] of being the agent of universe; and the "clearness" of soul is non-existence of experience [which is] attributed to it. Thus, when "clearness" of these two [i. e. of the principle of understanding and soul] has equally taken place, then Isolation,—perfect emancipation—ensues:‡

---

* उक्तसंयमबलादन्त्यायाम्भूमिकायामुत्पन्नज्ञानं तारकत्वगाधात्संसारपयोधेर्यो-
गिन इत्यान्वर्थिक्यासंज्ञया तारकमित्युच्यते । अस्य विषयमाह । सर्वाणि तत्व निम-
हदादीनि विषयोऽस्येति सर्वविषयम् । स्वभावश्चास्य सर्वथाविषयत्वं सर्वाभिरव-
स्थाभिः स्थूलस्वरूपसूक्ष्मादिभेदेन तैस्तैश्च परिणामैः सर्वेण प्रकारेणावस्थितानि
तत्त्वानि विषयोऽस्येति सर्वथाविषयम् । स्वभावान्तरमाह । अक्रममिति निःशेषनाना-
वस्थापरिणतभावग्रहणेनास्य क्रमो विद्यते इत्यक्रमम् ॥ सर्वंकरतलगतामलकवद्
युगपत् पश्यतीत्यर्थः ॥

† अस्मात् तारकात् किम्भवतीत्याह ।

‡ सत्वपुरुषावुक्तलक्षणौ तयोः शुद्धिसाम्ये कैवल्यम् । सत्त्वस्य सर्वकर्तृत्वाभि-
माननिवृत्त्या स्वकारणेऽनुप्रवेशः शुद्धिः । पुरुषस्य शुद्धिरुपचरितभोगाभाव इति
द्वयोः समानायां शुद्धौ कैवल्यमुत्पद्यते मोक्षो भवतीत्यर्थः ॥

THE

SANKHYA

OR

YOGA APHORISMS

OF

PATANJALI.

BOOK IV.

Now [the fourth book, which is called] Kaivalya Páda—book of Isolation—is commenced for the purpose of establishing, by consistent reason, the nature of Isolation, by means of expelling mistakes arisen from contrary determination. And there by mentioning various causes as birth &c., of the fore-mentioned perfections, he informs us that the meditation should, therefore be performed; and he states its subservience to Isolation.*

जन्मौषधिमन्त्रतपः समाधिजाः सिद्धयः ॥ १ ॥

Aph. 1. Perfections are produced by birth, herbs [of mysterious virtue,] incantations, penances and meditations.

Some "Perfections" [Siddhi, supernatural powers] are caused by birth alone; such as the motion of birds in the air and the like; or the knowledge &c., of Kapila and other saints, [or minuteness &c., of deities that were invested with them in their birth]. "Perfections" produced by herbs consist of elixirs and

* इदानीं विप्रतिपत्तिसमुत्थभ्रान्तिनिराकरणेन युक्त्या कैवल्यस्वरूपावस्थापनाय कैवल्यपादोऽयमारभ्यते । तत्र पूर्वोक्तसिद्धीनां नानाविधजन्मादिकारणप्रतिपादनद्वारेणै वम्बोधयति समाधिः कर्तव्य इति कैवल्यार्थत्वञ्चाह ॥

the like, that is, supernatural herbs in Pátála—the regions under the earth, [this perfection is obtained by persons who possess knowledge of these supernatural herbs or medicines]. "Perfections" produced by Incantations are well known [that is this perfection may be obtained by any one, who knows and repeats incantations]. Perfections produced by "Penances" are those obtained by Vishwámitra and others, [mendicants and performers of penances]. "Perfections" caused by "meditations" are such as have been described before.*

The [real] cause of perfections is meditation alone performed in the other births; Incantations and the rest are merely media or mediate causes [or occasional causes]. But then [it may be asked] how the meditation of other [former] births can be the cause [of perfection, for] in the case of Nandiswara and others the result is seen in this birth alone? To this he replies.†

जात्यन्तरपरिणामः प्रकृत्यापूरात् ॥ २ ॥

Aph. 2. The change into another class is from the supply of natures.

The change of class &c., of Nandishwara and others in this present life, was from the "Supply of Natures." That is, the natures of former births alone supply the modifications in this birth—viz., they [the former natures] cause changes of those [modifications] by changing them into different classes, &c.‡

---

* काश्चन जन्मनिमित्ता एव सिद्धयो यथा पक्ष्यादीनामाकाशगमनादयः । यथा वा कपिलादिमहर्षीणाञ्ज्ञानादयः । औषधिसिद्धयः पातालादौरसायनादयः । मन्त्र-सिद्धयः प्रसिद्धाः । तपः सिद्धयो यथा विश्वामित्रादीनाम । समाधिसिद्धयः पूर्वमेवोक्ताः ॥

† सिद्धीनां समाधिरेव हेतुर्जन्मान्तराभ्यस्तः । मन्त्रादीनांनिमित्तमात्राणि ननु नन्दीश्वरादीनां जात्यादिपरिणामोऽस्मिन्नेव दृश्यते तत्कथञ्जन्मान्तरसमाधेः कारणत्वं तत्राह ॥

‡ योऽयमिहैवजन्मनि नन्दीश्वरादीनां जात्यन्तरादिपरिणामः स प्रकृत्या पूरात् पाश्चात्या एव हि प्रकृतयोऽस्मिन् जन्मनि विकारानापूरयन्ति तान् जात्यन्तरादि-द्वारेण परिणामयन्ति ॥

[The meaning is this that the fact of change of class &c., as is seen in the case of Nandishwara &c., who was born a Brahman, and by worship of Siva was changed into a deity in that very life, can be accounted for by Nature—or modifications of Nature—i. e. in the case of Nandishwara the body and organs of sense belonging to him as a man and a Brahman were modified into the body and organs of sense of a deity, by supply of constituent particles of the body and organs of sense belonging to a deity].

But [even] then [it may be objected] merits and demerits are observed to be in process of being realised in this life : how then can it be maintained that the supply of natures is the cause? To this he replies :—

निमित्तमप्रयोजकम्प्रकृतीनां वरणभेदस्तु ततः क्षेत्रिकवत् ॥ ३ ॥

Aph. 3. The occasional is the non-efficient cause of natures : thereby there is removal of obscurations, as in the case of a husbandman [who removes the impediments to the irrigation of his fields].

"Occasional"—merit &c., is the non-efficient cause of the modifications of natures into other things, for a cause is not set in motion by an effect. Then where [it may be asked] is operation of the merits &c.? To this he replies :—*

Thereby is the removal of obscurations "as in the case of a husbandman." "Thereby" from the merits &c., which are realised, takes place "Removal" or destruction of whatever is obscurant—the obstacles—i. e., of works &c., because it is contradictory. On the removal of that obstacle, the natures themselves become efficient of the desired effect. He gives an example, like a husbandman, i. e., as a farmer or husbandman desiring to conduct water from one field to another merely re-

† ननु च धर्माधर्मादयस्तत्रक्रियमाणा उपलभ्यन्ते तत्कथम्प्रकृतीनामापूरणात्कारणमित्यत्राह ॥

* निमित्तं धर्मादि तत्प्रकृतीनामर्थान्तरपरिणामे न प्रयोजकं नहि कार्य्येण कारणम्प्रवर्तते । कुत्र तर्हि धर्मादेर्व्यापारस्तत्राह ॥

moves the impediments or obstacles [in tho way] of the water which being removed the water itself assumes the modification of profluence, but there is no exertion made by him of advance of water. Similarly is it to be understood of merit and demerit.*

When an ascetic assumes numerous bodies simultaneously, then from whence are so many minds [which are necessary for so many bodies] produced? To this he replies.†

निर्माणचित्तान्यस्मितामात्रात् ॥ ४ ॥

Aph. 4. The minds in the productions [ensue] from mere egoism.

The minds in the productions [that is, in the bodies which he produces for himself] of an ascetic created by himself, ensue as sparks arise simultaneously as modifications from fire, at his will from egoism alone, which is the general and original cause [of mind].‡

But [it may be objected] as there may be different purposes of so many, [different] minds, how can they produce one effect? To this he replies.§

प्रवृत्तिभेदे प्रयोजकञ्चित्तमेकमनेकेषाम् ॥ ५ ॥

Aph. 5. In different activities of [those] numerous [minds] one mind [of the ascetic] is the moving cause.

---

* वरणभेदस्तु ततः क्षेत्रिकवत् । ततस्तस्मादनुष्ठीयमानाद्धर्मादेर्यद्वरणमावरण-कधर्मादि तस्यैव विरोधित्वात् क्षयः क्रियते । तस्मिन् प्रतिबन्धे क्षीणे प्रकृतयः स्वयमभिमतकार्य्याय प्रभवन्ति । दृष्टान्तमाह । क्षेत्रिकवत् यथा कृषीवलः केदारात् केदारान्तरं जलं निनीषुर्जलप्रतिबन्धकावरणभेदमात्रङ्करोति तस्मिन् भिन्ने जलं स्वयमेव प्रसररूपं परिणामंगृह्णाति नतु जलप्रसरणे तस्य कश्चित् प्रयत्नः एवन्धर्मादेर्बोद्धव्यम् ॥ † यदाऽनेकशरीराणि युगपदेव गृह्णाति योगी तदा कुतस्तानि चित्तानि प्रभवन्तीत्याह ॥

‡ योगिनः स्वयं निर्म्मितेषु कायेषु यानि चित्तानि तानि मूलकारणादस्मिता-मात्रादेव तदिच्छया प्रसरन्ति । अग्नेर्विस्फुलिङ्गा इव युगपत् परिणमन्ति ॥

§ ननु बहूनाञ्चित्तानाम्भिन्नाभिप्रायत्वान्नैककार्य्यकर्तृत्वं स्यादित्यत्राह ॥

The "Moving cause"—i. e. that which actuates the different activities— various operations of those [different] minds, as a ruler, is the one mind of the ascetic and not a different element.*

The meaning is that as the mind like a ruler directs at will the sight, the hand &c., [i. e. other organs of sense and action] in his [the ascetic's] own body, so in like manner it does in regard to other bodies [i. e. with regard to the internal and external organs of sense belonging to other bodies].†

He [now] states the distinction of the mind produced by meditation from the minds produced by birth &c., [birth medicine, incantations and penances].‡

तत्र ध्यानजमनाशयम् ॥ ६ ॥

Aph. 6. Among these [minds produced by birth &c.], that which springs from meditation is without substratum.

Among those five kinds of minds springing from birth &c., [i. e. birth, medicines, incantations, penances and meditation] that which springs from meditation or reflection is without substratum—i. e. destitute of the basis of mental deposits of works.§

He [now] states that as the mind of the ascetic is free from afflictions and actions and is distinct, so his work also is likewise distinct [from that of others].||

कर्म्माशुक्लाकृष्णं योगिनस्त्रिविधमितरेषाम् ॥ ७ ॥

---

* तेषां चेतसाम्प्रवृत्तिभेदे व्यापारनानात्वे एकं योगिनश्चित्तम्प्रयोजकम्प्रेरकमधिष्ठातृत्वेन न भिन्नम तत्वम् ॥

† अयमर्थो यथात्मीयशरीरे मनश्चक्षुः पाण्यादीनि यथेच्छम्प्रेरयत्यधिष्ठातृत्वेन तथा कायान्तरेष्वपि ॥

‡ जन्मादिप्रभावचित्तात्समाधिप्रभवस्य चित्तस्य वैलक्षण्यमाह ॥

§ ध्यानजं समाधिजं यच्चित्तन्तत्पञ्चसु जन्मादिप्रभवचित्तेषु मध्येऽनाशयङ्कर्म्मवासनारहितमित्यर्थः ॥

|| यथेतरचित्तेभ्यो योगिनश्चित्तं क्लेशकर्म्मादिरहितं विलक्षणं तथा कर्म्मापि विलक्षणमित्याह ॥

Aph. 7. The work of an ascetic is neither pure nor dark, and that of others is of three kinds.

[There are four kinds of works (1) pure, [shukla] (2) dark, [krishna]; (3) pure and dark [shukla-krishna]; (4) neither pure nor dark [asukla-krishna]. Work such as sacrifice &c., which produces a good result is pure that which produces an evil or a bad result, such as the murder of a Brahman &c., is dark; that which is the commixture of both is [called] pure-dark.*

Of these the pure [work] is of those persons who give alms and perform penances and study the Veda; dark work is that which belongs to infernal beings; the pure dark work is of men. The work of ascetics is neither pure nor dark, for it does not produce any result, in consequence of the renunciation of results of their practice.†

He [now] states the result of this work.‡

ततस्तद्विपाकानुगुणनांमेवाभिव्यक्तिर्वासनानाम् ॥ ८ ॥

Aph. 8. Therefrom [results] manifestation of those mental deposits alone which are conformable to its fructification.

There are two kinds of mental deposits of works, (1) those which have their fruit in memory alone; (2) those which have for their fruit, rank [in the scale of being] longevity and enjoyment. Of these, [two kinds] those that have for their fruit, rank, longevity and enjoyment, have been described before.§

But of those that have for their fruit, memory, manifestation merely of those mental deposits takes place, which are adequate

---

* शुभफलदं कर्म यागादि शुक्लम्। अशुभफलदं ब्रह्महत्यादि कृष्णम्। उभयसङ्कीर्णं शुक्लकृष्णम् ॥

† तत्र शुक्लकर्म्म दानतपःस्वाध्यायादिमताम्पुरुषाणाम् । कृष्णकर्मनारकाणाम् । शुक्लकृष्णं मनुष्याणाम् । योगिनाम्फलत्यागेनानुष्ठानेन न किञ्चित्फलमारभते ॥

‡ अस्यैव कर्मणः फलमाह ।

§ इह द्विविधाः कर्म्मवासनाः स्मृतिमात्रफला जात्यायुर्भोगफलाश्च तत्र जात्यायुर्भोगफलाः पूर्वङ्कृतनिर्णयाः ।

and agreeable to the fructification of the work—that is those mental deposits of work become manifest, which are adequate and agreeable to this or that body [whether of man, deity or animal &c., originating in this or that work). The meaning is this, that by whatever work any body such as [of a deity &c.,] had previously originated [in work] after an interval of hundreds of years in commencing the same kind of body again, the mental deposits [of works] having for their fruit memory alone, re-appear in regard to new things alone. The others which are not agreeable thereto remain in subsidence. In this case the mental deposits [impressions produced by experience of hell &c.] become manifest.*

Having raised a doubt as to the possibility of the causal relation of these mental deposits or impressions [of mind], in order to show its possibility he states.†

जातिदेशकालव्यवहितानामप्यानन्तर्य्यं स्मृतिसंस्कारयोरेकरूपत्वात् ॥ ९ ॥

Aph. 9. There is an immediacy among these [impressions] though intercepted by rank [in the scale of being], place and time, because the recollection and the train of self-reproductive impression are identical [that is they are not different].

Of the transmigrating souls wandering in various births, when any one, having experienced some particular birth, after an interval of thousands of births, enters upon the same birth again, then the impressions [of mind, vasana], which, depending on the particular body &c.,—the cause of manifestation, were

---

* यास्तु स्मृतिमात्रफलास्तास्ततः कर्म्मणो यादृक्शरीरमारब्धं देवमनुष्यतिर्य्यगादिभेदेन तस्य विपाकस्य या अनुगुणा अनुरूपा वासनास्तासामेव तस्मादभिव्यक्तिर्वासनानाम्भवति । अयमर्थः येन कर्म्मणा पूर्वं देवतादिशरीरमारब्धं जात्यन्तरशतव्यवधानेन पुनस्तथाविधस्यैव शरीरस्यारम्भे तदनुरूपा एव स्मृतिफला वासनाः प्रकटीभवन्ति लोकोत्तरेष्वेवार्थेषु तस्य स्मृत्यादयो जायन्ते इतरास्तु सत्योऽप्यनभिव्यक्ता इवास्तिष्ठन्ति न तस्यां दशायां नरकादिशरीरोपभोगभवा वासना व्यक्तिमायान्ति ॥

† आसामेव वासनानां कार्य्यकारणभावानुपपत्तिमाशङ्क्य समर्थयितुमाह ।

manifested in that fore-experienced birth, and which disappeared [for some period] for want of that particular kind of cause of manifestation, do appear again on finding the same kind of the body &c.,—the cause of [their] manifestation. Thus, even on an interval of rank [Játi], place and time, there exists an immediacy—non-interval among these in accomplishing identical effects, viz., memory &c., because there is an identity [that is, there is no difference] between a memory and the train of self-reproductive thought. For example, from the work [merit and demerit] which is performed, the train of self-reproductive property in the shape of impression takes place in the intellectual principle. This is the germination of the fruit [of works] that is, of paradise and hell &c., or the existence of the works—sacrifice &c., in a state of power. The recollection of the agent takes place from the self-reproductive property of the power of experiencing this or that particular enjoyment; and from the recollection there is the experience of pleasure and pain, and from that experience spring up again the self-reproductive impression and recollection, &c. For one whose doctrine, memory and self-reproductive impression are different [things], the relation of cause and effect is very difficult for want of an immediacy. But in our view, when the experience itself becomes the self-reproductive impression and the self-reproductive impression changes into memory, then there is no difficulty of causal relation, because only one intellect or mind remains as a recollector.*

---

* इह नानायोनिषु भ्रमतां संसारिणां काञ्चिद्योनिमनुभूय यदा योन्यन्तरसहस्रव्यवधानेन पुनस्तामेव योनिम्प्रतिपद्यते तदा तस्याम्पूर्वानुभूतायां योनौ तथाविधशरीरादिव्यञ्जकापेक्षया वासना याः प्रकटीभूता आसंस्तास्तथाविधव्यञ्जकाभावात्तिरोभूताः पुनस्तथाविधव्यञ्जकशरीरादिलाभे प्रकटीभवन्ति। जातिदेशकालव्यवधानेऽपि तासां स्वानुरूपस्मृत्यादि फलसाधने आनन्तर्य्यं नैरन्तर्य्यमेव कुतः स्मृतिसंस्कारयोरेकरूपत्वात्। तथाहि अनुष्ठीयमानात्कर्म्मणश्चित्तसत्वे वासनारूपः संस्कारः समुत्पद्यते स च स्वर्गनरकादीनाम्फलानामङ्कुरीभावः कर्मणां यागादीनां शक्तिरूपतयावस्थानं। कर्तुश्च तथाविधभोग्यभोक्तृत्वस्वरूपसामर्थ्यसंस्कारात् स्मृतिः

Let there exist an immediacy and the causal relation among the impressions [of mind] but when a perception takes place the first time is it then caused by an impression or does it proceed with a cause? To clear up this doubt he states as follows:—*

तासामनादित्वमाशिषो नित्यत्वात् ॥ १० ॥

Aph. 10. They have eternity because the benediction is eternal.

"They" impressions "have" eternity—state of a thing not having a beginning—, hence it means that they are without a beginning because the benediction is eternal; that is, the benediction in the shape of the intense desire—i. e. special resolution, "May the causes of my pleasure exist always and may there never be separation of us from them" which is the cause of impressions, is eternal—i. e. has no beginning.†

The meaning is this,—that, when there is the proximity of the cause [i. e. impression] who can oppose the realization of the effects, that is of the perception and the self-continuant impressions? What is meant is this,—the intellect, modified by [various] perception and self-reproductive impression &c., and having the attributes of contraction and expansion, on

---

स्मृतेश्च सुखदुःखोपभोगस्तदनुभवाच्च पुनरपि संस्कारस्मृत्यादयः । एवञ्च यस्य स्मृतिसंस्कारादयो भिन्नास्तस्यानन्तर्य्याभावे दुर्लभः कार्य्यकारणभावः । अस्माकं तु यदानुभव एव संस्काराभवति संस्कारश्च स्मृतिरूपतया परिणमते तदैकस्यैव चित्तस्यानुसन्धातृत्वेन स्थितत्वात्कार्य्यकारणभावो न दुर्घटः ॥

* भवत्वानन्तर्य्यकार्य्यकारणभावश्च वासनानां यदा तु प्रथममेवानुभवः प्रवर्तते तदा किं वासनानिमित्त उत निर्निमित्त इति शङ्का व्यपनेतुमाह ॥

† तासां वासनानामनादित्वं न विद्यते आदिर्यस्य तस्य भावस्तत्तासामादिर्ना-स्तीत्यर्थः कुत आशिषो नित्यत्वात् । येयमाशीर्महामोहरूपा सदैव सुखसाधनानि मे भूयासुर्मा कदाचित् तैर्वियोगो मम भूयादिति यः सङ्कल्पविशेषो वासनानां कारणं तस्य नित्यत्वादनादित्वादित्यर्थः ॥

finding this or that cause of manifestation— i. e. the fructification [of works], is diversified by different effect.*

Having raised the doubt, since they [impressions] are infinite how is it possible to get rid of them, he declares the means for their removal.†

हेतुफलाश्रयालम्बनैः संगृहीतत्वादेषामभावे तदभावः ॥ ११ ॥

Aph. 11. As [they are] collected by cause, effect, substratum and support [therefore] on non-existence of these, non-existence of the impressions takes place.

The cause of impressions is internal perception, and of this i. e. of perception, desire &c. [i. e. desire, aversion &c.] and of these [i. e. of desire &c.] ignorance; this is the immediate and mediate cause; the "effect" is body &c. and memory &c. "substratum" is the intellectual principle [or mind]; and the; "support" of impressions is the same as that of perception [i. e. the object—the object perceived, that is whatever object being present any impression is excited, that object is the support of that impression].‡

Therefore, as all the impressions are collected by the cause, effect, substratum and support, on non-existence of this cause &c. that is, while these are rendered useless like a burnt seed by knowledge and asceticism, the impressions, for want of root, do not spring up—i. e. do not produce [their] effect; this is their non-existence.§

---

* एतदुक्तम्भवति कारणस्य सन्निहितत्वादनुभवसंस्कारादीनां कार्य्याणाम्प्रवृत्तिः केन वार्य्यते । अनुभवसंस्काराद्यनुविद्धं सङ्कोचविकाशधर्मिचित्तं तत्तदभिव्यञ्जकविपाकलाभात् तत्तत्फलरूपतया परिणमत् इत्यर्थः ॥

† तासामानन्त्याद्धानंकथं सम्भवतीत्याशङ्क्य हानोपायमाह ॥

‡ वासनानामन्तरानुभवो हेतुस्तस्याप्यनुभवस्य रागादयस्तेषामविद्या इति साक्षात् पारम्पर्य्येण च हेतुः । फलं शरीरादिः स्मृत्यादि च । आश्रयो बुद्धितत्त्वमालम्बनं यदेवानुभवस्य तदेव वासनानाम् ॥

§ अतस्तैर्हेतुफलाश्रयालम्बनैरनन्तानामपि वासनानां संगृहीतत्वात् तेषां हेत्वादीनामभावे ज्ञानयोगाभ्यां दग्धबीजकल्पत्वे विहिते निर्मूलत्वाच्च वासनाः प्ररोहं यान्ति न कार्य्यमारम्भन्त इति तासामभावः ॥

It may be asked: Since it is observed that the intellect is in momentary transition, and a difference is proved, inasmuch as the impressions are called into being not simultaneously, according to the relation of cause and effect, how can there be unity in the intellect? In answer to this he states.*

अतीतानागतं स्वरूपतोऽस्त्यध्वभेदाद्धर्म्माणाम् ॥ १२ ॥

Aph. 12. That which is past and that which is to come does exist in its proper nature, for the course of properties is different.

Production of things not existing is not reasonable, because their relation with existence is impossible, no relation of a hare's horn &c. [that is of anything chimerical and impossible] with existence has been anywhere observed. In the case of a non-entity, regarded as an effect, with what design do the causes proceed to act? No one exercises activity having observed a non-existing object; otherwise there would be a contradiction also among existences [inasmuch as if the non-existent became existent, the existent might become non-existent]; there is no relation of a non-existence. Whatever has an existence of its own proper nature, how can that assume a state of non-entity—i. e. non-existence? That is, it can never assume the contrary shape.†

Therefore, as destruction of existences is impossible and production of non-existences is not possible, the subject of the attributes, though modified by different properties arranged according to their three-fold nature, their three-fold time, stand-

---

* ननु प्रतिक्षणं चित्तस्य नश्वरत्वोपलब्धेर्वासनानां तत्फलानाञ्च कार्य्यकारणभावेनायुगपद्भावित्वाद्भेदे कथमेकत्वमित्याशङ्क्य एकत्वसमर्थनायाह ॥

† इह ह्यसताम्भावानामुत्पत्तिर्न युक्तिमती तेषां सत्वसम्बन्धायोगान्नहिशशविषाणादीनांक्वचिदपि सत्वसम्बन्धोदृष्टः । नीरुपाख्ये च कार्य्ये किमुद्दिश्य कारणानि प्रवर्तन्ते नह्यसन्तं विषयमालोच्य कश्चित्प्रवर्तते सतामपि विरोधात् । नाभावसम्बन्धोऽस्ति । यत्स्वरूपेण लब्धसत्ताकं तत्कथं नीरूपाख्यतामभावरूपतां भजते न विरुद्धं रूपं स्वीकरोतीत्यर्थः ॥

ing in their respective courses [of past, present and future] do not abandon their forms; but while standing in the present course they acquire only their perceptibility. The difference of courses such as past and future &c., belongs exclusively to the properties. And the relation of cause and effect is stated in this series in the same manner only.*

Therefore it cannot be denied that one sole intellect continues as the subject of attributes until final emancipation.†

Of what kind are these subjects of attributes? To this he replies:—‡

ते व्यक्तसूक्ष्मा गुणात्मानः ॥ १३ ॥

Aph. 13. These individualised and subtile [objects] consist of qualities.

These same subjects of attributes consist of—i. e. are of the nature of the qualities—that is they are modified forms of the qualities, purity, passion and darkness, existing in the different forms of gross and subtile. For concomitance—attendance of all individuals or entities differing as internal and external has been seen with purity, passion and darkness, full of pleasure, pain and indifference; and what is seen as concomitant with any thing, that is seen to be the modified form of that, just as jars &c., which are concomitant with earth, are modified forms of earth.§

---

* तस्मात्सतां नाशासम्भवादसतां चोत्पत्त्यसम्भवात् तैस्तैर्धर्मैर्विपरिणममानो धर्मी सदैवैकरूपतयैवावतिष्ठते धर्मास्तु त्रैविध्यकत्वेन त्रैकाल्यत्वेन व्यवस्थिताः स्वस्मिन्नध्वनि व्यवस्थिता न स्वरूपं त्यजन्ति वर्तमानेऽध्वनि व्यवस्थिताः केवलं योग्यतां भजन्ते । तस्माद्धर्माणामेवातीतानागताद्यध्वभेदस्तेनैव रूपेण च कार्य्य-कारणभावोऽस्मिन्दर्शने प्रतिपद्यते ॥

† तस्मादपवर्गपर्यन्तमेकमेव चित्तं धर्मितयानुवर्तमानं न निन्होतुं पार्यते ॥

‡ त एते धर्मधर्मिणः किंरूपा इत्यत आह ।

§ ये एते धर्मधर्मिणः प्रोक्तास्ते व्यक्तसूक्ष्मभेदेनावस्थिता गुणाः सत्त्वरजस्त-मोरूपास्तदात्मानस्तत्स्वभावास्तत्परिणामरूपा इत्यर्थः । यतः सत्त्वरजस्तमोभिः सुखदुःखमोहमयैः सर्वासां बाह्याभ्यन्तरभेदभिन्नानाम्भावव्यक्तीनामन्वयोऽनुगमो दृ-श्यते यच्च यदन्वयि तत्तत्परिणामरूपं दृष्टं यथा घटादयो मृदन्विता मृत्परिणामरूपाः ॥

If these three qualities are the material causes of everything, how is the expression "one subject of attributes" to be employed? Having raised this doubt he states:—*

परिणामैकत्वाद्वस्तुतत्त्वम् ॥ १४ ॥

Aph. 14. Unity of thing results from unity of modification.

Although there are three qualities, still unity—i. e. sameness of thing is spoken of, for there is unity of their [the qualities'] modification, characterised by the relation of secondary and primary, viz., in some cases purity is secondary, in others passion and in others darkness. For instance in the example, this is earth, this is air &c., [earth is a modification of the quality of darkness and the air is a modification of that of passion].†

It may be objected that the object may be called one or many if it differs from the cognition, but when the cognition itself, from the influence of impressions, existing in the relation of cause and effect, appears in different shapes, how then can it be so called? To this he replies:—‡

वस्तुसाम्ये चित्तभेदात्तयोर्विविक्तः पन्थाः ॥ १५ ॥

Aph. 15. The course of these two [that is, the thing and the object] is distinct, for there is a diversity of thoughts regarding one thing.

"Of these two"—i. e. of the knowledge and thing "The course is distinct"—i. e. the path is different. Why? Inas-

---

* यद्येते त्रयो गुणाः सर्वत्र मूलकारणं कथमेको धर्मीति व्यपदेशः इत्याशङ्क्याह ॥

† यद्यपि त्रयो गुणास्तथापि तेषामङ्गाङ्गिभावलक्षणो यः परिणामः क्वचित्सत्त्वमङ्गी क्वचिद्रजः क्वचित्तम इत्येवं रूपस्तस्यैकत्वाद्वस्तुनस्तत्त्वमेकत्वमुच्यते । यथेयं पृथिवी अयं वायुरित्यादि ॥

‡ ननु च ज्ञानव्यतिरिक्ते सत्यर्थे वस्त्वेकमनेकं वा वक्तुं युज्यते यदा विज्ञानमेव वासनावशात्कार्य्यकारणभावेनावस्थितं तथा तथा च प्रतिभाति तदा कथमेतच्छक्यते वक्तुमित्याह ।

much as there is a diversity of thoughts regarding one thing —i. e. even in regard to the same thing that is being perceived such as a woman &c., difference of thoughts in the shape of pleasure, pain and indifference has been observed among various observers. For instance, on seeing a lovely and beautiful woman pleasure arises in an amorous person, aversion in her rival, and disgust in an ascetic; and thus, since various thoughts take place even in regard to one thing, how can a thing be an effect of the principle of thought? For were it the effect of one thought, the thing would appear uniformly.*

Besides if a thing were an effect of mind then if that mind were engrossed by another object, that thing would be nothing. If it be replied, "Be it so," we deny this; for then how could this same thing be perceived by many others? And as it is perceived, therefore it is not an effect of the thinking principle. If it be replied that that thing is created by many simultaneously, then there should be a difference between a thing that is created by many, and a thing which is created by one. And if the difference is not admitted then there being difference of causes and non-existence of difference of effect, the universe would become causeless or uniform.†

What is to be stated is this, that even the cause being different, if the effect is not different, the universe created by

---

* तयोर्ज्ञानार्थयोर्विविक्तः पन्था विविक्तो मार्ग इति यावत् कथं वस्तुसाम्ये चित्तभेदात् समानेऽपि वस्तुनि स्त्र्यादावुपलभ्यमाने नानाप्रमातॄणां चित्तस्य भेदः सुखदुःखमोहरूपतया समुपलभ्यते । तथाहि । एकस्यां रूपलावण्यवत्यां योषित्युपलभ्यमानायां सरागस्य सुखमुत्पद्यते सपत्न्यास्तु द्वेषः परिव्राजकादेर्घृणेत्येकस्मिन्नपि वस्तुनि नानाविधचित्तोदयात्कथञ्चिन्न कार्य्यत्वं वस्तुन एकचित्तकार्य्यत्वे वस्त्वैकरूपतयैव भासेत ॥

† किञ्च चित्तकार्य्यत्वे वस्तुनो यस्य चित्तस्य यद्वस्तुकार्य्यं तस्मिन्नार्थान्तरव्यासक्ते चित्ते तद्वस्तु न किञ्चित्स्यात् । भवत्विति चेन्न तदेव कथमन्यैर्बहुभिरुपलभ्यते उपलभ्यते च तस्मान्नचित्तकार्य्यम् । अथ युगपद्बहुभिः सोऽर्थः क्रियते तदा बहुनिर्मितस्य तस्यार्थस्यैकनिर्मिताद्वैलक्षण्यं स्यात् । यदि च वैलक्षण्यं नेष्यते तदा कारणभेदे सति कार्य्यभेदस्याभावे निर्हेतुकमेकरूपं वा जगत्स्यात् ॥

many causes may be of one and the same form; or in consequence of its not following the difference of causes it would be independent and causeless. And if it is so [it may be asked] why does the same object which consists of three qualities not produce cognitions full of pleasure, pain and indifference in one percipient? We reply that this is no valid objection. For as the object consists of three qualities the mind likewise consists of three qualities, and the merits, demerits are its [the mind's] accessories in the production of an object [in different shapes] from the manifestation of these [merits, demerits &c.] manifestation of mind takes place in such and such a form. Thus when the woman is in the presence of an amorous person, his mind, auxiliary to which is merit, undergoing modification through the predominance of purity, becomes full of pleasure. The mental state of the rival alone likewise through the predominance of passion subsidiary to which are wealth and merit, becomes full of pain. The mental state of the irate rival through the predominance of darkness, accessory to which is violent demerit, becomes full of dullness. Therefore the sensible object is different from the sensation. Therefore there is thus no identity between the sensation and its object. There is no relation of cause and effect, inasmuch as there is a contradiction. For [were it not so] it would follow that even there being a difference of cause there would be non-existence of difference of effect. Thus it is established that the object is distinct from the cognition.*

---

* एतदुक्तं भवति सत्यपि भिन्ने कारणे यदि कार्य्यस्याभेदस्तदा समग्रं जगन्नानाविधकारणजन्यमेकरूपं स्यात् कारणभेदाननुगमनात् स्वातन्त्र्येण निर्हेतुकं वा स्यात्। यद्येवं कथं तेन त्रिगुणात्मनार्थेनैकस्यैव प्रमातुः सुखदुःखमोहमयानि ज्ञानानि न जन्यन्ते मैवं यथाऽर्थस्त्रिगुणस्तथा चित्तमपि त्रिगुणं तस्य चार्थप्रतिभासोत्पत्तौ धर्माधर्मादयः सहकारिणस्तदुद्भववशस्तस्य तेन तेन रूपेणाभिव्यक्तिस्तथा च कामुकस्य सन्निहितायां योषिति धर्मसहकृतं चित्तं सत्वस्याङ्गितया परिणममानं सुखमयम्भवति तदेवार्थधर्मसहकारिरजसोऽङ्गितया दुःखरूपं सपत्नीमात्रस्य भवति तीव्राधर्मसहकारितया तमसोऽङ्गित्वेन कोपनायाः सपत्न्या मोहमयं भवति तस्माद्विज्ञानव्यतिरिक्तोऽस्ति ग्राह्योऽर्थः॥ तदेवं विज्ञानार्थयोर्न तादात्म्यं विरोधान्न

If this, the cognition, being the illuminator is perceptive by nature, and the object being liable to be illuminated is naturally perceptible, why then does not perception and recollection of all objects take place simultaneously? In order to obviate this difficulty he states.*

तदुपरागापेक्षित्वाच्चित्तस्य वस्तुज्ञाताज्ञातम् ॥ १६ ॥

Aph. 16. An object is known or unknown to the mind inasmuch as the tint of the object is required [to it].

An external object is known and unknown from the tint of the object—i. e. from bestowing its shape upon the mind. The meaning is that every thing when taking place requires an apparatus [of conditions]. The cognition of blue &c., when taking place requires a tint from the object derived through the channel of the organs of sense as its accessory cause; for a different object could not be perceived because that has no relation [with the knowledge]. Thence the same object which tinged the intellect with its colour—or bestowed its shape upon it, is brought by the cognition into use [as known]; and the object that has not given its shape is not used as known. And recollection takes place in regard to that object alone, which has been previously perceived and regarding which an object by resemblance &c., exciting the self-reproductive thought becomes the accessory cause of it (recollection). Thus perception of all things does not take place simultaneously. Therefore there is no contradiction.†

कार्य्यकारणभावः कारणाभेदे सत्यपि कार्य्यस्याभेदप्रसङ्गादिति ज्ञानाद व्यतिरिक्तस्यार्थस्य व्यवस्थापितम् ॥

* यद्येवं ज्ञानश्चेत्प्रकाशत्वाद्ग्रहणस्वभावमर्थश्च प्रकाश्यत्वाद्ग्राह्यस्वभावस्तत्कथं युगपत्सर्वानर्थांश्च गृह्णाति न स्मरति चेत्याशङ्क्य परिहारं वक्तुमाह ॥

† तस्यार्थस्योपरागादाकारसमर्पणाच्चित्ते बाह्यं वस्तु ज्ञातमज्ञातञ्च भवति । अयमर्थः सर्वः पदार्थ आत्मलाभे सामग्रीमपेक्षते नीलादिज्ञानञ्चोपजायमानमिन्द्रियप्रणालिकया समागतमर्थोपरागं सहकारिकारणत्वेनापेक्षते व्यतिरिक्तस्यार्थस्य सम्बन्धाभावाद्ग्रहीतुमशक्यत्वात् ततश्च येनैवार्थेनास्य ज्ञानस्य स्वरूपोपरागः कृत-

If, thus the percipient soul also does not perceive yellow at the same time when it perceives blue, then incidentalness—i. e. liability of becoming modified in perceiving the shape [of the object] becomes necessary to the soul inasmuch as it is a percipient. To remove this doubt he states :—*

सदा ज्ञाताश्चित्तवृत्तयस्तत्प्रभोः पुरुषस्यापरिणामित्वात् ॥ १७ ॥

Aph. 17. The modification of the mental states are always known, because the presiding spirit is not modified.

These modifications of the thinking principle in the shape of changes and misconceptions are always—at all times known to the governing principle—the soul conscious of the mental state, because the soul whose essence is consciousness is not modified—does not undergo a modification. For if the soul also be modified then the modifications [or the mental states] being occasional cannot possibly be known at all times. What is meant is this—what is knowable in the interior to the soul existing always as a ruling principle in the form of consciousness is the clear Pure element, which also is constantly permanent, and by whatever object it is tinged, that object is reflected in the intelligence. And when the shadowing of consciousness takes place it is proved that the soul is always percipient. Thus there cannot be doubt that the soul is modifiable. But it may be objected that if the mind itself from the prevalence of the Pure element is illuminant, and illumination being illuminant of itself and of other objects illuminates itself as well as the objects, then the business [or

---

स्तमेवार्थज्ञानं व्यवहारयोग्यतां नयति। ततश्च सोऽर्थो ज्ञात इत्युच्यते येनाकारो न समर्पितः स न ज्ञातत्वेन व्यवह्रियते यस्मिंश्चानुभूतेऽर्थे सादृश्यादिनाऽर्थः संस्कारमुद्बोधयन् सहकारिकारणतां प्रतिपद्यते तस्मिन्नेवार्थे स्मृतिरुपजायते इति न सर्वत्र ज्ञानं नापि स्मृतिरिति न कश्चिद्विरोधः ॥

* यद्येवम्प्रमातापि पुरुषो यस्मिन् काले नीलं संवेदयते तस्मिन्नेव काले पीतमताश्चित्तवत्तस्यापि कादाचित्कग्रहीतृरूपत्वादाकारग्रहणे परिणामित्वम्प्राप्तमित्याशङ्क्य परिहारं वक्तुमाह ॥

the process] is accomplished by that alone, what need is there of another percipient! To remove this doubt he states:—*

न तत्स्वाभासं दृश्यत्वात् ॥ १८ ॥

Aph. 18. It is not self-illuminative inasmuch as it is cognisable.

If mind is not self-illuminative—the illuminator of objects, in other words it is perceptible by the soul. If it be asked why: we reply that it is so because it is perceptible, and that which is perceptible is cognisable by the pecipient as a jar &c. And the mind [or thinking principle] is perceptible therefore it is not self-illuminative.†

But it may be objected that this argument is not attended by that which is to be proved, for it is not established that the perception is cognisable. Moreover it is by means of the consciousness of knowledge that activities of souls in acquiring good and avoiding evils are observed. For instance "I am angry" "I am afraid" and "I have a desire in regard to this object" &c., do not take place with being known to the understanding. To refute this, he states:—‡

---

* या एताश्चित्तस्य परिणामविपर्ययादिरूपा वृत्तयस्तास्तत्प्रभोस्तस्य चित्तस्य ग्रहीतुः पुरुषस्य सदा सर्वकालमेव ज्ञेयास्तस्य चिद्रूपतयाऽपरिणामात् परिणामित्वाभावादित्यर्थः ॥ यदाऽसौ परिणामी स्यात्तदा परिणामस्य कादाचित्कत्वात्तासां चित्तवृत्तीनां सदा ज्ञातृत्वं नोपपद्यते । अयमर्थः पुरुषस्य चिद्रूपस्य सदैवाधिष्ठातृत्वेन व्यवस्थितस्य यदन्तरङ्गं ज्ञेयं निर्म्मलं सत्वं तस्यापि सदैवावस्थितत्वाद्येन येनार्थेनोपरक्तम्भवति तथाविधस्य दृश्यस्य सदैव चिच्छायासङ्क्रान्तिसद्भावस्तस्यां सत्यां सिद्धं सदा ज्ञातृत्वमिति न कदाचित्परिणामित्वाशङ्का । ननु च चित्तमेव सत्वोत्कर्षाद्यदि प्रकाशकं प्रकाशश्च स्वपरप्रकाशरूपत्वादात्मानमर्थम्प्रकाशयतीति तावतैव व्यवहारसमाप्तिः किम्ग्रहीत्रन्तरेणेत्त्याशङ्कामपनेतुमाह ।

† तच्चितं स्वाभासं दृश्यप्रकाशकम्भवति पुरुषवेद्यम्भवतीति यावत् कुतो दृश्यत्वाद्यत्किञ्चिद्दृश्यं तद्द्रष्टृवेद्यं यथा घटादि वेद्यञ्च चित्तं तस्मान्न स्वाभासम् ॥

‡ ननु च साध्याविशिष्टोऽयं हेतुर्दृश्यत्वमेव चित्तस्यासिद्धं किञ्च स्वबुद्धिसंवेदनद्वारेण पुरुषाणां हिताहितप्राप्तिपरिहाररूपाः प्रवृत्तयो दृश्यन्ते तथा हि क्रुद्धोऽहं भीतोऽहमत्र मे राग इत्येवमाद्या संविद् बुद्धेरवेदनान्नोपपन्नेत्त्याशङ्क्य निरसितुमाह ॥

एकसमये चोभयानवधारणम् ॥ १९ ॥

Aph. 19. Attention to two [objects] cannot take place simultaneously.

The cognition of an object is that which makes it capable of being regarded as such and such; viz., that such and such an object is cause of pain or pleasure; and the perception of understanding is the making possible the notion of "ego," in the form of pain and pleasure—i. e. painful or happy. These two kinds of process cannot take place simultaneously at the time of the perception of any object, for there is a contradiction; two contradictory processes being simultaneously impossible. Hence it is stated that as it is impossible to perceive both its own shape and an object at the same time, the understanding is not self-illuminative. Moreover as the two results of these two processes are not perceived; being directed towards the external object and not existing in itself, the perception of understanding [cognition] does not take place; consequently the result existing in the object takes place but not that which exists in itself [the soul.]*

But it may be said, Let the cognition not be self-perceptive, still it may be perceived by another cognition. He rejects this:-†

चित्तान्तरदृश्ये बुद्धिबुद्धेरतिप्रसङ्गः स्मृतिसङ्करश्च ॥ २० ॥

Aph. 20. If one perception be cognisable by another then there would be the further necessity of cognition of cognition and a confusion of recollection also would take place.

---

* अर्थस्य संवित्तिरिदं तया व्यवहारयोग्यतापादनम् । अयमर्थः सुखहेतुर्दुःखहेतुर्वेत्यर्थः । बुद्धेश्च संविदहमित्येवमाकारेण सुखदुःखरूपतया व्यवहारयोग्यतापादनम् । एवं विधश्च व्यापारद्वयमर्थप्रत्यक्षताकाले न युगपत् कर्तुं शक्यं विरोधाद्धि विरुद्धयोर्व्यापारयोर्युगपत् सम्भावोऽस्ति अत एकस्मिन् काले उभयस्य स्वरूपस्यार्थस्य चावधारयितुमशक्यत्वाच्च चित्तं स्वप्रकाशमित्युक्तम्भवति किञ्चैवंविधव्यापारद्वयंनिष्पाद्यफलद्वयस्यासंवेदनाद्बहिर्मुखतयैवार्थनिष्ठत्वेन चित्तस्य संवेदनाभावादर्थनिष्ठमेव फलं न स्वनिष्ठमित्यर्थः ।

† ननु माभूद्बुद्धेः स्वयंग्रहणं बुद्ध्यन्तरेण भविष्यतीत्याह ।

If one notion be perceived by another [and not by itself] then this notion also being unable to illuminate another notion, another cognition must be assumed for the perception of that, and another for the perception of that, and so on. Thus there would be a regress adinfinitum [of notions], and an object would not be perceived even in the whole life of a man. And while the knowledge is uncertain the object cannot be known. And confusion of recollections also would take place. On a notion taking place regarding a colour or taste, endless other notions would take place in order to perceive this. And when by the train of self-reproductive thought or mental impressions many recollections may be produced simultaneously, then as the notion of object is not terminated the perceptions and recollection taking place simultaneously, and it being impossible to know regarding what object the recollection took place, confusion of recollections would take place. And thus it would not be known that this recollection is conversant above colour, and this conversant about taste.*

Having raised the doubt that if the notion is not self-illuminative, and it is not perceived by another notion, how then is it that the processess in the form of "knowledge of an object" are spoken of? He states his own opinion :—†

चितेरप्रतिसङ्क्रमायास्तदाकारापत्तौ स्वबुद्धिसंवेदनम् ॥ २१ ॥

Aph. 21. The self-knowledge of cognition takes place when

---

* यदि हि बुद्धिर्बुद्ध्यन्तरेण वेद्येत तदा साऽपि बुद्धिः स्वयम्बुद्ध्यन्तरम्प्रकाशयितुमसमर्थेति तस्या ग्राहकं बुद्ध्यन्तरङ्कल्पनीयं तस्याप्यन्यदित्यनवस्थानात्पुरुषायुषेणाप्यर्थप्रतीतिर्न स्यान्नहि प्रतीतावप्रतीतायामर्थः प्रतीतो भवति । स्मृतिसङ्करश्च प्राप्नोति रूपे रसे वा समुत्पन्नायाम्बुद्धौ तद्ग्राहिकाणामनन्तानां बुद्धीनामुत्पत्तेर्बुद्धिजनितैः संस्कारैर्यदा युगपद्बह्व्यः स्मृतयः क्रियन्ते तदाऽर्थबुद्धेरपर्य्यवसानाद्बुद्धिस्मृतीनां युगपदुत्पत्तेः कस्मिन्नर्थे स्मृतिरियमुत्पन्नेति ज्ञातुमशक्यत्वात् स्मृतीनां सङ्करः स्यादितीयं रूपे स्मृतिरियं रसस्मृतिरिति न ज्ञायेत ॥

† ननु च बुद्धेः स्वप्रकाशत्वाभावे बुद्ध्यन्तरेण चासंवेदने कथमयं विषयसंवेदनरूपो व्यवहार इत्याशङ्क्य स्वसिद्धान्तमाह ॥

the intelligence [soul] which is non-transeunt acquires the shape of understanding.

The soul as being the thinking principle is intelligence, which is non-transeunt, that is, it has no transition or passing into another place; that is to say, it is not confounded with any other thing. The qualities [Purity, Passion and Darkness] in the modification characterised by the relation of secondary and primary pass over into the primary quality—*i. e.* they assume its proper nature as it were, or as the atoms in a state of transition give form to an object in the external world; not so the power of intellection, for that always remains uniform, inasmuch as it exists in itself. Hence when understanding in the vicinity of it [the soul] acquires the nature of intelligence, then it becomes like intelligence. And when the power of intelligence reflected upon the modification of understanding becomes undistinguishable from it—*i. e.* from the modification of the understanding, then the self-knowledge of understanding takes place.*

He now proceeds to state that the self-knowing understanding by its power of perceiving all objects is sufficient to accomplish all purposes:—†

द्रष्टृदृश्योपरक्तं चित्तं सर्वार्थम् ॥ २२ ॥

Aph. 22. The thinking principle (i. e. intellect) tinged by the knower and the knowable is the totality of objects.

---

* पुरुषश्चिद्रूपत्वाच्चितिः साऽप्रतिसंक्रमा न विद्यते प्रतिसंक्रमोऽन्यत्रगमनं यस्याः सा तथोक्ताऽन्येनासङ्कीर्णेतियावत् । यथा गुणा अङ्गाङ्गिभावलक्षणे परिणामेऽङ्गिनङ्गुणमुपसंक्रामन्ति तद्रूपतामिवापद्यन्ते यथा वा लोके परमाणवः प्रसरन्तो विषयमारूपयन्ति नैवाश्चितिः शक्तिस्तस्याः सर्वदैवैकरूपतया स्वप्रतिष्ठत्वेन व्यवस्थितत्वादतस्तत्सन्निधाने यदा बुद्धिस्तदाकारतामापद्यते चेतनेवोपजायते बुद्धिवृत्तिप्रतिसंक्रान्ता च यदा चिच्छक्तिर्बुद्धिवृत्त्याविशिष्टतया सम्पद्यते तदा बुद्धेः स्वस्यात्मनो वेदनम्भवतीत्यर्थः ॥

† इत्थं स्वसंविदितं चित्तं सर्वार्थग्रहणसामर्थ्येन सकलव्यवहारनिर्वाहक्षमम्भवतीत्याह ॥

The "knower" is the soul, tinged by it, means when the understanding has assumed its (the soul's) proper nature in contiguity with it. "Tinged by the knowable"—or the object means, when it (the mind) has assumed the modification in the shape of an object. Then that (the mind) itself becomes competent to perceive all objects. As only pure crystals, mirrors and the like are capable of receiving a reflection, so also the "quality of purity" not over-powered by "Passion" and "Darkness," being the pure is capable to receive the reflection of the intelligence [soul]; not so Passion and Darkness, for they are impure. Then the pure quality of purity, wherein the shapes of Passion and Darkness are subsided, being primary or not associated, exists always modifying in one form like a fixed apex of the lamp-flame, by its efficacy of receiving the reflection of intelligence (soul) until the attainment of liberation. As motion in iron is produced in the vicinity of a loadstone, in the same manner the manifestable intelligence of the quality of purity (understanding) is manifesaed in the proximity of the soul in the shape of intelligence.*

Hence in this system of philosophy there are two powers of intelligence, [1] the ever-rising, and [2] the manifestable. The ever-rising power of intelligence is the soul. And the manifestable power of intelligence is the "quality of Purity" (understanding) i. e. the intelligence manifestable in the con-

* द्रष्टापुरुषस्तेनोपरक्तं तत्सन्निधाने तद्रूपतामिव प्रापन्नं । विषयोपरक्तगृहीतविषयाकारपरिणामं यदा भवति तदा तदेव सर्वार्थग्रहणसमर्थं जायते । यथा निर्मलस्फटिकदर्पणाद्येव प्रतिबिम्बग्रहणसमर्थमेवं रजस्तमोभ्यामनभिभूतं सत्वं शुद्धत्वाच्चिच्छायाग्रहणसमर्थम्भवतीति न पुनरशुद्धत्वाद्रजस्तमसी । तदा न्यग्भूतरजस्तमोरूपमङ्गितया सत्वं निश्चलप्रदीपशिखाकारं सदैवैकरूपतया परिणममानं चिच्छायाग्रहणसामर्थ्यादामोक्षप्राप्तेरवतिष्ठते यथाऽयस्कान्तसन्निधाने लोहस्य चलत्वमाविर्भवत्येवञ्चिद्रूपपुरुषसन्निधानेसत्वस्याप्याभिव्यङ्ग्यमभिव्यज्यते चैतन्यम् । अतएवास्मिन्दर्शने द्वे शक्ती नित्योदिताऽभिव्यङ्ग्या च नित्योदिताचिच्छक्तिः पुरुषस्तत्सान्निधाने अभिव्यक्त्याऽभिव्यङ्ग्यञ्चैतन्यंसत्वमभिव्यङ्ग्या चिच्छक्तिः । तदेतच्चित्तमेव द्रष्टृदृश्योपरक्तं विषयविषयिनिर्भासं चेतनाचेतनस्वरूपापन्नं सर्वार्थमित्युच्यते ॥

tiguity of the soul—are ever-rising power. Therefore the understanding alone, tinged by the knower and knowable—appearing as object and subject—i. e. assuming the shape or nature of both intelligent and unintelligent, is called the totality of objects.

But it may be asked: The adumbration of a clear object of finite extension has been seen in a pure thing, like the shadow of the face in a looking glass: how does the adumbration of perfectly pure and infinite soul take place in the impure quality of Purity—understanding? To this it may be replied thus. You say this not knowing the nature of adumbration. The manifestation that takes place in the vicinity of the soul, of the manifestable power of intelligence residing in the "quality of Purity" is called adumbration; and of whatever kind the power of intelligence residing in the soul is, reflection of same takes place upon it. As for what has been said: How is the perfectly pure soul reflected upon the impure "quality of Purity?" this also is inconsistent. For the sun &c. is seen to be reflected in water &c. which is dificient in purity. And as for what has been said that reflection of an infinite does not take place, this too is inconsistent. For a reflection even of ether which is infinite is seen in a mirror, &c.*

---

* ननु प्रतिबिम्बनं निर्मलस्य नियतपरिमाणस्य निर्मले दृष्टं यथा मुखस्य दर्पणेषु अत्यन्तानिर्मलस्य व्यापकस्य च पुरुषस्यानिर्मलसत्वे कथम्प्रतिबिम्बनमुत्पद्यते। उच्यतेप्रतिबिम्बनस्य स्वरूपमनवगच्छता भवतेदमभ्यधायि। यैव सत्वगताया अभिव्यङ्ग्यायाश्चिच्छक्तेः पुरुषस्य सान्निध्येऽभिव्यक्तिः सैव प्रतिबिम्बनमुच्यते यादृशी च पुरुषगताचिच्छक्तिस्तच्छाया तत्राप्याविर्भवतीति, यदप्युक्तमत्यन्तानिर्मलः पुरुषः कथमनिर्मले सत्वे प्रातिसंक्रामतीति तदप्यनैकान्तिकम्। नैर्मल्यादपकृष्टेपि जलादावा दित्यादयः प्रतिसंक्रान्ताः समुपलभ्यन्ते॥

यदप्युक्तमपरिच्छिन्नस्य नास्ति प्रतिसंक्रान्तिरिति तदप्यनुपपन्नम्॥

व्यापकस्याप्याकाशस्य दर्पणादौ प्रतिसंक्रान्तिदर्शनात्॥ एवञ्च न कदाचिदनुपपत्तिः प्रतिबिम्बदर्शनस्य। ननु सात्विकपरिणामरूपे॥ बुद्धिसत्त्वे पुरुषसन्निधानाभिव्यङ्ग्या चिच्छक्तिर्बाह्याकारसंक्रान्ता पुरुषस्य सुखदुःखरूपो भोगइत्युक्तम्। तदनुपपन्नम्। तदेव चित्तसत्वं॥ प्रकृतावपरिणतायाः कथं सम्भवति किमर्थञ्च तस्याः

Thus there is no contradiction in the observation of such reflection. But then it may be objected that it has been stated that the power of intelligence which is manifestable in contiguity with the soul in the understanding—i. e. the modification of the "quality of Purity," reflected in the form of an external object is called the soul's experience in the shape of pleasure or pain. This also is unreasonable. For how is that understanding possible when nature is not modified, and to

---

परिणामः । अथोच्यताम्, पुरुषस्यार्थोऽपि भोगसम्पादनतया कर्तव्यमतः पुरुषार्थकर्तव्यतया तस्या युक्त एव परिणामः । नन्नोपपन्नम् । पुरुषार्थकर्तव्यताया एवानुपपत्ते । पुरुषार्थो मया कर्तव्य इत्येवं विधोऽध्यवसायः पुरुषार्थकर्तव्यतयोच्यते जडायाश्चप्रकृतेः कथम्प्रकृतमेवैवंविधोऽध्यवसायः । आस्तिचेदध्यवसायः कथं जडत्वम् । अत्रोच्यते । अनुलोमप्रतिलोमलक्षणपरिणामद्वये सहजं शक्तिद्वयमस्ति ॥ तदेवपुरुषार्थकर्तव्यतयोच्यते सा चाचेतनाया अपि प्रकृतेः सहजैव तत्र महदादिमहाभूतपर्य्यन्तोऽस्या बहिर्मुखतयाऽनुलोमः परिणामः पुनः स्वकारणानुप्रवेशद्वारेणास्तान्तः प्रतिलोमः परिणामः इत्थं च पुरुषभोगसमाप्तेः सहजशक्तिद्वयक्षयात् कृतार्था प्रकृतिर्न पुनः परिणाममारभते । एवंविधायाश्च पुरुषार्थकर्तव्यतायां जडायाः प्रकृतेनकदाचिदनुपपत्तिः । ननु यदीदृशीशक्तिः सहजैव प्रधानस्यास्ति तत्किमर्थं तदर्थिभिर्मोक्षाय यत्नः क्रियते । मोक्षस्य चानर्थनीयत्वे तदुपदेशकस्य शास्त्रस्याप्यानर्थक्यम् । उच्यते । योऽयम्प्रकृतिपुरुषयोरनादिर्भोग्य भोक्तृत्वभावलक्षणः सम्बन्धस्तामिन् सति व्यक्तचेतनायाः प्रकृतेः कर्तृत्वाभिमानाद् दुःखानुभवे सति कथमियमात्यन्तिकी दुःखनिवृत्तिर्मम स्यादिति भवत्येवाध्यवसायोऽतोदुःखनिवृत्युपायोपदेकशास्त्रोपदेशापेक्षाऽस्त्येव प्रधानस्य । तथाभूतमेव कर्मात्मरूपं बुद्धिसत्वं शास्त्रोपदेशस्य विषयः । दर्शनान्तरेष्वप्येवंविध एवाविद्यास्वभावः शास्त्रेऽधिक्रियते स च मोक्षाय यतमान एवंविध एव शास्त्रोपदेशं सहकारिणमपेक्ष्य मोक्षाख्यम्फलमासादयति सर्वाण्येव च कार्य्याणि प्राप्तायां समग्रायां सामग्र्यामात्मत्नं लभन्ते ॥

अस्य च प्रतिलोमपरिणामद्वारेणोत्पाद्यस्य मोक्षाख्यस्य कार्य्यस्येदृश्येव सामग्री प्रमाणेन निश्चिता प्रकारान्तरेणानुपपत्तेरतस्तां विना कथम्भवितुमर्हति अतःस्थितमेतत्संक्रान्तविषयोपरागमभिव्यक्तचिच्छायं बुद्धिसत्वं विषयनिश्चयद्वारेण समग्रां लोकयात्रां निर्वाहयतीति । एवंविधमेवचित्तं परे भ्रान्ताः स्वसंवेदनं चित्तं चित्तमात्रञ्जगदित्येवं ब्रुवाणाः प्रतिबोधिता भवन्ति ॥

what purpose would such modification take place? To this we may reply: "Nature" has to provide fruition for the soul, therefore inasmuch as she must afford the aim of the soul, her modification is necessary. This is not right. For it is not possible that she should compass the end of the soul. For Nature's determination to effect the end of the soul is called the provision of the aim of the soul. How is such a resolution compatible with an unintelligent "nature," and if there is a resolution in nature, how then is she unintelligent? To this it is replied: There are two innate powers in the two modifications characterised by successiveness and regressiveness, the same are called the fulfilment of the end of the soul: and these modifications are easy for unintellignt nature also. Its [the nature's] successive modification is from understanding &c. up to the gross elements, she being then directed outwards; again by means of subsiding into the respective courses, the modification which is called regressive modification recedes into egotism. Hence the experience of the soul being completed, and in consequence of the cessation of the two innate powers, nature having realised her end undergoes no further modification.

The necessity of providing the end of the soul being as afore-stated, there is no contradiction involved in the unintelligence of nature. But it may be asked that if such a power does naturally exist in nature, why do those seekers of it make efforts to attain emancipation, and if the liberation is not aimed at, then the system also which lays down precepts for it must be declared useless. This is replied to thus: The eternal relation of the soul and nature characterised as the relation of experiencer and experienced. being admitted, the fact of the intelligence of nature follows, and then there being an experience of pain in consequence of her supposing herself an agent, the resolution: How shall absolute cessation of pain take place in me? takes place; hence the system that lays down precepts for the means of removing pain is required by nature. Such an understanding [the modified state of the quality of purity] in the shape of active soul is the object of the instruction by this system. In other philosophical systems also such a habit of nature has been made the subject [that is, has been described]. And this endeavouring to attain emancipation, having found such an auxiliary as the precepts of the system, realises the effect or result called emancipation. All effects take their form [i. e. are produced] on receiving their whole apparatus: The apparatus of this effect called emancipation, which is producible merely by regressive modification, has been proved to be the same [as stated] for it cannot be produced in another way. Therefore how can it take place without that? Consequently it is established that the "quality of purity" in the understanding tinged by the object and in which the shadowing of the intelligence [soul] has taken place, carries on all processes of the universe. Certain erroneous thinkers who suppose their own mind self-conscious, and maintain that the whole universe is pure mind, are hereby informed that the nature of the mind is such as we have described it.

But it may be questioned. If all purposes are accomplished by the mind thus described, why then should an experiencer be acknowledged? With reference to this doubt he declares as follows :—*

तदसंख्येयवासनाभिश्चित्रमपि परार्थं संहत्यकारित्वात् ॥२३॥

Aph. 23. Though variegated by innumerable impressions (mental deposits) it exists for the sake of another, because it operates in association.

It—the mind—or understanding, though variegated—assuming various forms by innumerable mental impressions, exists for the sake of another—that is, it accomplishes the aim of another—i. e. of the governing principle, which aim is characterised as experiencer, experience, and emancipation. If we be asked why, we reply that it is because it operates in performing

---

* ननु यद्येवंविधादेव चित्तात्सकलव्यवहारनिष्पत्तिः कथम्प्रमाणशून्योद्रष्टाऽभ्युपगत इत्याशङ्कायां द्रष्टुः प्रमाणमाह ॥

the aim in association—conjointly—i. e. together with another; whatever performs operations in association with another is observed to exist for the sake of another as a seat, or bed; and the qualities of purity, Passion and Darkness assuming modification in the shape of understanding operate in association; hence they exist for the sake of another. And that other is the soul.*

He now proceeds to ascertain what isolation i. e. the aim of the system, is, by the ten following aphorisms.†

विशेषदर्शिन आत्मभावभावनाविनिवृत्तिः ॥ २४ ॥

Aph. 24. The cessation of the (false) notion regarding the soul takes place in him who knows the difference.

Thus the difference between soul and mind being proved, whoever observes their peculiarity, that the one is different from the other, the idea of such a one knowing the proper nature of the mind, as to the understanding being tne soul, ceases. That is to say, the false notion that the mind itself is the knower and experiencer is removed.‡

What happens when this has taken place? To this he replies:—§

तदा विवेकनिम्नं कैवल्यप्राग्भारं चित्तम् ॥ २५ ॥

A*ph.* 25. Then the mind becomes deflected towards discrimination and bowed down towards [or by] Isolation.

---

* तदेव चित्तं सङ्ख्यातुमशक्याभिर्वासनाभिश्चित्रमपि नानारूपमपि परार्थं परस्य स्वामिनो भोक्तृभोगापवर्गलक्षणमर्थं साधयतीति कुतः संहत्यकारित्वात संहत्य सम्भूय मिलित्वाऽर्थक्रियाकारित्वात् यद्यत्संहत्यार्थक्रियाकारि तत्परार्थं दृष्टं यथा शयनासनादि । सत्वरजस्तमांसि च चित्तलक्षणपरिणामभांजि संहत्याकारीणि यश्च परः स पुरुषः ॥

† इदानीं शास्त्रफलं कैवल्यं निर्णेतुं दशभिः सूत्रैरुपक्रमते ॥

‡ एवं सत्वपुरुषयोरन्यत्वे साधिते यतस्तयोर्विशेषम्पश्यति । अयमस्मादन्य इत्येवं रूपं विशेषं जानाति । तस्य विज्ञातचित्तस्वरूपस्य चित्ते याआत्मभावभावना साविनिवर्तते । चित्तमेवकर्तृज्ञातृ भोक्तृ इत्यभिमानो निवर्तते इत्यर्थः ॥

§ तस्मिन् सति किम्भवतीत्याह ॥

The mind of the ascetic which was inclined towards Ignorance, and directed towards, i. e. bowed down towards, objects, and had the experience of objects for its fruit, is now turned towards discrimination, i. e. comes into the right path and is directed inwards "Isolation"—i. e. has Isolation for its result, or is passessed of the germ of Isolation.*

Now by describing the causes of the impediments, which occur to the mind flowing in [the path of] discrimination, he mentions the means of abandoning those [obstacles]:—†

तच्छिद्रेषु प्रत्ययान्तराणि संस्कारेभ्यः ॥ २६ ॥

Aph. 26. In the intervals thereof other thoughts arise from the self-continuant impressions.

Different thoughts characterised by non-abstraction, which arise in the intervals in the vacuities in the mind of the ascetic abiding in meditation, spring up in the shape of "I" "mine" &c. from the former impressions of the mind produced by the perceptions of non-abstraction, though now extenuated.‡ Therefore such thoughts must be abandoned by extirpating their causes. This is what is to be stated.

He now states that the methods of abandoning these are as they have been described before:§

हानं तेषां क्लेशवदुक्तम् ॥ २७ ॥

Aph. 27. The means of the avoidance of these are explained to be as in the case of the affiictions.

---

* यदस्याज्ञाननिम्नं बहिर्मुखं विषयोपभोगफलंचित्तमासीत्तदिदानीं विवेकनिम्नं विवेकमार्गमंतर्मुखंकैवल्यप्राग्भारं कैवल्यफलं कैवल्यप्रारम्भं वा सम्पद्यत इति ॥

† अस्मिंश्च विवेकवाहिनिचित्ते येऽन्तरायाः प्रादुर्भवन्तिः तेषां हेतुप्रतिपादनद्वारेण त्यागोपायमाह ॥

‡ तस्मिन् समाधौ स्थितस्य छिद्रेष्वन्तरालेषु यानि प्रत्ययान्तराणि व्युत्थानरूपाणि ज्ञानानि तानि प्राग्भवेभ्यो व्युत्थानाऽनुभवजेभ्यः संस्कारेभ्योऽहं ममेत्येवंरूपाणि क्षीयमाणेभ्योऽपि प्रभवन्ति । अंतःकरणोच्छित्तिद्वारेण तेषां हानं कर्तव्यमित्युक्तं भवति ॥

§ हानोपायश्च पूर्वमेवोक्तइत्याह ॥

The abandonment of the train of the self-reproductive thoughts must be made in the same manner as the methods described before for the avoidance of afflictions, ignorance &c. That is, as they [the afflictions] being consumed in the fire of knowledge do not acquire germination again in the soil of the mind, like burnt seeds, so also the train of the self-productive thoughts [does not continue.]*

He mentions the method of that kind by which, when meditation has been consolidated by the non-production of other thoughts, any particular kind of ascetic attains excellence in meditation.†

प्रसंख्यानेऽप्यकुसीदस्य सर्वथा विवेकख्यातेर्धर्म्ममेघः समाधिः ॥ २८ ॥

Aph. 28. If the ascetic is not desirous of fruit [or is not inert] even when the perfect knowledge has been attained, [then] the meditation, [technically called] Dharma-Megha, cloud of virtue, takes place from the entire discriminative knowledge.

"Perfect knowledge" means, knowing the nature differing from each other of all elements in whatever order they exist; even, when this knowledge has taken place if the ascetic has not the desire for the fruit, or is not inactive, then, by means of the discriminative knowledge being entirely consolidated on non-production of other thoughts, the meditation, that is called "Dharma-Megha" cloud of virtue is attained. It is called the cloud of virtue, because it irrigates or waters the highest virtue, which is called "ashukla-krisha" neither white nor black, and is the provider of the chief aim of the soul.‡

---

* यथा क्लेशनामविद्यादीनां हानं पूर्व्वमुक्तं तथा संस्काराणामपि कर्तव्यं यथा तेज्ञानाग्निस्पृष्टा दग्धबीजकल्पा न पुनश्चित्तभूमौ प्ररोहं लभन्ते तथा संस्कारा अपि ॥

† एवम्प्रत्ययान्तरानुदये स्थिरीभूते समाधौ यादृशस्य योगिनः प्रकर्षसमाधिप्राप्तिर्भवति तथाविधमुपायमाह ॥

‡ प्रसंख्यानं यावतां तत्वानां यथाक्रमं व्यवस्थितानाम्परस्परविलक्षणस्वरूपपरिभावनं तस्मिन् सत्यप्यकुसीदस्य फलमलिप्सोः प्रत्ययान्तराणामनुदये सर्वप्रकार विवेकख्यातेः परिशेषाद्धर्म्ममेघः समाधिर्भवति । प्रकृष्टमशुक्लकृष्णम्परमपुरुषार्थसाधकं मेहति सिञ्चतीति धर्ममेघः ॥

What results from that? To this he replies.*

ततः क्लेशकर्म्मनिवृत्तिः ॥ २९ ॥

Aph. 29. Therefrom takes place removal of the afflictions and works.

"Therefrom" from the meditation called "Dharma-Megha," springs up the removal of the afflictions, from Ignorance up to the tenacity [of mundane existence] and of the works of three kinds, differing as white &c. [*i. e.*, white, black, and neither white nor black] by means of the extirpation of their respective antecedent causes from the arising of the knowledge.†

What takes place after these have been removed? To this it is replied —‡

तदा सर्वावरणमलापेतस्यज्ञानस्यानन्त्याज्ज्ञेयमल्पम् ॥ ३० ॥

Aph. 30. Then from infiniteness of the knowledge free from the impurity of all its obscurations, the knowable appears small.

"Then" after the removal of the afflictions and works. The knowable becomes small, *i. e.* the object of little estimation or calculation, because knowledge, freed from these, that is void of the obscurations, *i. e.* afflictions [Ignorance &c.] which obscure the mind, becomes infinite, unlimited, like the sky when the clouds have departed. That is the ascetic knows all that is knowable without any trouble.§

He states what takes place after this :—‖

ततः कृतार्थानाम्परिणामक्रमसमाप्तिर्गुणानाम् ॥ ३१ ॥

* तस्माद्धर्म्ममेघात्किम्भवतीत्याह ॥

† ततो धर्म्ममेघात्क्लेशानामविद्यादीनामभिनिवेशान्तानां कर्म्मणाञ्चशुक्लादिभेदेन त्रिविधानाञ्ज्ञानोदयात्पूर्वपूर्वकारणनिवृत्त्या निवृत्तिर्भवतीत्यर्थः ॥

‡ निवृत्तेषु तेषु किम्भवतीत्याह ॥

§ आव्रियते चित्तमेभिरित्यावरणानि क्लेशास्तेभ्योऽपेतस्य तद्विरहितस्य ज्ञानस्य गतघनगगननिभस्यानन्त्यादनवच्छेदाज्ज्ञेयमल्पमल्पगणनास्पदम्भवति । अक्लेशेनैव सर्वं जानातीत्यर्थः ॥

‖ ततः किमित्याह ॥

Aph. 31. Thereupon takes place the termination of the succession of the modification of the qualities which have done what was to be done [or which have realised their end.]

"Thereupon" after this takes place the termination, *i. e.* complete cessation, *i. e.* non-production of the succession, to be described hereafter, of modification, in succession and regression up to the attainment of the aim of the soul, characterised by their relation of existing [qualities] as primary and secondary, of the qualities, *i. e.* "Purity" "Passion" and "Darkness" which have done what was to be done, *i. e.* which have effected the soul's aim, characterised as experience and emancipation.*

He now defines the order above mentioned.†

क्षणप्रतियोगी परिणामापरान्तनिर्ग्राह्यः क्रमः ॥ ३२ ॥

Aph. 32. The order is counterpart of the moment, perceptible in the latter end of the modification.

"Moment" is a very small portion of time; the counterpart of that, means, perceptible in the latter end of the modification [of time, or moment] differing from one [preceding] moment. That is whatever is perceived by calculative cognition after the moments have been perceived, the same thing is called the order of moments. It cannot be perceived if the moments are not perceived.‡

He now states the general nature of "Isolation"—the result.§

पुरुषार्थशून्यानाम्प्रतिप्रसवः कैवल्यंस्वरूपप्रतिष्ठा वाचितिशक्तिरिति॥३३॥

---

* कृतो निष्पादितो भोगापवर्गलक्षणः पुरुषार्थः प्रयोजनं यैस्ते कृतार्था गुणाः सत्वरजस्तमांसि तेषाम्परिणाम आपुरुषार्थसमाप्तेरनुलोम्येन प्रातिलोम्येन वाङ्गाङ्गिभावस्थितिलक्षणस्तस्य योऽसौ क्रमो वक्ष्यमाणस्तस्य परिसमाप्तिरपुनरुद्भव इत्यर्थः॥

† क्रमस्योक्तस्य लक्षणमाह ॥

‡ क्षणोऽल्पीयान् कालस्तस्य योऽसौ क्रम एकक्षणविलक्षणपरिणामापरान्तनिर्ग्राह्योऽनुभूतेषु क्षणेषु पश्चात् सङ्कलनबुद्ध्या यो गृह्यते स क्षणानांक्रम उच्यते। नह्यननुभूतेषु क्षणेषु क्रमः परिज्ञातुं शक्यः ॥

Aph. 33. The re-absorption of those [qualities] void of the aim of the soul, or the abiding of the power of intelligence in its own nature, is Isolation.

The re-absorption is the regressive modification of the qualities which have consummated the ends of the soul characterised as fruition and emancipation. On the consummation thereof there is non-production of modification; in other words, the state of the intellectual faculty, on the cessation of identity [with objects,] abiding in its own proper nature, is called "Isolation."‡

---

§ इदानीम्फलभूतस्य कैवल्यस्यासाधारणं स्वरूपमाह ॥

‡ समाप्तभोगापवर्गलक्षणपुरुषार्थानां गुणानां यः प्रतिप्रसवः प्रतिलोमपरिणामः समाप्तौ विकारानुद्भवो यद्वा वा चिच्छक्तेर्वृत्तिः सारूप्यनिवृत्तौ वृत्तिमात्रेऽवस्थानं तत्कैवल्यमुच्यते ॥ इति ॥

END.

APPENDIX.

General extracts, selected from various books, are appended to this treatise, with the object of showing how all Eastern and other thinkers agree on those vital questions of Life and Death, which have perplexed the greatest minds of Europe and America. When we find that "Doctors disagree" in the West, we turn with relief to the philosophical beliefs which originated in this country and were unanimously adopted by the sages of China, Persia, Arabia, Egypt, Greece, &c. &c. These beliefs, though supplanted more or less by the materialistic dogmas of Europe, have still lived through all changes, and we trust the time is come to bring them forth more vividly than ever before the public. It may be said, passingly, that the Himàlayan Brothers, the "Adepts", have proved an unrecognised but all important factor in any real spiritual progress both in India and elsewhere. It is a hopeful sign of the times that the utility of the systems of philosophy, inaugurated by Patanjali, Kapila, Màha Muni *Shankaráchárya* and other philosophers of the East, are more and more acknowledged, and taken advantage of by people to whom Western thought has ceased to be all in all; and it may fairly be inferred that India will once more assume the leading position in the world of Metaphysical truth, and achieve a spiritual renaissance of the world.

(*Extracts from tke Vishnu Smriti,*) *Chap. XCVII.*

1 Sitting with the feet stretched out and crossed so as to touch the thighs, with the right hand (stretched out and) resting upon the left, with the tongue fixed in the palate and without bringing the one row of teeth in contact with the other, with the eyes directed to the

tip of the nose, and without glancing at any of the (four) quarters of the sky, free from fear, and with composure, let him meditate upon (Purusha), who is separate from the twenty-four entities.*

2 He who is eternal, beyond the cognisance of the senses, destitute of qualities, not concerned with sound, tangibility, form, savour or odour, knowing everything, of immense size.

3 He who pervades everything, and who is devoid of form.

4 Whose hands, and feet are everywhere, whose eyes, head, and face are everywhere, and who is able to apprehend everything with all the senses.

5 Thus let him meditate.

6 If he remains absorbed in such meditation for a year, he obtains the accomplishment of Yoga (concentration of the thought and union with the Supreme).

7 If he is unable to fix his mind upon the being destitute of form, he must meditate successively on earth,

---

* The twenty-four (it should be twenty-five) entities are stated in the Sánkhya to consist of the root-principle (Múlaprakriti), the seven productions evolved from it (Vikritayah), the sixteen productions evolved from these, and Purusha (the soul), who is neither producer nor produced.

(1) The first "root-principle" is composed of the three qualities in equipoise: sattwa, rájasa, and tamas. The most accurate rendering of these terms is "pure, unimpassioned virtue", "passion", and, "depravity inclining to evil".

(2) The "great entity" (Mahat) is the cause of apprehension.

(3) The "self-consciousness" (Ahankára) is the cause of referring all objects to self.

(4) The "subtile elementary particles" (tanmátrás) are identical with sound, tangibility, form, taste and odour.

(5) The eleven senses, i. e., the organs of perception and action: the nose, eye, skin, tongue and ear, are the five organs of perception; hand, feet, arms, parts of generation, and tongue, are the five organs of action; and the mind.

(6) The five grosser elements (ether, air, fire, water, and earth) are productions (from the former entities).

Purusha, who is neither producer nor produced, is the twenty-fifth entity.

water, fire, air, ether, mind, intellect, self, the indistinct (avyakta), and Purusha: having fully apprehended one, he must dismiss it from his thoughts and fix his mind upon the next one in order.

8 In this way let him arrive at meditation upon Purusha.

9 If unable to follow this method also, he must meditate on Purusha shining like a lamp in his heart, as in a lotus turned upside down.

10 If he cannot do that either, he must meditate upon Bhagwat Vásudeva (Vishnu), who is adorned with a diadem, with ear-rings, and with bracelets, who has the (mystic mark) Shrivatsa, and a garland of wood-flowers on his breast, whose aspect is pleasing, who has four arms, who holds the shell, the discus, the mace, and the lotus-flower, and whose feet are supported (and worshipped) by the earth.

11 Whatever he meditates upon, that is obtained by a man (in future-existence): such is the mysterious power of meditation.

12 Therefore must he dismiss every thing perishable from his thoughts and meditate upon what is imperishable only.

13 There is nothing imperishable except Purusha.

14 Having become united with him (through constant meditation), he obtains final liberation.

15 Because the Great Lord pervades the whole universe (pura), as he is lying there (shete), therefore is he denominated Purusha by those who reflect upon the real nature (of the Supreme spirit).

16 In the first part and the latter part of the night must a man bent on contemplation constantly and with fixed attention meditate upon Purusha Vishnu, who is destitute of (the three) qualities (Sattva, rajas, tamas) and the twenty-five entities.

17 He (or it) is composed of the entities, beyond the cognisance of the senses, distinct from all the (other) entities, free from attachment (to the producer, &c.) supporting every thing, devoid of qualities and yet enjoying (or witnessing the effect of) qualities.

18 It exists without and within created beings (enjoyed and as enjoyer), and in the shape both of inmoveable things (such as trees and stones) and of moveable things (such as water or fire) it is undistinguishable on account of its subtility; it is out of reach (imperceptible), and yet is found in the heart.

19 It is not distinct from creation, and yet distinct from it in outward appearance; it annihilates and produces by turns (the world), which consists of everything that has been, that will be, and that is.

20 It is termed the light of the sidereal bodies, and enemy of darkness (ignorance), it is knowledge, it should be known, it may be understood (by meditation), it dwells in every man's heart.

21 Thus the 'field,' knowledge (or meditation) and what should be known, have been concisely declared; that faithful adherent of mine, who makes himself acquainted therewith, becomes united to me in Spirit.

Buddhist Scriptures from the Chinese philosophy of the Tian-Tai School by Mr. Samuel Beal.)

The sytem of Chi-kai was founded on the principles advocated in the Tchong-Lun. (Pránуamúla Shástra Tika) written by Nagarjuna, which rejects all antitheses, and endeavours to find the central truth or central method in the conciliation of antinomies. The true method is found neither in book-learning nor external practice, nor ecstatic contemplation, neither in the exercise of Reason, nor the reveries of fancy; but there is a middle condition, a system which includes all and rejects none, to which all others gravitate, and in which alone the soul can be satisfied. The term "Chi-kwan" by which the *Tian Tai* system is generally known, has been sometimes translated by the words "fixed contemplation;" but, as we shall find from the work itself the true meaning of the phrase is "knowledge and meditation," implying that both the one and the other are necessary for arriving at perfection. This idea is also plainly referred to in the Dhammapada (372), "Without knowledge "there is no meditation, without meditation there is no know-"ledge; he who has knowledge and meditation is near "Nirvâna" (vide Max Muller's version of Buddha Ghosha's Parables, CLX).

With reference to the phrase "Chi-kwan", the perface to the work, viz, the "Siau-chi-kwan" written by Chi-kai in the Siu-shan Temple in the Tian-tai hills, and reprinted from the Canon in A. C. 1798, states that it means precisely the same as "ten-hwui" (absolute wisdom), or tsih-chau (passive-splendour, a common phrase for the supreme condition of "Nirvána", a condition which admits of effulgency united with passivity), or as "mingtsing" (brightness and rest). [From this we gather that "Chi-kwan" denotes that condition of being, which admits of a union of knowledge and meditative repose.]

Chi-kai begins his work with the following well known Gatha.

"Scrupulously avoiding all wicked actions,
Reverently performing all virtuous ones,
Purifying this intention from all selfish desire,
Is the doctrine of all the Buddhas".

(He then proceeds)—"Although a man may earnestly desire to enter the path to "Nirvana", and studiously pursue the directions of the various discourses (*Shastras*) on the subject, he may nevertheless miss altogether attaining his desired aim. Now the two laws contained in the idea of "Chi-kwan" are simply these: that which is spoken of as "Chi" (fixity) is the first mode (or gate to Nirvana), and consists in overcoming all the entanglements of mind; that which is called "Kwan" (meditation) is the Rest which follows or accompanies the separation of mind from all external influences. Once "fixed," a man will tenderly foster the good principles of knowledge (heart-knowledge). Possessed of true meditation, a man has gained the mysterious art of liberating his spiritual nature (his soul). The first is the excellent cause of absolute mental repose, whilst the second is the fruitful result of Supreme Wisdom. A man perfect in Wisdom and in meditation, he is throughly provided by his own advantage to advantage the world. Hence, the *Lotus of the Law* says :—"Buddha, self-established as the great vehicle, was thus himself an attainable Law (for others), himself adorned with the might of meditation and wisdom, by these was enabled to save mankind.

So these two powers are like the two wheels of a chariot, or the two wings of a bird; a man who practises himself in both, forthwith destroys the power of error; hence the Sutra says :—"If a man with a one-sided aim acquire merit by meditation, and do not learn wisdom, he is called 'foolish'; and if he learn wisdom without practising meditation, he is called 'deluded'." And another Sutra says :—" A Shravaka, because he has great power of self-composure, does not necessarily arrive at (see) the Nature of Buddha; nor does Shi-chu Bodhisatwa, although by the power of wisdom he may arrive at (or see) the Nature of Buddha necessarily understand the Nature of all the Budha Tathagatas". But whoever has completely mastered both the practice of meditation and the acquirement of wisdom, that man has accomplished his great aim, and shall certainly arrive at Nirvana.

Now, for the purpose of assisting those who wish to practise these two principles ("Chi-kwan"), we have put together the following brief sections :—

I Accomplishment of external means. These are five. (1) Observing the Precepts (i. e., the ten commandments,) purely and perfectly : there are three classes of persons who keep the Precepts, who are not the same.

(a) If a man, before becoming a disciple of Buddha, has not been guilty of the five sins, murder, adultery, theft, slander (falsehood of any sort), drunkenness, and, after meeting with a Teacher, has adopted the five additional Rules and taken refuge in Buddha, the Law, and the Church; if such a man having left his house and received ordination, persuade others to follow his example, and himself live blamelessly in his profession, this man belongs to the superior class of those who observe the Precepts. Such a man, engaging in the practice of "chi-kwan", will arrive at the condition of Buddha as easily as a pure garment is dyed by the dyer.

(b) The second class of persons are those who having received ordination, continue in their duty as to chief matters, but yet offend in some minor points, and so have occasion constantly to practise the rules of penance; these are like cloth covered with defilement, which must be washed before it is dyed.

(c) The third class of persons are those who, after ordination, have transgressed wilfully. Under the Little Vehicle there was no room for such persons to repent; but, under the system of the Great Vehicle, they may recover themselves.

Those, who, having sinned thus, seek for Recovery by Repentance, must observe the following rules :—

(a) They must revive their faith in rewards and punishments.

(b) They must encourage in themselves a feeling of deep shame for their sin.

(c) They must be filled with a sense of reverence and fear.

(d) They must desire to destroy occasions of sins; or, as the Law says, "shape their conduct according to Religion".

(e) They must confess their sins without reserve.

(f) They must cut off all sinful inclinations (or heart-leanings to sin).

(g) They must excite in themselves a jealously for Religion (the Law, or desire to protect the Law).

(h) They must promote in themselves a desire to see all men arrive at salvation.

(i) They must constantly invoke "all the Buddhas".

(j) They must consider the "deadness" (unproductiveness) of the nature of sin.

If a man is able to observe these ten Rules, and at the same time attend scrupulously to the external duties of Religion—such as adorning the altar, cleaning his person, and clothed in pure garments, scattering flowers and burning incense in honor of the three gems, as the Law directs—thus doing, for a week, for three weeks, for a month, three months, till a whole year be past—finding then that he has thoroughly repented of his crime, and that the hold of evil is utterly destroyed in him, then he is Fixed (i. e. restored to purity). But by what marks may he know that the power of evil is destroyed? If the disciple, at the time when he has thus repented with all his heart, realise the vanity (light profit) of earthly engagements, (of body and heart), obtain propitious dreams, and moreover experience (observe) the various indications of inward spiritual tokens, and awake to a sense of the development of virtuous principles and, as he sits in contemplation, perceive his body to be as a cloud or a shadow, and thus gradually attain to the limits of the *dhyanas*, and if again he thoroughly understand the character of the enlightened condition of mind which exhibits itself by immediate recognition of sacred truth, so that on opening the Scriptures their true meaning at once flashes into the heart, and in consequence of this condition he enjoys true Peace, by such proofs as these he may assuredly know that the root of his sin, which led to transgression and spiritual deadness is utterly destroyed. From this time forth, resolutely holding to the Laws of purity called Sîla (perfect compliance with all the rules of the Vinaya), he may then practise the way of Samadhi, (i. e., prepare himself for arriving at spiritual perfection), as the torn and dirty robe, when mended and washed, is again fit for use.

But, if a man has broken the great commandments, and so fear prevents him from arriving at "fixed contemplation" (complete abstraction of mind), and he does not follow the directions ot the Sacred Books in framing his religious life; yet if he be only sensible of a profound reverence in the presence of the three Gems, (the Tri-ratna—Buddha, the Law, the Church), search out and bring to light his former sins, cut off the secret springs of it that entwine his heart, and, as he sits in reflection continually, realize the nature of sin as being empty (vain or dead), and so concentrate his thoughts on the Buddhas of the ten religions, (i. e., "all the Buddhas," or the "Supreme"), and when he breaks off from his meditations, immediately resorts with perfect intention to the burning of incense, and bodily worship, and with contrite heart recite the precepts and intone the sacred Books of the Great conveyance, and so the obstacles that prevented his religious advancement,and the causes of his grievous sin, be gradually overcome and destroyed, because of this, arriving at purity, the power of contemplation will expand and increase. Hence the Sutra called the Miau-shing-teng (Surangama Samâdhi) says: "If a man, because he has transgressed the greater commandments, be filled with fear, and desiring to destroy the power of sin, seek to do so by the practice of intense thought, which, after all, being imperfect, is ineffectual to the desired end, such a man ought to take up his abode in a desert spot (live in a pansal,) and, holding his mind in check, continne to sit and recite the Scriptures of the Great Vehicle, till he find the entire weight of sin removed and destroyed, and the various powers of abstract contemplation, self-originated, come into his possession."

II. The second external means relates to clothing and food. Now, with respect to the first, there are three rules. (1) That which relates to the one garment worn by the great teachers of the Snowy Mountains (the school of the Haimavatas ?), barely sufficient to cover the body, (who) by excluding themselves from the society of men, aimed to perfect themselves in the virtue of endurance (patience, *kshanti*). (2) That which relates to Kasyapa, or the school of Kasyapiyas, which is the same as that of the Aryastha viras, from whom the Haimavatas proceeded), who always observed the Dhuta rules about dress, which require that only such garments shall be used as are made from cloth defiled in various ways, and of these only three of a prescribed length. (3) That which relates to those who live in very cold countries, and who are of imperfect powers of endurance—to these Tathagata allowed other garments besides the three, and other things in strict moderation.

With respect to food there are four rules. (1) That which relates to the great professors of the higher order, who live in mountain depths remote from men, and feed on vegetables and fruits according to their season. (2) That which relates to those who continually observe the Dhutā rules in reference to the food they have begged. (3) The food allowed to an Aranyaka (hermit) to be received from his Danapati (patron). (4) The pure food allowed to the priesthood when living in community.

III. The third external means relates to the possession of a pure place of abode. With refernce to the word "hien" as signifying a place of abode, (pansala ?), it is a place where no business is transacted, and where there are no contentions or disputes; so it is called a peaceable place; there are three descriptions of such places, (1) in some deep mountain ravine, remote from human intercourse; (2) in some forest resort, (Aranya) where the Dhuta rules may be followed; this place must be at least three or four li (half a mile or more) from a village, so as to be removed from any sound of worldly business or contention; (3) in a spot at a distance from a place where laymen live, in the midst of a quiet Sangharama; all these places are called peaceable and calm abodes.

IV. The fourth external means relates to freedom from all worldly concerns and influences. There are four things to be avoided under this head. (1) To desist from all share in ruling or governing a people, so as not to incur any responsibility connected with the mode of discharging the trust. (2) To desist from all worldly friendships, and all social or family connections. (3) Not to follow any trade or art, whether of medicine, sorcery or other persuasion. (4) To desist fram all professional engagements connected with worldly learning, discussion, instruction, and so on.

V. The fifth external means relates to the promotion of all virtuous knowledge, of which there are three divisions. (1) Taking care of all religious books. (2) Endeavouring to promote agreement amongst religious persons, so that there shall be no division or confusion. (3) Endeavouring to transmit and inculcate, by every expedient of mind and action, the true principles of virtuous knowledge.

We have thus briefly glanced at the five sorts of preparatory observances requisite for the final acquisition of Chi-Kwan.

2. ON CHIDING THE EVIL DESIRES.

These evil desires are five : every one who enters on the practice of meditation with a view to perfect himself in the system called "Chi-Kwan," must overcome these desires. They are commonly known in the world as the lust after beauty, sound, smell, taste and touch ; by the delusive influences of these passions men (different worldly teachers) foster in themselves the growth of concupiscence (तृष्णा), but if they are able to understand thoroughly the folly (sin) of such indulgences, so as not to permit their existence in their own case, this is called "Chiding the evil desires."

The first effort is to be made against the lust after beauty ; that is to say, the beautiful form of man or woman : the painted eyes, the graceful neck, the bright-red lips, the pearl-white teeth ; and also the various attractive colors of worldly treasures, such as blue and yellow, red and white &c., all which are the causes of besotment, and by producing a frenzy of love result in every kind of evil कर्म. So it was Bimbasara Raja who was born in his enemy's country as a mistress in the harem of Avambra on account of his lustful propensities ; so also Udayana Raja, besotted by lust, cut off the hands and feet of the five hundred Rishis, and thus incurred every kind of retributive punishment.

The second effort is to be made against the lust of sound, in which is included the love of music, whether of the lute or guitar, or the musical Bamboo pipes, or of golden instruments (gongs or cymbals) or of the musical stone, and of the voice of singing men or singing women; all these are calculated to produce a clouded and besotted mind in the case of those who hear them, and so result in an evil Karma. Thus it was the five hundred Rishis who dwelt in the Snowy mountains, by listening to the singing of the Gandharva Nymphs, lost their power of mental abstraction, and their hearts became beclouded and confused. Thus, and in other ways we may know the evil consequences of fondness for "Sound".

The third effort is to be made against fondness for perfumes such as the perfumed persons of men or women, or the smell of food, or the seasonings of food; in short, every kind of pleasant aroma which foolish men delighting in, forthwith are entangled in the trammels of lust. Thus it was that Bhikshu dwelling beside the Lotus-tank, perceiving the delicious scent of the flowers, his heart was filled with lust, and so he fell in love with the Spirit of the Tank, (the Naiad), and incurred the gravest guilt (caused a great scandal). Is it right, then, to be careless about this matter, when by it such consequences may ensue? Surely this consideration should cause those who are indifferent (asleep) to rouse themselves. By these and other considerations we may learn the evil consequences of fondness for perfumes.

The fourth effort is to be made against the lust of taste, that is to say, the taste of bitter, sour, sweet, salt, fresh and so on; all species of highly flavoured and tasty meats and drinks; fondness for such things will cause the mind to become cloudy and impure, and so create every kind of evil Karma, like the Sramanera, (novice), who was so infatuated with the love of cream, that at the end of his life he was born again as one of the small insects that live in cream. By these and other considerations we may learn the evil consequences of fondness for delicate or tasty food.

The fifth effort is to be made against the love of touch that is to say, the soft or silky feel of a person's body; or love of anything warm in cold weather, or any thing cold in warm weather; in short, all those pleasant sensations arising from contact which overcome the judgment of foolish and ignorant men, and raise up within them, as a result, a Karma opposed to religion, as in the case of the Rishi Yih-Koh (Ekashringa), who, by the power of this lust, lost his spiritual capabilities, and became the courtezan Ganika (Ki-King). By this and other considerations we may learn the evil consequences resulting from this love of touch.

These considerations respecting the forbidden desires are taken from the discourses of the Great-conveyance (Maha yana) School; and in these also we find the following:—

Alas! for the miseries which all creatures endure constantly, from these five desires! And still they seek after their indulgence, and are never satisfied! These five desires conduce to our continuance in misery, as fuel, which revives and supports fire. These five desires can bring no satisfaction, as a dog gnawing a rotten bone; they produce quarrels and fights, as birds contending for a bit of flesh; they burn, as the flame of a torch when the wind is contrary burns the hand; they are poisonous, as the poison of snakes; their benefit is no more than that of a dream; they last but for a moment, as the spark from the flint, and are utterly vain!—The wise man, again, considers them as hateful robbers, which hold in their bonds the foolish men of the world till they die, and after death, entail on them endless miseries; these lusts are shared in common with the beasts; by their indulgence we are brought into the condition of abject slavery; these miserable lusts immerse us in the filth of the three worlds. I, then, preparing the exercise of *dhyana*, (religious abstraction) should drive away, these hindrances, as robbers are driven away and expelled according to the Gathas in the Dhyana Sutra,

"We are still tangled in the coil of Life and Death,
Because we still indulge our taste for sinful pleasure;
We treasure up for ourselves vengeance when we die;
Vain as these pleasures are, they entail nothing but sorrow," &c.

3. CASTING AWAY HINDRANCES.

The hindrances here spoken of are five; viz, covetousness, anger, sloth, restlessness and unbelief. In the previous section we spoke of desire for external gratifications, the object being in one of the five categories of sense. But now we are speaking in brief, of the desires which are originated in the mind itself, viz, when engaged in the practice of religious duties; (1) A covetous desire; for instance, after complete wisdom; the thoughts about this will so intertwine as to becloud and impede the virtuous intentions (heart) and result in the production of an imperfect wisdom. For consider! if the animal desires, strengthening in the heart are able (as it were) to consume the body, how much more will not the fire, which the heart itself produces by its desires, burn up every virtuous principle? The man who encourages this covetous disposition banishes reason, and drives it away; he makes the foundation of misery ever broader and broader; the heart that entertains it can never approach the border of wisdom, as it is said in the following Gàthas which relate to the subject;

"The man who has entered on the path of Reason, ashamed and wearied (of sin)
Who has taken the alms-bowl, able to confer happiness on all creatures,
How can such a one again become subject to covetous desires,
Or be soiled and besotted by the five passions?
Having once let go the indulgence of such things,
He discards them, nor ever looks back.
The man who returns to the gratification of these desires,

Is like a fool returning to his vomit;
For these desires, whilst the search lasts, are bitter,
And when gratified bring distraction and fear,
And when not obtained result in disappointment and chagrin.
There is no foundation for any happiness in them.
Such is the misery of these Desires!
But when a man has been able to give them all up,
Having gained the joys of deep mental abstraction,
There is no room left for any further delusion".

Then the second hindrance to be cast away is "anger": this is indeed the origin of all religious failure; the cause of a man's falling into every evil way of existence. It is the enemy of all peace, and the great robber of the virtuous heart; the fruitful source of the gravest sins of the mouth. For thus it is the disciple, when, sitting in the very act of religious contemplation, thinking on such and such a man, considers thus in his mind: "that man is a continual nuisance to me and to my friends; he seems to court my enmity;" and then he considers about past circumstances, and future ones, and so he is filled with vexation, and this generates anger, and this produces hatred and this results in a determination to retaliate; thus it is anger beclouds the heart, and so it is called a "hindrance," and should be cast away at once; and so Sakra Devana in a verse puts this question to Buddha:—

"What is it destroys tranquillity and joy?
What is it destroys all contentment?
What is the root of bitterness (poison),
Which destroys every virtuous principle?"

To which Buddha replied in the following verse:—

"Destroy anger, there will be Rest and joy;
Destroy anger, there will be contentment
Anger is the root of bitterness (poison);
Anger destroys every virtuous principle".

Thus we may gather just this, that we ought to cultivate a loving and patient disposition, and by destroying and forsaking every remnant (of anger), induce a perfect tranquillity of mind.

The third hindrance is slothful indolence. The darkness that dwells within the heart is called sloth, and the heaviness, which pervades every part of the corporeal system, inviting to sleep and laziness, this is called indolence; and hence the name slothful indolence. It is this disposition that prevents all present or future attainment of solid happiness, and stands opposed both to the happiness of heaven and the attainment of Nirváña, so great is the destructive power of this wicked principle. So that whilst the other hindrances cause one to lose ground, this indolence makes one like a dead person unable to hold any ground, and for this reason it is difficult to extirpate and destroy—as Buddha, when enlarging on this very subject in the presence of the Bodhisatwas, says in verse:—

> "Rise from thy bed! embrace not the stinking corpse of sleep!
> Suppose the arrows of grievous disease penetrated thy body,
> "And the whole collection of miseries consequent thereon, could there then be peaceful Rest?" &c.

Thus, by various arguments, he chides the hindrance of slothfulness, and warns us, by shortening our hours of rest, to get rid of the cloudy influences that darken the mind, and, if necessary, to devote ourselves, more and more to the practice of fixed contemplation, in order to curb and destroy the inclination to indolence.

The fourth hindrance to be cast away is restlessness and vexation. This restlessness is threefold: (1) Restlessness of body; when one cannot be still in any position, but there is a constant inclination to get about something else, either to walk about, or to sit, or to change position. (2) Restlessness of the vocal organs, as when one is always humming or singing, or chattering or arguing. (3) Restlessness of mind, as when one is always thinking how to excel in worldly knowledge.

This is the "love of change" of which we speak, destructive of all true religion; for if the mind of the religious person cannot be firmly fixed in contemplation, when governed by the ordinary rules used by men for this purpose, how much less when this restlessness is allowed to dissipate its strength? It is like trying to hook a mad elephant, or to restrain a camel without catching him by the nose as the Gatha says;—

> "You have shaved your head and assumed the soiled garments (of a priest;)
> You have taken the earthen alms-dish, and gone begging your daily food.
> What pleasure, then, can there be now in indulging yourself in restlessness?
> For if you let loose and indulge such feelings as these you lose all profit in Rielgion.

Surely, then, to lose all profit in religion, and at the same time all worldly pleasures, such a condition is a sad one! and that which causes it should be, once for all, cast away. But what is the vexation of which we spoke? This vexation fills up the measure of the "Hindrance" of Restlessness. How is it, then? At the time when this restlessness is indulged, the influences of religion are no longer felt, and therefore when the man afterwards desires to practice fixed contemplation, he finds himself overpowered by vexation on account of his former conduct, and so sorrow obscures the mind; hence this name of "obscuration", or "hindrance". Now this vexation or sorrow, caused by transgression, is of two kinds: (1) The sorrow which we have just mentioned. (2) Sorrow for some grievous sin, the recollection of which causes continual remorse, the arrow of which sticks fast in the soul, and cannot be removed. As the Gatha says:

> "Doing what we ought not to do,
> Not doing what we ought to do,
> The fire of regretful sorrow which (now) burns,
> In after ages (leads to ruin) and misery,

But if a man is able to repent of his sin,
And to complete his repentance, there is no more grief.
In this way heart is restored to peace;
But repentance not fulfilled, there is the constant recollection of sin,
Whether of omission or commission,
And this is just the condition of the Fool,
Not repenting with all his heart,
Not doing what he is able to do.
He completes the sum of his evil deeds,
And he cannot but do that which he ought not."

The fifth hindrance to be rejected is the cloud of unbelief. This unbelief obscuring the mind, there can be no hearty faith in any religious duty, and there being no faith, then there is no advantage to be got by any religious profession (Law of Buddha). We may compare the case of such a man to that of a person without hands in the middle of a Treasure mountain;—having no hands, what use to him are the treasures? Such is the character of this unbelief. There are three kinds of unbeliefs—(1) That sort of doubt about oneself which leads a man to think thus: "All my faculties are dark, and dull; the pollution of sin in my case is very great; I am unlike any one else". Thinking thus about himself, a man in the end will be unable to attain perfection. If he desires to prepare himself for this perfection, he must not undervalue his own condition; for whilst sojourning in the present world, it is difficult to ascertain, what principles of virtue there may be within the heart. (2) There is a second kind of unbelief, viz., that which relates to one's Religious Teacher, as if a man were to say: "My teacher has no dignified ways with him, or peculiar marks of excellency; he cannot, then, possess any great religious endowments, how then can he instruct me"? Such doubts as these will effectually prevent any advance in the way of समाधी (*Samadhi*); we should desire, therefore, to exclude the idea, for as it is said in the Mahayana Shastra, "A stinking leather-purse may contain much gold; if, therefore, we would have the gold we must not fling away the purse". The disciple should even argue even thus: "My master, although he is not perfectly pure, is yet able to promote in my mind the love of Religion (Buddha)". (3) There is a third kind of unbelief which relates to the Law: for this is the argument, "that the mind of man, which is naturally so taken up with worldly concerns, can never with faith and reverence undertake religious duties; and that there can be no sincerity in such profession. But what then? (such a) doubt is the very principle of failure, as is said in the Gatha—

> The man who, travelling along a precipitous road,
> Doubts whether he can proceed or not,
> Is like the man who, living in the midst of the realities of life (religious virtues)
> Doubts of their truth.
> Because he doubts he cannot deligently inquire
> After the true marks of that which is.
> This unbelief, born from folly,
> Is the evil product of an evil heart,
> For virtue and vice are true;
> And so life and death and Nirvana are true
> There can be no doubt about these.
> Cherishing the principles of unbelief,
> The King of Death and the infernal lictors will bind you,
> As a Lion seizes the deer,
> So that there can be no rescue.
> There will be doubts as long as we reside in the world.
> Yet, pursuing with joy the road of virtue,
> We ought, like the man who observes the rugged path along the precipice,
> Gladly and profitably to follow it.

Thus those who have faith will enter into all the profit of a religious life; whilst those who have no faith, even when living in the profession of religion, will profit nothing. By all these considerations, therefore, we should learn at once to cast away the hindrance of unbelief.

But why should we reject only these, it may be asked, out of so many hindrances which exist? Because, we reply, in these* five all others are included. The disciple, therefore, who gets rid of these five is like the man who is suddenly freed from the burden on his back, or a diseased man restored to health, or a starving man brought to a place of abundant food or a man who escapes unhurt from a band of robbers; so the man freed from these hindrances finds his heart, restored to rest, filled with calm and peace. Whereas the heart, enthralled by these faults, is like the sun, or the moon obscured by clouds, or when covered by the hand of the असुर, (Asurá) unable to shed forth any light, or shine with any degree of brightness.

4. HARMONISING THE FACULTIES.

The disciple, when he first engages in the practice of religious contemplation,* desiring to prepare his life in agreement with the laws of all the Buddhas, must first arm himself with a firm resolve to save all creatures, vowing that he will himself seek to obtain the wisdom of the Supreme Buddha. Firm as adamant in this resolve, pressing forward with all courage and determination, regardless of his own individual life, if he thus goes on perfecting himself in Religion, and in the end not turning back, then afterwards when sitting in devout meditation, keeping before his mind none but right reflections, he will clearly apprehend the true condition of all phenomenal existence; without any distinct recognition of that which is called

---

* तृष्णा, राग, मोह, दंभ, अहंकार, अथवा काम, क्रोध, लोभ, मद, मत्सर.

* The distinction between ध्यान (Dhyana) and समाधी (Samadhi) is best given in the words of Patanjali "Restraint of the body, retention of the mind and meditation, which thence is exclusively confined to one subject, is ध्यान (Dhyana); the idea of identification with the object of such meditation, so as if devoid of individual Nature is समाधी (Samádhi)". *Vishnu Puran*, 658 n.

excellent (virtue) or the contrary; disregarding the knowledge of all that which depends on the exercise of the senses; perceiving that all things, in their nature imperfect, are mixed up with grief and vexation; that the three worlds are the result of birth and death; and that all things in the three worlds do but result from the Heart—his experience will be that which is stated in the Dasabhumi Sutra. "The three worlds have no other originator but the 'one self' (heart)—if a man knows that this 'self' has no individual nature, then all phenomena (Conditions) will appear to him unreal; and thus, his heart being without any polluting influence (envelope) there will be a clear end of all power possessed by Karma to reproduce in his case 'life or death'."

Having arrived at this point, the disciple ought to advance to the further practice of right preparation.

Now what do we mean by "harmonising the faculties?" We mean just what the potter does to the clay before he places it on his wheel; he cleanses it from all inpurities, and brings it to a proper consistency; or as the musician, who tunes the strings of his lute to a proper concord:—so the disciple prepares his heart. Now, for the purpose of thus harmonising his faculties there are five duties requiring attention, which, properly performed, will make the attainment of समाधि (Samádhi) easy; but not observed, will cause many difficulties in the way of attaining virtuous principles.

The first duty regards "food;" and with respect to this the rule is that one's individual desires should be regulated according to reason: if a man overfill himself, then the vapours quickly rise and the body swells, and the various pulsations, not proceeding regularly, the mind becomes darkened and burthened, and there is no rest whilst sitting in reflection. If a man eats too little, then the body becomes emaciated, the heart is in suspense and the thoughts become feeble and disconnected. So that in either case there is no way for the accomplishment of "Samadhi."

Thus, for those who enter on the practice of Samádhi, attention to food is the first, and most important requisite, as the Sutra says:

The bodily functions being in healthy exercise, the Reason (religious knowledge) advances, knowing how to practise moderation in food and drink.

Occupying his solitary pansal, in uninterrupted contentment,
His heart at rest and joyously persevering in the Religious life,
"Such is the teaching of all the Buddhas (with respect to their followers)."

The second thing to be adjusted is "sleep;" for sleep is the delusive covering of ignorance, and cannot be tolerated. Too much sleep prevents all right apprehension of the "Holy Law;" and, moreover, destroys all religious merit. It causes the heart to become dark, and uproots every virtuous principle. But by regulating the hours of sleep, both the mind and the animal nature are purified and cleansed; the memory becomes distinct, and so it is possible to compose the heart within the sacred limits which make it possible to experience the enjoyment of Samádhi. And so the Sutra says: "By not yielding to the influences of sloth, either one night or two (i. e. at the present or some future time) rejecting and not listening to its bewitchments, the life is cleansed and there is nothing further to attain." Think, then, of the fire of destruction (death) which will burn up the world and all in it, and so early every morning seek to deliver yourself, and yield not to sloth!

The third, fourth and fifth adjustments relate severally to the body, the breath, and the mind.

With respect to the body: care must be taken that no violent exertion be used previous to entering on the exercise of "meditation," lest the breath should be agitated, and the mind in consequence be unsettled; composing the body to a state of perfect quiet, first of all, the mat must be placed in a properly retired spot, where the disciple may remain quiet and free from interruption for a considerable time. After this the legs must be properly arranged; if the mode called "pwan-kea," be adopted, then the left leg is placed above the right and drawn close into the body, so that the toes of the left foot be placed evenly on the right thigh and those of right foot on the left thigh. But if the "ts'iuen-kea" mode of sitting be preferred, then the right leg is uppermost.

Next, the clothes must be properly arranged and spread out, so that during the period of "meditation" they shall not fall off. Then the hands ought to be composed, i. e., the palm of the left hand placed in the hollow of the right; corresponding to the position of the legs; then placing them, thus arranged in close contact with the body, let the heart be at rest!

The next requirement is to straiten the body. Having first of all stretched the joints seven or eight times, so that, as the An-mo Law directs, the hands and feet may not become dead, let the spine be perfectly straight, neither curved nor humped the head and neck upright; the nose exactly plumb with the navel, neither awry, nor slanting, nor up nor down, but the whole face straight and perfectly fixed.

Next with regard cleansing the mouth, the rules about coarse and impure breathing are these: on opening the mouth to disperse the breath there should be no rough or sudden exhalation, but gently and smoothly, and whilst the breath is passing out consider that in different parts of the body there are pulsations that admit of no exit (?); after dispersing the breath shut the mouth, then breathe gently in through the nose until three inspirations have been made, or if the breath be well adjusted then one inspiration is sufficient. Afterwards, the mouth being closed, the teeth and lips scarcely separated, let the tongue remain pressing on the upper ledge of the teeth, then open the eyes just enough to perceive the exterior light. Thus, retaining the body in an upright sitting posture, the head and the four limbs immovable and perfectly fixed—such are the rules respecting the body on entering on "fixed contemplation".*

* The various rules respecting the postures of the योगी (Yogi) may be consulted विष्णु पुराण (Vishnu Puran,) 653, &c. And also Mr. Spier's Ancient India, pp. 430, 431.

Next with respect to "breathing" .There are four kinds of respiration: 1st. Windy respiration; 2nd, A gasping respiration; 3rd, Emotional breathing; 4th. Pure respiration. The first three modes are unharmonised conditions; the last is harmonised. What, then, is the condition denoted by "windy respiration". It is when, at the time of sitting down to engage in meditation, the breath passing in and out of the nostrils may be perceived by the noise it makes: this is wind. Then what is gasping? It is when, sitting down to engage in "meditation", although there be no noise in breathing, yet the respiration is broken and uneven, as though it came not through a clear passage: this is gasping. What, then, is emotional beathing? This is when, sitting down to meditate, although there be no noise, or gasping, still the respiration is not equable or smooth: this is emotional breathing. And lastly, what is proper respiration? This is when there is neither noise nor gasping, nor uneven breathing, but the respiration is calm, and regular, the sign of an equable and well balanced mind: this is proper respiration. The first kind of respiration produces confusion of mind; the second produces an interrupted condition of thought; the third tends to distress the mind; the last alone leeds to "fixity". So that when sitting in meditation, if any of the three former methods of breathing be detected, they are signs of what is named "want of harmony" in the exercise (use) of religious duties. Moreover, with respect to the "heart", we observe that if there be any anxiety or distress of mind, this is an impediment in the way of Samâdhi. If, then, we desire to "harmonise" the heart, we must observe three things. 1st. To put down, and destroy all that distresses our peace of mind. 2nd. To have the substance of the body (limbs) freely and easily arranged. 3rd. To take care that the breathing is gentle and smooth as through a hair tube. Breathing in this way, all distress of mind must be overcome, and therefore the heart may be easily composed to "fixed contemplation."

Lastly, with respect te "harmonising" the mental faculties,

there are several schemes for doing this: on entering, being fixed, and leaving the condition of absolute rest. On entering Samádhi, all confused thoughts must be suppressed and harmonised so that they cannot get the upper hand. And next, there must be some fixed object for the eye to gaze on when the mind is dead or fickle. Now, this deadness of mind consists in a want of recollection and a general indisposition to exertion in which case the disciple must compel his attention to a particular point, as at the end of the nose, forcing his mind to engage with determination on the influences which occupy it (or should direct it), and not wander away from them for a moment. This is the way to overcome deadness.

And, now what is fickleness or flightiness of mind? It is when at the time of sitting down to "meditate," the mind is swayed to and fro, and the body ill at ease, influenced by exterior circumstances of various descriptions: this is flightiness. In such a case, the mind ought to be bound down to repose in the middle of the body, as it were in the navel, and all the wandering thoughts be centred in one point; the mind will then be easily composed and fixed.

But beyond this, though there be no "deadness," or "levity" of heart, there may be a "momentary excitement," or a "careless condition." The first arises from some such cause as this. Whilst engaged in contemplation, the mind suddenly fixes on the idea that now because of such or such an effort "Samádhi" is coming on, and so there be a feeling of excitement or hysteria. Such a state of mind should be suppressed, and overcome by reflecting that all the influences of the animal spirits (or passion nature) all flow from the differences which exist in the interior parts of our constitution. (?) If the heart is affected with carelessness, resulting from an inward satisfaction on account of progress, then the body will be ill-adjusted, the mouth full of spittle, and, in consequence, a general bewilderment will ensue—to remedy this the body must be gathered up, and, by a sudden effort, the mind centred in the subject that engages its attention.

With regard to the Rules which relate to the government of the mind when engaged in the actual enjoyment of Samadhi, the only observation necessary is, to take care that neither body, breath, nor mind be allowed to relax from their state of discipline, so as to risk the interruption of the tranquillity enjoyed.

On emerging from Samádhi, a man ought first to scatter, or dissipate the influences which bind his heart; by opening his mouth, and letting go his breath, and then loosen the hundred secret springs (pulses or feelings) with him. After this, let him gently move his brow and pass his hand over his head; then separating his feet, he may stretch them in any direction, and afterwards rub the whole of his body with his hand. Then he may open his eyes and go free.

Thus one should proceed on breaking the spell of "meditation"—by attending to trifles all deviation from the right standard is avoided. And so the Gatha says :—

"There are steps and grades in advancing towards a condition of rest,

Not disregarding slight indiscretions, but by exact attention,

Like a horse well broken in and trained, we stand still or we go on as desired".

The *Lotus* of the Good Law also says: "All the Bodhisatwas of this great congregation have equally attained their present condition by diligent conduct, earnest perseverance, rightly entering on, engaging in and quitting countless myriads conditions of Samadhi, &c.

(*Instruction of Buddha.*)

Buddha said to Vatsa, illustrious youth! diligently and earnestly striving after the condition of Samata (Repose) and that of Vipasina (clear sight), then you may advance through every stage of mental advancement, until you arrive at the condition of Buddha himself. *Beal's Buddhist Scriptures.*

(*Extracts from Dabistan.*)

The Persian Mobed Khoda Jai, in the "cup of Rai Khusro" a commentary on the text of the poem of the venerable Azar Kaivan, thus relates: "He who devotes himself to walking in "the path of God, must be well skilled in the medical sciences, "so that he may rectify whatever predominates or exceeds in "the bodily humours: in the next place, he must banish from "his mind all articles of faith, systems, opinions, ceremonials, "and be at peace with all: he is to seat himself in a small and "dark cell, and gradually diminish the quantity of his food." The rules for the diminution of food are thus laid down in the *Sharistan* of the holy doctor *Ferzanah Bahram*, the son of *Farbâd*: "From his usual food, the pious recluse is every day "to subtract three direms, until he reduces it to ten direms "weight: he is to sit in perfect solitude, and give himself up "to meditation". Many of this (Sepasiyan) sect "have brought themselves to one direm weight of food: their principal devotional practice turning on these five points: namely, fasting, silence, waking, solitude, and meditation on God. Their modes of invoking God are manifold, but the one most generally adopted by them is that of the *Muk Zhûp*: now in the *Azanan* or *Pehlevi Mâk* signifies "four", and Zhúp a "blow"; this state of meditation is also called *Char Sang*, "the four weights", and *Char Kub*, "the four blows". The next in importance is the Siyá Zhup, "the three weights" or "three blows." The sitting postures among these devotees are numerous; but the more approved and choice are limited to eightyfour; out of these they have selected fourteen; from the fourteen they have taken five; and out of the five two are chosen by way of eminence: with respect to these positions, many have been described by the *Mobed Sarush* in the *Zerdusht Afshár*: of these two, the choice position is the following:—The devotee sits on his hams, cross-legged, passing the out side of the right foot over the left thigh, and that of the left foot over the right thigh, he then passes his hands behind his back, and holds in his left hand the great toe of the right foot, and in the right hand the great toe of the left foot, fixing his eyes intently on the point of the nose: this position they call *Farnishin*, "the splendid seat", but by the Hindu Jogies it is named the Padmasan or "Lotus seat". If he then repeat the *Zekr-i-Mukyhub*, he either lays hold of the great toes with his hands, or if he prefer, removes his feet off the thighs, seating himself in the ordinary position, which is quite sufficient—then, with closed eyes, the hands placed on the thighs, the armpits open, the back erect, the head thrown forward, and fetching up from the navel with all his force the word *Nist*, he raises his head up: next, in reciting the word *Husti*, he inclines the head towards the right breast: on reciting the word *Magar*, he holds the head erect; after which he utters *Yezdan*, bowing the head to the left breast, the seat of the heart. The devotee makes no pause between the words thus recited; nay, if possible, he utters several formularies in one breath, gradually increasing their number. The words of the formulary (*Nist* husti Magar Yezdan) "there is no existence save God" are thus set forth. "Nothing exists but God;" or, "There is no God, but God;" or, "There is no adoration except for what is adorable;" or this. "He to whom worship is due is pure and necessarily existent;" or, "He who is without equal, form, color, or model." * * * In the inward meditation, the worshipper regards three objects as present: "God, the heart and the spirit of his Teacher;" whilst he revolves in his heart the purport of this formulary: There is nothing in existence but "God" but if he proceeds to the suppression of breath, which is "called the knowledge of Dam and *Sûmrad*," or the science of breath, and imagination, he closes not the eyes, but directs them to the tip of the nose, as we have before explained under the first mode of sitting: this institute has also been recorded in the *Surud-i-Mastan*.

It is thus recorded in the *Zerdusht Afshár*; the worshipper having closed the right nostril, enumerates the names of God from one to sixteen times, and whilst counting draws his breath upwards; after which he repeats it twenty-two times, and lets the breath escape out of the right nostril, and whilst counting propells the breath aloft; thus passing from the six Khâns, or stages to the seventh; until from the intensity of imagination he arrives to a state in which he thinks that his soul and breath bound like the jet of a fountain to the crown of the head: they enumerate the seven stages, or the seven degrees in this order: 1st, the position of sitting; 2nd, the hips; 3rd, the navel; 4th, the pine-heart; 5th, the windpipe; 6th, the space between the eyebrows; and 7th, the crown of the head. As causing the breath to mount to the crown of the head is a power peculiar to the most eminent persons; so, whoever can convey his breath and soul together to that part, becomes the Vicegerent of God. According to another institute, the worshipper withdraws from all sensual pursuits, sits down in retirement, giving up his heart to his original world on high, and without moving the tongue, repeats in his heart, Yezdan! Yezdan! or, God! God; which address to the Lord may be made in any language, as Hindi, Arabic, etc.

Another rule is, the idea of the Instructor: the worshipper imagines him to be present and is never separated from that thought, until he attains to such a degree, that the image of his spiritual guide is never absent from the mind's eye, and he then turns to contemplate his heart: Or he has a mirror before his sight, and beholds his own form, until, from long practice, it is never more separated from the heart, to which he then directs himself: or he sits down to contemplate his heart, and reflects on it as being in continual movement. In all these cases, he regards the practices of the suppression of the breath as profitable for the abstraction of thought: an object which may also be effected without having recourse to it.

Another rule is, what they call *Azád Awd*, or "the free voice," in Hindi, *Anahid*; and in Arabic, *Sant Mutluk*, or "the absolute sound." Some of the followers of Mohammed relate, that it is recorded in the traditions that a revelation came to the venerable prophet of Arabia resembling "the tones of a bell" which means the "Sant Mutluk" which Hafiz of Shiraz expresses thus.

"No person knows where my beloved dwells;
"This much only is known, that the sound
of the bell approaches."

The mode of hearing it is after this manner: the devotees direct the hearing and understanding to the brain, and whether in the gloom of night, in the house, or in the desert hear this voice, which they esteem as their *Zikker*, or "address to God."

Then having opened the eyes and looking between the eyebrows, a form appears. Some of these who walk in the path of religious poverty among the followers of Mohammed (On whom be benedictions!) asserts that the expression *Kab Kausain*, "I was near two bows' length," alludes to this vision. Finally, if they prefer it having closed the eyes for some time, they reflect on the form which appeared to them on looking between the eyebrows; after which they meditate on the heart; or without contemplating the form, they commence by looking into the heart; and closing both eyes and ears, give themselves up entirely to meditation on the heart abandoning the external for the internal: whoever can thus contemplate obtains all that he wants.

Finally the searcher after the Being who is without equal or form, without color or pattern, whom they know and comprehend in the Persian under the name of "*Izad*," in Arabic, by the blessed name of "*Allah*," and in Hindi as "*Para Brahma Nârâyana*," contemplates him without the intervention of Arabic, Persian, Hindi, or any other language, keeping the heart in his presence, until he, being rescued from the shadows of doubt, is identified with God. The venerable *Mauldvi Jami* says on this head.

"Thou art but an atom, He, the great Whole;
But if for a few days thou meditate with care
On the whole, thou becomest one with it.

(Vol. I, pp. 73 to 83.)

Now the terms *Murcouh khab*, *Murdop Khass*, and *Sàonós*, are terms applied by the Sipàsián to the following mode of sleeping: the devotee rests (having thrown his legs beneath him,) on his knees, pressing to the ground both heels as far as the great toe: and applying the extremities of the knees to the earth, he keeps his seat on the same; he is then to lie on his back, keeping the points of his fingers on his head; after this he is to look entirely between the eyebrows, and carry into practice the *Habs-i-dam*, or imprisonment of the breath. The Darvesh Subahani, one of the great Sufees, used to say: " Such was the sleep of the prophets." They also say: "The prophets of old used to sleep on their backs, with their faces directed towards the Heavens:" which is the same as the position before described.

(Vol. I, p. 111.)

Ashur Beg Karamanhi is also one of those who obtained the gift of spiritual intelligence through *Far Zanah Bahram*, the son of Farhad, notwithstanding the total absence of regular studies; by the exertion of his innate powers, he, like the other *Yekanah Bin*, " Seers of one God," attained communion with God. In the year of the Hijira 1044 (A. D. 1636,) the author conversed with him in Kashmir, and inquired into the nature of his intercourse with Bahram. He answered: "I went by " way of experiment to Farzanah, and he thus directed me: " whether alone or in a crowd, in retirement or in public, every " breathing which issues forth must proceed from the head; " and on this point there must be no inattention. He also " said: guard the internal breath as long as thou canst, direct- " ing thy face to the pineformed heart, until the invocation be " performed by the heart in the stomach; also thy invocation " should be thus: God! God! Meditate also on this sentiment: " O Lord! none but thou forms the object of my desire! When " I had duly practised this, and found its impressive influence, " then from the bottom of my heart I sincerely sought God.

"After some time he enjoined me to practice the *Tawajjah-i-Talkin*, turning to instruction: that is: keep thy soul in the "presence of God, divested of letters and sounds, whether Ara- "bic or Persian, never removing thy mind from the pine-formed "heart. By conforming to these instructions, I have come at "last to such a state, that the world and its inhabitants are "but as a shadow before me; and their very existence as the "appearance of the vapour of the desert."

(Vol. I, p. 135.)

Mahmud Beg Timan in the year of the Hijira 1048, (A. D. 1637), whilst in Kashmir, coming out of his cell one day, saw before him a wounded dog, moaning piteously; as the animal was unable to move, he therefore sold the only two objects he possessed; his carpet for prayer and his rosary, with the proceeds of which he purchased remedies for the dog. That same year, he said to the author: "On the first day of turning my "heart to the mental invocation of God, I had scarcely perform- "ed it ten times, when an evident influence was manifested: "at the moment of the first part, called *Nafi*, of the sentence, "my human existence disappeared. At the time of the second, "called *Asbat*, a determined sign of Divine grace became "visible: My sentence was this: "There is no God". (Vol. 1., pp, 135-136.

(*Extract from Ward's account of the Hindus*)

Pythagoras taught that "in the pursuit of wisdom, the ut- "most care must be taken to raise the mind above the domi- "nion of the passions, and the influence of sensible objects "and to disengage it from all corporeal impressions, that it may "be inured to converse with itself, and to contemplate things "spiritual and divine. Contemplative wisdom cannot be com- "pletely attained, without a total abstraction from the ordi- "nary life".

(Extracts from the Dialogue of Plato.)

In the book named Phœdo, Socrates said in answer to Simmias; "But does not purification consist in this, as was said "in a former part of our discourse, in separating as much as "possible the soul from the body, and in accustoming it to "gather and collect itself by itself on all sides apart from the "body and to dwell, as far as it can both now and hereafter "alone by itself delivered as it were from the shackles of the "body."

(Vol. I, page 66.*)*

(Extracts from Hours with the Mystics by R. A. Vaughan, B. A.)

The Neo-Platonist was accustomed to call every other branch of science the "lesser Mysteries:" this inward contemplation, the climax of Platonism, is the *great* mystery, the inmost, highest initiation. Withdraw into thyself, he will say, and the adytum of thine own soul will reveal to thee profounder secrets than the cave of Mithras. So that this *Mysticus* is emphatically the enclosed, self withdrawn, introverted man. This is an initiation which does not merely, like that of Isis or of Ceres, close the lips in silence, but the eye, the ear, every faculty of perception, in inward contemplation or in the ecstatic abstraction of the trance.

So then it is an effort man is to make—in harmony with the matter-hating principles of this school to strip off the Material and sensuous integuments of his being, and to reduce himself to a purely spiritual element. And in thus ignoring the follies and the phantasms of appearance—as they call the actual world—the worshipper of pure Being believed himself to enjoy at least a transitory oneness with the object of his adoration.

(Vol. I, p. 21.)

The aim of the mystic, if of the most abstract contemplative type, is to lose himself in the Divine Dark—to escape from every thing definite, every thing palpable, every thing human, into the Infinite Fullness; which is, at the same time, the 'intense insane'. The profoundest obscurity is his highest glory: he culminates in darkness: for, is not the deathlike midnight slumber of the sense, he will ask us, the wakeful noonday of the spirit? (Vol. I, p. 14.)

'Mystic,' according to Dionysius the Areopagite, is not merely a sacred personage, acquainted with the doctrines and participator in the rites called mysteries, but one also who (exactly after the Neo-Platonist pattern) by mortifying the body, closing the senses to every thing external, and ignoring 'every intellectual apprehension', attains in passivity a divine union, and in ignorance a wisdom transcending all knowledge.

(Vol. I, p. 22.)

Philo wrote to Hephœstion that in calm retirement and contemplation we are taught that we know like only by like, and that the foreign and lower world of the sensuous and the practical may not intrude into the lofty region of divine illumination.

He also stated that a man ought at least to have evinced some competency for the discharge of the social duties before he abandons them for the divine. First the less, then the greater. (Vol. I, p. 72.)

Contemplation of the Divine Essence is the noblest exercise of man; it is the only means of attaining to the highest truth and virtue, and therein to behold God is the consummation of our happiness here. (Vol. I, pp. 73-74.)

Plotinus in his epistle to Flaccus wrote thus :—'Purify your soul from all undue hope and fear about earthly things, mortify the body, deny self,—affections as well as appetites, and the inner eye will begin to exercise its clear and solemn vision.

The wise man recognises the idea of the Good within him. This he develops by withdrawal into the Holy-Place of his soul. He who does not understand how the soul contains the Beautiful within itself, seeks to realize beauty without, by laborious production. His aim should rather be to concentrate and simplify and so to expand his being; instead of going out into Manifold; to forsake it for the One, and so to float upwards towards the divine fount of being whose stream flows within him.

(Vol. I, p. 87.)

The region of truth is not to be investigated as a thing external to us, and so only imperfectly known. It is *within* us. Here the objects we contemplate and that which contemplates are identical—both are thought. The subject cannot surely know an object different from itself. The world of ideas lies within our intelligence. Truth, therefore, is not the agreement of our apprehension of an external object with the object itself. It is the agreement of the mind with itself. Consciousness, therefore, is the sole basis of certainty. The mind is its own witness. Reason sees in itself that which is above itself as its source; and again, that which below itself as still itself once more.

You ask, how can we know the Infinite? I answer, not by reason. It is the office of reason to distinguish and define. The Infinite, therefore, cannot be ranked among its objects. You can only apprehend the Infinite by a faculty superior to reason, by entering into a state in which you are your finite self no longer, in which the Divine Essence is communicated to you. This is Ecstacy. It is the liberation of your mind from its finite consciousness. Like only can apprehend like; when you thus cease to be finite you become one with the Infinite. In the reduction of your soul to its simplest self, its divine essence, you realise this Union, this Identity.

But this sublime condition is not of permanent duration. It is only now and then that we can enjoy this elevation (mercifully made possible for us) above the limits of the body and the world. I myself have realised it but three times as yet, and Porphyry hitherto not once. All that tends to purify and elevate the mind will assist you in this attainment, and facilitate the approach and the recurrence of these happy intervals. There are, then, different roads by which this end may be reached. The love of beauty which exalts the poet; that devotion to the One, and that ascent of science which makes the ambition of the philosopher; and that love and those prayers by which some devout and ardent soul tends in its moral purity towards perfection. These are the great highways conducting to that height above the actual and the particular, where we stand in the immediate presence of the Infinite, who shines out as from the deeps of the soul. (Vol. I, pages 85 and 88.)

Porphyry—With Porphyry author of a treatise on Abstinence the mind does not lose, in that state of exaltation, its consciousness of personality. He calls it a dream in which the soul, dead to the world, rises to an activity that partakes of the divine. It is an elevation above reason, above action, above liberty, and yet no annihilation, but an ennobling restoration or transformation of the individual nature. (Vol. I, page 103.)

According to Iamblichus, God is a Non-Being, who is above all being. He is apprehended only by negation. When we are raised out of our weakness, and on a level with God, it seems as though reason were silenced, for then we are above reason. We become intoxicated with God, we are inspired as by the nectar of Olympus. He teaches philosophy as the best preparation for Quietism. (Vol. I, page 112.)

Dionysius the Areopagite says :—Our highest knowledge of God, therefore, is said to consist in mystic ignorance. In omninescience we approach Omniscience. This Path of Negation is the highway of mysticism. It is by refraining from any exercise of the intellect or of the imagination by self-simplification, by withdrawal into the inmost, the divine essence of our nature—that we surpass the ordinary condition of humanity, and are united in ecstasy with God. (Vol. I, page 125.)

Knowledge has three degrees. Opinion, Science, Illumination. The means or instrument of the first is sense; of the second, dialectic ; of the third, intention. To the last, I subordinate reason. It is absolute knowledge founded on the idenity of the mind knowing with the object known.

St. Theresa. There are, in her scale, four degrees of prayer. The first is *simple mental prayer*,—fervent, inward, self withdrawn ; not exclusive of some words, nor unaided by what the mystics called discursive acts, i. e., the consideration of facts and doctrines prompting to devotion. In this species there is nothing extraordinary. No mysticism, so far.

Second degree :—*The prayer of quiet* called also *Pure contemplation.* In this state the Will is absorbed, though the Understanding and Memory may still be active in an ordinary way. Thus the nun may be occupied for a day or two in the usual religious services, in embroidering an altar-cloth, or dusting a chapel ; yet without the Will being engaged. That faculty is supposed to be as it were bound and taken up in God. This state is a supernatural one. Those who are conscious of it are to beware lest they suffer the unabsorbed faculties to trouble them. Yet they should not exert themselves to protract this 'recollection.' They should receive the wondrous sweetness as it comes, and enjoy it while it lasts, absolutely passive and tranquil. The devotee thus favoured often dreads to move a limb, lest bodily exertion should mar the tranquillity of the soul. But happiest are those who, as in the case just mentioned, can be Marys and Marthas at the same time.

Third degree :—*The prayer of union*; called also *Perfect Contemplation.* In this prayer, not the will only, but the Understanding and Memory also, are swallowed up in God. These powers are not absolutely inactive; but we do not work them, nor do we know how they work. It is a kind of celestial frenzy—a sublime madness, says Theresa. In such a transport she composed her ecstatic hymn, without the least exercise of the understanding on her part. At this stage the contemplatist neither thinks nor feels as a human being. The understanding is stunned and struck dumb with amazement. The heart knows neither why it loves, nor what. All the functions of the mind are suspended. Nothing is seen, heard, or known. And wherefore this sudden blank? That for a brief space (which seems always shorter than it really is) the Living God may, as it were take the place of the unconscious spirit—that a divine vitality may for a moment hover above the dead soul, and then vanish without a trace; restoring the mystic to humanity again to be heartened and edified, perhaps for years to come, by the vague memory of that glorious nothingness.

Fourth Degree :—*The prayer of a reparture, or Ecstasy.* This state is the most privileged, because the most unnatural of all. The bodily as well as mental powers are sunk in a divine stupor. You can make no resistance, as you may possibly, to some extent, in the Prayer of Union. On a sudden your breath and strength begin to fail; the eyes are involuntarily closed, or, if open, cannot distinguish surrounding objects; the hands are rigid, the whole body cold. (Vol. II, pages 141 and 143.)

Cornelius Agrippa. In his treatise *On the Three fold way of knowing God,* he shows how, by Divine illumination, the Christian, may discern the hidden meanings of a New Testament, as the cabbalist evolves those of the Old. It teaches the way in which the devout mind may be united to God, and, seeing all things in Him, and participating in his power, may even now, according to the measure of faith, foretell the future and control the elements. (Vol. II, p. 39.).

Theophrastus Paracelsus gives prominence to two new ideas which greatly modify and facilitate the researches of theosophy. One of these is the theory of divine manifestation by *Contraries,* —teaching (instead of the old division of Being and Non-Being) the development of the primal ground of existence by antithesis, and akin, in fact, to the principle of modern speculative philosophy, according to which the Divine Being is the absorption *(Aufhebung)* of those contraries which his self-evolution, or *lusus amoris,* has posited. This doctrine is the key-note in the system of Jacob Behmen. The other is the assumption that man—the micre-cosm, is as it were, a miniature of the macro-cosm—the great outer world, &c. &c. (Vol. II, Pages, 49 & 50).

Paracelsus extolls the power of faith to penetrate the Mysteries of Nature, and shows how a plain man, with his Bible only, if he be filled with the Spirit and carried out of himself by divine communication, may seem to men a fool, but is in truth *more* wise than all the doctors.

Jacob Behmen consulted the writings of Schwenkfeld and Weigel in his despondency. Weigel bids him to withdraw into himself and await, in total passivity, the incoming of the divine Word, whose light reveals unto the babe what is hidden from the wise and prudent. By the same writer he is reminded that he lives in God, and taught that if God also dwell in him, then is he even here in Paradise—the state of regenerate souls. (Vol. II, pages, 65 & 66).

(*Quietists.*)

The Hesychasts or Quietists (in the fourteenth century) of Mount Athos, we are told, in accordance with the prescription of their early teachers, said that there was a Divine light hid in the soul and they seated themselves daily in some retired corner and fixed their eyes steadfastly for a considerable time upon the middle of their belly or navel, and in that situation they boasted that a sort of Divine light beamed forth upon them from the mind itself, which diffused through their soul wonderful delight, and on this account they were called *Ousadouvxoi*. (*Beal's Buddhist Scripture*, page 151.)

(*Extracts from Peary Chand Mittra's work on Soul.*)

Swedenborg saw the intimate connection between thought and vital life. He says—"Thought commences and cor-"responds with respiration. The reader has before attended "to the presence of the heaving over the body; now let him "*feel* his *thoughts*, and he will see that they too heave with the "mass. When he entertains a long thought, he draws a long "breath; when he thinks quickly, his breath vibrates with "rapid alternations; when the tempest of anger shakes his "mind, his breath is tumultous; when his soul is deep and tran-"quil, so is his respiration; when success inflates him, his lungs "are as timid as his concepts. Let him make trial of the con-"trary; let him endeavour to think in long stretches, at the "same time that he breathes in fits, and he will find that it is "impossible; that in this case the chopping will needs mince "his thoughts. Now this mind dwells in the brain, and it is "the brain, therefore, which shares the varying fortunes of the "breathing. It is strange that this correspondence between the "states of the brain or mind and the lungs has not been admit-"ted in science, for it holds in every case, at every moment."

This subject engaged his special attention and he discovered the correspondence between respiration and thoughts and emotions, and thus he discovered the links between the body and the soul. He says—"Inward* thoughts have inward breaths,

* The observation of Swedenborg, the great Seer of modern times, explains the philosophy of the प्राणायाम *Prânâyâm* of the Indian Yogis.

"and purer spiritual thoughts have spiritual breaths hardly "mixed with material."

The philosophy of this (Yoga) exercise is that it tranquillises the mind. Directions for different modes of sitting are given. Adopting Bhadrásana or Siddhásana the Yogi should exercise his will power to go beyond the brain, and mingle with the आकाश sky. He should think that he is with the sky or the sky is within him while thus exercising to control the vital bondage, and to elevate the brain, the Yogi should meditate on the Divine Light.

His attitude should thefore be *Khechari*,† or towards the sky which means that he may gradually succeed in looking *upward*. Another teaching is that the Yogi, while in the exercise of Pránáyám should concentrate his will force on the region between the two eye-brows, or on the point of his nose, it being necessary to fix his will on one object only, which is called Savikalpa and gradually becomes Nirvikalpa, or on no object.

The teaching of the Vishnu Purana is—"By ths union of "prayer and meditation, let him behold soul in himself." Prayer is to be not in words, but in the psychic exercise or the exercise of the will power, that it may transcend the brain and reach the infinite world. This will result in the absorption of the knower, knowledge, and knowable in the soul. The knower is the intellectual coat, knowledge is the mental coat, and knowable is the elemental product through the senses, all coming under the domain of the mind, where all bondage is.

By such meditation the mind is overwhelmed with light. It ceases to dream.

Another instruction contained in the Gita is—"He who having closed up all the doors of his faculties, looked up his mind in his own breast, and fixed his spirit in his head, standing firm in the exercise of devotion, repeating in silence "*Om*" the mystic sign of Brahma, thence called 'Ekakshar,' shall, on

---

† He who can keep his mind and breathing calm, and can see without effort, practises "*Khechari.*".

his quitting this mortal frame, calling upon me, without doubt, go the journey of supreme happiness."

In the golden (luminous) highest sheath, the knowers of the soul know the Brahma, who is without spot, without part, who is pure, who is the light of lights.—*Mandukya.*

Pránáyám leads to reverie or abstraction and is followed by *Pratyáhára* or the suspension of the senses and the non-reception of external impressions. This state is followed by *Dháraná* or abstraction from breath, mind and natural wants and tranquillity from all sensul disturbances. It is the somnambulistic state which is followed by *Dhyána*, the clairvoyant state. *Samádhi* or *Nirvána* or the spiritual state is the last state.

These different states may be created by Yoga or spiritual agency. The effect of both is the development of the psychic power. They may not be lasting in the natural body, but the *Samádhi* state is the culmination of the different antecedent states, and when once created, it does not disappear.

Sànkhya says—"Yoga prepares the soul for that "absorbed contemplation by which the great purpose of "deliverence is to be accomplished." It further says, that such power, however transcendent, is not sufficient for the attainment of beatitude, i. e., union with the Divine power, or in other words, the attainment of the soul-state. The Vedánta says that, "When the knowledge of God is less perfect, the Yogi possesses transcendent powers." But this is not the finality of this life. Theosophy is therefore the end. Yoga and Spiritualism are the means.

The Budhists aimed at the state of "void," or raising the brain so that it might be free from impression. This state in Yoga is called *Manomayi*, or above the mind state. The Rev. Mr. Charles Kingsley says—"Empty thyself and God will fill thee."

The powers of the subtile body, according to the Sánkhya Darshana, are eight-fold, viz:—1, *Animá*: 2, *Mahimá* 3, *Laghimá*; 4, *Garimá*; 5, *Prapti*; 6, *Prákámya*; 7, *Vasitwa*; 8, *Isitwa*. These powers consist in shrinking into a minute form to which thing is pervious, or enlarging to a gigantic body, or assuming levity (rising along side a sun-beam to the solar orb), or possessing unlimited extension of organs (as touching the Moon with the tip of a finger), of irresistible will (for instance sinking into the earth as easily as in water) and dominion over all beings animate and inanimate, faculty of changing the course of nature, ability to accomplish everything desired. The first four powers relate to the body and motion. The fifth predicting future events, understanding unknown languages, curing diseases, divining unimpressed throughts, and understanding the language of the heart. The sixth is the power of converting old age into youth ; the seventh is the power of mesmerising human beings and beasts, and making them obedient ; it is the power of restraining passions and emotions. The eighth is the spiritual state ; the absence of the above seven proves that in this state the Yogi is full of God.

Mr. J. J. Morse of Boston in his work called "Inspirational and Trance-speaking," says—"For ordinary purposes, it is well "to divide mediumship into two distinct classes, viz, the physical "and psychological ; or perhaps, more correctly speaking, material and mental phenomena." After writing at some length on this subject he has stated the results of his own personal experiences in this matter as under :—

"The first essential I recognize is the closest possible "approximation to absolute health, bodily and mentally. The "second condition is, that I should be surrounded with harmonious persons, and congenial influences. These conditions "being present, I seat myself at the desk, and try to absent my "mind from my surroundings. The first feeling I experience "is usually a species of electric current passing mildly and gently "down the arms, on the outward sides, culminating in a shock "as it reaches the hand. The current appears to spread, to react upwards, and to permeate the brain, more especially the "superior or upper portions. The regions of Ideality, Sublimity, Benevolence, Veneration, Causality, Eventuality, Comparison, and also firmness, and constructiveness, are more or "less excited. The current, I have mentioned, induces a plea-"sant, soothing effect; and a stupor, accompanied by a sensa-"tion of falling backwards into nothingness, terminates my "consciousness. The entire series of operations, though, always "give me the idea that they have more of the nervous than the "muscular connected with them. My return to consciousness "is seemingly like rising up out of a deep void, accompanied "by a buzzing, dizzy sensation in the head, sometimes accom-"panied with severe bodily fatigue, but more frequently with "nervous exhaustion. You will therefore perceive that my "mediumship partakes more of the nervous and mental than of "the Muscular and Automatic. * * * The value of trance-"mediumship is a means of communicating with the inhabitants "of the spirit-world."

(*Extracts from Seership, Guide to soul-sight, by P. B. Randolph.*)

But what is true clairvoyance? I reply, it is the ability, by self-effort or otherwise, to drop beneath the floors of the outer world, and come up,as it were, upon the other side. *** It is the *Light* which the seer reaches sometimes through years of agony, by wading through oceans, as it were, of tears and blood. It is an interior unfoldment of native powers culminating in somnambulic vision through the mesmeric processes, and the comprehension and application of the principles that underlie, and overflow human nature and the physical universe, together with a knowledge of the principia of the vast spirit-sea whereon the worlds of space are cushioned. Thus true clairvoyance *generally* is knowledge resulting from experiment born of agony, and purified by the baptism of fire.

Never begin a course of experiments unless you intend to carry them on to certain success. To begin a course of magnetic experiments, and become tired in a fortnight because you do not succeed, is absurd. Mesmeric circles are, all things considered, probably the quickest way to reach practical results in a short time.

In the attempt to reach clairvoyance, most people are altogether in too great a hurry to reach grand results and in that haste neglect the very means required, permitting the mind to wander all over creation—from the consideration of miserable love affair of no account whatever, to an exploration of the mysterious enshrouding the great nebulæ of Orin or Centauri. Now that won't do. If one wants to be able to peruse the life-scroll of others, the *first* thing learned must be the *steady* fixing of mind and purpose, aim and intent upon a *single* point, wholly void of other thought or object. The *second* requirement is, *Think the thing closely*; and *third, will steadily, firmly,* to know the correct solution of the problem in hand, then the probabilities are a hundred to ten that the vision thereof, or the *Phantorama* of it, will pass before you like a vivid dream; or it will flash across your mind with resistless conviction of truth.

(*Extract from Statuvolism or artifical somnambulism by William Baker Fahnestock, M. D.*)

Various methods have been employed by different operators to induce artificial somnambulic state. The plan adopted and practised by Mesmer and his pupils has already been detailed in a preceding chapter of this work. Those of modern magnetizers are scarcely less absurd than that employed by Mesmer and his immediate followers.

Some operators of the present day, who believe in a magnetic influence, still pursue the ludicrous method of sitting down opposite to the patient, holding his thumbs, staring into his eyes, and making passes &c, until the desired object is effected.

Others, who believe looking to be essential, direct the patient to look at some object intently until the lids close and the patient becomes unconscious.

Very few, however, can be induced to enter the state by any of the above ways, and those who do, usually fall into the *sleeping condition* of this state, and are generally dull, listless, and seldom good clairvoyants.

The most rational, certain, and pleasant way of inducing this state which I have discovered is the following :—

When persons are desirous of entering this state, I place them upon a chair where they may be at perfect ease. I then request them to close the eyes at once, and to remain perfectly calm at the same time that they let the body lie perfectly still and relaxed. They are next instructed to throw their minds, to some familiar place—it matters not where, so that they have been there before and seem desirous of going there again, even in thought. When they have thrown the mind to the place, or upon the desired object, I endeavour, by speaking to them frequently, to keep their mind upon it; viz: I usually request them to place themselves (in thought) close to the object or person they are endeavouring to see, as if they were really there, and urge them to keep the mind steady, or to form an image or picture of the person or thing in their mind, which they must then endeavour to see. This must be persevered in for some time, and when they tire of one thing, or see nothing, they must be directed to others successively, as above directed, until clairvoyance is induced. When this has been effected the rest of the senses fall into the state at once or by slow degrees—often one after another, as they are exercised or not—sometimes only one sense is affected during the first sitting. If the attention of the subject is divided, the difficulty of entering the state perfectly is much increased, and the powers of each sense while in this state will be in proportion as that division has been much or little.

Almost every subject requires peculiar management, which can only be learned by experience or a knowledge of their character, &c. Much patience and perseverance is often required to effect it; but if both be sufficiently exercised, the result will always be satisfactory—if not in one sitting, in *two or more.* I have had several to enter this condition after twenty (20) sittings, and had them to say, that "if they had not interfered, and let things take their course, they would have fallen into it in the first sitting". This shows that those who do not enter it in one or two sittings, must do something to prevent it.

Many persons have entered the state in the above manner who could not do so in any other; although repeated trials had been made to effect it.

(*Extracts from Mental Medicine by the Rev. W. F. Evans.*)

The method of inducing interior perception, long practised by the magicians of the East, was by gazing at an ink-spot. Steadily looking at some small object or figure on the ceiling of the bedroom, will induce sleep, when a person is inclined to wakefulness. This I have often tried with success. The sleep in this case may be partly somnambulic, but is extremely tranquil, and refreshing. The late Dr. Gregory gives the same testimony, from his own experience regarding it.

As previously directed in the instructions given respecting the induction of the interior sensitive state by another, let the patient assume an easy position, and be quiet and passive, A recumbent posture is a good one. Then direct the attention to some object, so situated as to require the eyes to be somewhat elevated in order to see it. Abstract the attention from everything else, and gaze steadily at it, with the eyes partly closed for a few moments. As soon as the eyes feel a tendency to close entirely, and the room seems dark, or the vision blurred and obscured, shut them at once. Continue to gaze mentally at the same object, after the eyes are closed, and you will find that you can see it nearly as well as before. This is an interior vision and the dawning of spiritual pereception or vision independent of the external organs of sight. Continue perfectly passive and quiet. You are now in the state of sleep-waking, and on the boundary of both worlds. It is a condition of mental exaltation of quickened perceptions, and great psychological sensitiveness. If it is your wish to become mentally perceptive, direct your thoughts to some distant and familiar object or person, or to some place where you would *love* to be. You will perceive objects with the interior eye, as certainly and as really as you ever saw them with the outward organ. You will perceive not only what you have seen before, but what now exists though you never before saw it. The accuracy of this you may be able to test, if you desire it. I have done it many times, and found it as reliable as our ordinary vision. While in this state, you can, by an effort of will, transfer the interior sense of vision to any distance,—even to other continents. For this wonderful power is not subject to the limitations of time or space. It is not imagination merely,—it is a real interior or spiritual perception. The power we call imagination may be, and without doubt often is an inward seeing. All the senses may act independently of their material organs, and be transferred to any distance. By fixing the attention upon the organ of hearing, and listening, you can sometimes hear what persons, many miles away are saying. The sound is distinctly heard, though not with the outward ear. In fact, incredible as it may appear, their very thoughts become audible. This has been called clairaudience. The same is true of the sense of smell, and even taste. It is only the mind asserting its freedom from material restraints. A little practice, and a due share of perseverance, will render all this easy, and you will be able to enter upon this state without any preliminary process of gazing. Some, undoubtedly, will succeed better than others; but no one need fail entirely.

CONCENTRATION.

"There is but one step from the sublime to the ridiculous."

CONCENTRATION of the mind means the permanent predominance of one set of ideas or thoughts over the rest. Our mind is so constituted that it has a natural tendency to be lost in the labyrinth of the senses. Guided by unlimited desires, the mind hovers over a thousand and one objects of sense, and the attention being thus divided, the mental energy o spent is not productive of far reaching results. Biographies of great men show that the real difference between them and the common herd lies in the power of concentration of thought. Scientists, philosophers and wise men acquire such a wonderful control over the mind that they can, at will, immerse themselves in their special subjects, with all-absorbing attention. To discover great and grand truths, we must set the whole mental energy in one direction only. If we want to act up to any grand and sublime ideal, the ideal should be made to stand out in bold relief before the mind's eye. It is a curious fact that a mental impression, if sufficiently strong and lasting, is capable of reacting on the system, and this reaction has been found to mould even the physical frame in a peculiar way. The process known as *Bhrámarikaran*, in our Shastras, is an instance exemplifying the truth of the assertion, and modern gynecologists have in a manner corroborated the observation of our ancient and revered *Rishis* by describing the effect of terror or any lasting mental impression on the human organization. The effect of fright, caused by the sight of a *Kanch-poka* (beetle) on the delicate organisation of a *Telá-poka* (cockroach) is so great that in course of time (two or three weeks) the insect known as the cockroach is transformed into a beetle. This fact has come under my personal observation. In gynecological works various instances are recorded of the effect of fright on pregnant women, this effect being transmitted to the unborn offspring whose features were moulded accordingly. If, then, a mental impression is so powerful and its effects so very far-reaching, there can be no doubt that, by proper culture and training, we can bring the mind to such a state that only one set of impressions will be permanently predominant in it, and the results of such impressions will be proportionate to their intensity.

The practice of concentration of thought, if carried out steadily for sometime, is seen to produce (1) psychic exaltation, (2) perceptive exaltation, and (3) moral exaltation. But the mere exaltation of the psychic, perceptive and moral faculties, is not of itself an indication of the success of such practice. For, in the incubation period of insanity, these faculties are first exalted and then perverted. There is no hard and fast line of demarcation between sanity and insanity. We cannot, with any degree of certainty, define the limit where sanity ends and insanity begins. Dr. Johnson has traced, with the hand of a master, the insidious advances of diseased thought. He says :—

"Some particular train of ideas fixes upon the mind, all other intellectual gratifications are rejected : the mind in weariness or leisure recurs constantly to the favorite conception and feasts on the luscious falsehood, whenever it is offended with the bitterness of truth. By degrees the reign of fancy is confirmed. She grows first imperious and, in time, despotic. These fictions begin to operate as realities, false opinions fasten upon the mind and life passes in dreams of rapture or of anguish."

Dr. Winslow speaks on the same subject as follows :—

"An attentive observer, tracing the first period of the evolution of a fixed idea, witnesses one of the most curious spectacles imaginable. He sees a man the prey of a disposition imposed by insanity, striving from time to time to rid himself of it, but ever falling back under its tyrannical influence, and constrained by the laws of his mind to seek for some form under which to give it a body and a definite existence. He will be seen successively to adopt and to repel divers ideas which present themselves to him and laboriously striving to deliver himself of a delirium which shall be the expression, the exact image of an internal condition, of which he himself, after all, suspects not the existence. This first phase in the evolution of the fixed idea, this gradual and progressive creation of delirium, constitutes the period of incubation of insanity."

In insanity, too, the psychical faculties are first exalted. Tasse composed his most eloquent and impassioned verses during paroxysms of insanity. Lucretius wrote his immortal poem 'De regnum Natura' when suffering from an attack of mental aberration. Alexander Crudden compiled his 'Concordance' whilst insane. Some of the ablest articles in "Aiken's Biography" were written by a patient in a lunatic asylum. The perceptive faculties also, are, in the insane, first exalted and then perverted. Illusions of the senses and delusions of the mind are sometimes noticed among the incipient symptoms of acute affections of the encephalon, finally insanity and other cerebral disease often manifest themselves, in their early stages, by exaltations and perversions of the moral sense.

These two states of the mind then, are found to be closely related to each other. There is only a single step intervening between the 'sublime' and the 'ridiculous,' and that step is self-control. Directly the will ceases to exercise a proper influence over the understanding and the emotions, the mind loses its healthy balancing power. In insanity the power of self-control is weakened or altogether lost by a voluntary and criminal indulgence of a train of thought which it was the duty of the individual, in the first instance, to resolutely battle with control and subdue. But in the practice of concentration, the power of self-control is immeasurably enhanced. Evil thoughts are never allowed to cast their phantasmal shade across the clear mental horizon. But if this practice be carried out without due regard being paid to the collateral subjects of self-purification and unselfishness, and without the guidance of a master, the chances are that the mental equilibrium is overturned and it degenerates into the ridiculous. Religious fanaticism, sectarian bigotry, superstition and credulity, are the natural outcome of a want of self-control. How important it is to trace the connection between a total want of sensibility in regard to those impressions which affect the salvation of man from misery and bondage, and a super-exalted sensibility in regard to such matters. Both are, to a great extent, dependent on certain unhealthy conditions of the body. In my opinion, the attention of the physician should be particularly directed to the physical conditions of the functions of organic life, when he witnesses instances of a specially exalted or depressed condition of the religious feelings, not clearly traceable to the operation of the sixth principle in man. I am aware that there is a disposition on the part of those who take an *ultra*-spiritual view of the mind's operations to exaggerate truths which ultimately grow into dangerous lies.

"What cheer," says Emerson, "can the religious sentiment yield, when that is suspected to be secretly dependent on the seasons of the year and the state of the blood." "I knew," he continues, "a witty physician who found theology in the biliary duct and used to affirm that if there was disease of the liver, the man became a Calvinist, and if that organ was healthy he became a Unitarian." In reply to this piece of pleasantry, I would observe that many a man has considered himself spiritually lost whilst under the mental depression caused by a long continued hepatic and gastric derangement; and instances occur of persons imagining themselves to be condemned to everlasting punishment, or that they are subjects to Satanic visitation, or hold personal communion with Moses and Jesus Christ, owing to the existence of visceral disease and a congested condition of some one of the great nervous centres. "It is probable," says Dr. Cheyne, "that they, who have formed a lively conception of the personal appearance of Satan from prints or paintings, had the conception realised in nervous and febrile diseases, or after taking narcotic medicines, and it is but charitable to believe that Popish legends, which describe victories over Satan, by holy enthusiasts, have had their origin in delusions of the mind, rather than they were pious frauds."

Self-control then, is the prime factor which serves to distinguish the 'sublime' from the 'ridiculous,' and to keep the mind within legitimate bounds. But in order to ensure success in the practice of concentration of the mind, it were well to have a clear conception of the import of the term self-control. It is not enough merely to keep control over this or that passion, over this or that wrongful action, but by self-control we should learn to keep complete and full control over all the passions, evil thoughts and deeds that together form our lower nature. There is nothing so difficult as to keep constant and unremitting watch and ward over our ignoble self. The practice of negative virtues is none the less serious or difficult than the performance of active charity and benevolence. If we relax the stern wakefulness of reason and will—even for a single moment—if we allow the insidious advances of even one impure thought for a single moment, there is no knowing into what ignoble depths we may be hurled. Once admission is granted to an unhallowed sentiment, it seldom fails to strike root in congenial soil. Man being a composition of the Seraph and the Beast, what heart has been, at all times, free from malevolent passion, revengeful emotion, lustful unnatural feeling and, alas! devilish impulses? Is not every bosom polluted by a dark, leprous spot, corroding ulcer or centre of moral gangrene? Does there not cling to every mind some melancholy reminiscence of the past which throws, at times, a sombre shade over the chequered path of life? We may flatter our pharisaical vanity and human pride by affirming that we are free from these melancholy conditions of moral suffering and sad states of mental infirmity, but we should be belying human nature if we were to ignore the existence of such, perhaps only temporary, evanescent and paroxysmal conditions of unhealthy thoughts and phases of passion.

There are four great obstacles that stand in the way of the practice of concentration of thought, and these are termed in Sanskrit (1) *Vikshepa*, (2) *Rasáswádan*, (3) *Kasháya*, (4) *Laya*.*

(1) *Vikshepa* is that natural tendency of the mind which makes it ever and anon fly from a fixed point. This habitually diffusive tendency of the mind is one of the causes of our bondage. The practice of concentration is recommended in our *Shastras*, with the primary object of counteracting this evil tendency. But the apparently insurmountable nature of this tendency is never manifested so strongly as when we try to battle with it. Every

* In attaining to *Nirvikalp Samadhi* the reader is reminded that these four obstacles appear with but slight modifications.

beginner knows how frequently his mind unconsciously wanders away from the groove wherein he has been so assiduously striving it. Exert yourself to the best of endeavours to keep the image standing clearly before you, it gets blurred and indistinct in almost no time, and you find, to your utter discomfiture, the mind diverted into quite an unexpected and unlooked-for channel. The channels through which the mind thus slips away stealthily, afford it impressions either of pleasurable or painful character, and according to the predominance of the one or other, the second and third obstacles are said to present themselves. (2) *Ràsàswàdan*, therefore, is that state of the mind in which it broods over pleasurable ideas. Our mind is in such intimate sympathy with those impressions which are called pleasurable, that when it once reverts to a train of similar ideas, it is very hard to turn it away from them and fasten it upon the point from whence it wandered. (3) *Kasháya*, again, is that condition in which the mind is lost in the recollection of unpleasant thoughts—thoughts whose withering influence and death-like shadow over the mind, have been many a time the cause of blighting, saddening and often crushing the best, kindest and noblest of human hearts; (4) the last, though not the leastof the obstacles to abstract contemplation and concentration of thoughts, is what is termed *Laya* or passivity of the mind.

In fact, all these obstacles might be reduced to two categories of (1) *Vikshepa* and (2) *Laya, i.e.* Diversion of the attention and total passivity of the mind, the other two being included in the first. *Laya*, or passivity of the mind, is that state in which the mind is perfectly blank, and which, if continued for a short time merges into sleep. This state of the mind, induced during contemplation, is replete with dangers and should be perseveringly guarded against. It is a state which presents an opportunity to any passing elementary, or what is worse, it may offer the best conductivity to the 'magnetism of evil.' The best remedy against all these obstacles is an iron will to overcome them, and a dogged and persistent drill and discipline of the mind in the shape of the daily and intelligent obervance of our *Nitya Karma.*

SHREE KSHIROD SHARMA, F. T. S.